Gay Happiness

How to Get It

Complements of

Lee Dodé, Ph.D.

and

830 Fleming Street • Key West, FL 33040
305-294-3931

Arete Publishing
Key West

ISBN: 0-96630540-X

Printed in the United States of America
Typesetting and design by Solares Hill Design Group, Key West
Cover design by Dina Coyle, Dina Designs, Key West

Published by
Arete Publishing
Post Office Box 4382
Key West, Florida 33041-4382

My thanks to
Connie Gilbert, Nancy Wozniak, and Jackie.

Author's note

This book contains a variety of subjects and opinions not only about the gay lifestyle, but about the values of meaningful living. The book is the author's opinion of some solutions and there are many questions without solutions. You already have developed your own personal philosophy and you may agree or disagree with the author's knowledge through his experiences. Your experiences and/or knowledge may be different. As the subjects are presented, write down your agreement or disagreement. This process is an easy way to better know yourself, and you have it on paper.

Lee Dode'

"I think rank discrimination against anyone is deplored."
Supreme Court Justice Ruth Bader Ginsberg

Gay life existed in back alleys and sex dens, public toilets, and wild get-togethers with strange associations, steet walkers, hustlers, pimps and whores. Gays were victims. They were to be used and discarded. They weren't much good for anything except the obvious.

The United States began to reason that all mankind is equal even though some were different, not "normal". There were the white European majority of Italians, Swedish, French and English, the minorities of Orientals, blacks, and Indians, the freeing of the blacks, and women acquiring rights to become equal. There were the emotionally inflicted. The handicaped.

Then there were the "fairies" whose history include being murdered, punished, beaten, operated upon, tortured, bled, and castrated, but who wanted to be a respected minority. The terminology of "abnormal", "perverts", "fairies", "queers" roll off lips of respectable people. How could the gays compare themselves to someone respectable? How could these devious, anti-God, sex fiends be equal?

The "queers" were. They took disadvantages and turned them into advantages. They moved to larger cities and became respectable with jobs. They favored education and became active in business; gained money, power, respectablilty. They created their own lifestyle. That is what the "fags" wanted.

The right to design our lives.

I was born in the early twentieth century in the United States, white, mid-western, and of average intelligence. I was born or I became gay.

I fought an obligation to myself, to succeed or fail, to live as honestly as I wanted, as happily and successfully as I could. That was up to me; I was my own designer.

I have watched this progression of the gays fighting for their rights at every step along the way for over sixty years. The gay men and lesbians have made their lives more meaningful, and in combining with other minorities of blacks, women, Orientals, etc., to have our laws reflect the lack of discrimination against all, the freedom to develop the idea that all men are created equal with equal rights and protection under the law.

We are now an active part of politics, business, and many other occupations. Some have identified themselves as gay, their sexuality, and taken pride in their accomplishments. Many found strength in being backed by laws. We created families and communities. We fought ignorance and bigotry. At the end of the twentieth century, we are still at war, but we have won many battles.

Having watched myself and my generation fumble over being gay with ignorance often leading, I have made happiness in the changing world of the gay lifestyle. My strength is that I created many of my own problems, and learned to understand some of the answers, evaluated my role, and was successful and very happy. I want to push the knowledge and these experiences into the next century.

The future looks bright for the gays. We can prove our worth and contribution to community and country. We can fight those who will not allow us to be individual with minority views, but with American values. We must accept and demonstrate pride in our accomplishments. We must always check ourselves.

We have the right to design our own lives, and the right to be happy.

Lee Dodé

Table of Contents

The forming of being gay   1

The realization of being gay   31

The adjustment of being gay   67

The maturing of being gay   139

The wisdom of being gay   201

And death.   221

Footnotes   239

THE FORMING OF BEING GAY

From a genetic sperm and an egg, we are created and we grow for nine months inside the mother. We hear different sounds, we acquire health and nourishment, we inherit certain psychological characteristics and, perhaps, other things. We grow within the only world we have ever known, and we are born.

The world outside is a mysterious place of new sounds, smells, sensations, and impressions, and we draw attachments for those who meet our needs of health and well being. We grow dependent upon them, and we learn that they meet our demands. Some mental and physical characteristics are inherited and created within the child of the couple, and that family unit is responsible for the child's introduction into a new world. The baby grows independent and gains control of the world around the child. The baby's world starts to stretch to the world around the room, then a couple of rooms, then the yard, and on. The child's world becomes greater, and control of the objects within his world becomes larger. The child starts thinking independently and constantly is applying learned techniques that adapt the child's own personality to the world through trial and error, those things that are good or bad.

The baby grows into a world of brothers and sisters or neighbors, and learns to adjust. The world of the mother and then the mother and father and then the mother, father, and siblings and then adding neighbors and relatives, the world grows into many other people. Then there is Sunday school or preschool or school and the surroundings become broader, and finally into the school years.

And inside the egg and the sperm joined together is a person; a person with a heart, a will, a brain, a direction, an ambition and a satisfaction which will all materialize within the coming few years, eventually to end up in a person who thinks, hopes, and dreams, who fantasizes, imagines, and creates, a person alive with the wonder of the world and all that is in it. From an egg and a sperm.

MY BODY

You have been given a magnificent piece of equipment with which to work; a human body. The functions of it are so complicated that it will undoubtedly take a whole life to figure it out, and you will not succeed even then in understanding it. Each little part has a function. Most wonderfully, it is perfectly timed, inter-dependent, and complex, and it works beautifully for most people.

This highly technical body also has a brain about which we know very little. It seems to control the functions of the body. It has an unbelievable memory bank. It can execute a command rapidly, respond instantaneously. It holds the conscious and the sub-conscious minds. It controls reasoning and physical action. It allows the display of emotions.

Into this technical miracle has been placed a person who should give it the possibility of everlasting existence. Whatever soul or spirituality is if it exists, it does so in the most fantastic of machines; the human body.

Since we have grown up with the body we have, we take it for granted. We nourish it when it demands although often with the wrong fuel. We use it constantly, in consciousness as well as in sleep. When something goes wrong with it or it does not behave in the manner in which we expect it to behave, we have human mechanics which try to hide the trouble or treat the problem, and we call these physicians or medical doctors. When the functions of the brain aside from the physical happen, we try to treat the problems with what we call psychiatrists or psychotherapists or sociologist and a whole list of other specialists. We leave the soul to ministers or priests or religious mechanics. Man is proficient in fixing many of his parts, but there are things he does not know and time that he chooses not to waste.

One failure of man is his appreciation of the body, the appreciation of the function and beauty of his own human structure, the magnificent machine that we have been given.

(How arrogant of us to assume that this marvelous piece of equipment, beautiful inside and out, can be enhanced by man tattooing it, sticking pins and hooks through it, and destroying the natural beauty of it. You wouldn't use cheap gas or gas substitutes such as alcohol, drugs and stimulants in a new car, nor would you put decals on the outside. You would do what was best for the new car to see that it works efficiently. Why would you harm or alter the body you are going to have for possibly 80 or more years?)

WAS I BORN GAY ?

There continues to be a great deal of medical investigation into the development of the child that is yet to be born, the nine months from conception to birth, within the mother. Some Oriental countries count the nine months within the mother as part of the learning process, and when the child is born, it is its first birthday.

We know that the unborn baby is sensitive to light and sound from the outside world. We know there is an emotional link from the mother to the prenatal child. High anxiety profiles of mothers produce children with high anxiety. We know of a limited amount of inherited factors as in the genes, factors like blood type, hair color, hemophilia, etc. are transferred to the child through both the father and mother. We can test to see if the unborn child is going to be a boy or a girl. Although we can identify the sex of the prenatal baby, we cannot identify the sexuality of the unborn child. To my knowledge, most physicians and scientists believe that genetic homosexuality identification is still a theory, yet and maybe never to develop into fact.

The quest to discover a genetic basis of homosexuality may lead to drastic measures. "Many people assume that if we discover there is a genetic basis for homosexuality, it will lead to the acceptance of homosexuals ... But it's just as reasonable to believe that if we find the markers for homosexuality, the discovery will be used to eliminate sexual diversity. [1]

Although still theory, some physicians feel that a child that is born after the mother has gone through an abortion has a greater chance of being gay than one born to a woman who has not had an abortion. This has never been carefully studied.

WHAT IS A GAY PERSON?

A gay person is a boy or girl, man or woman, who desires to be emotionally, physically, and psychologically (feelings, body and mind) more responsive to his/her own sex than he/she is to the opposite sex.

We do not know at what age these emotions happen. Many will say the emotions are set into the baby before he/she is born (genetic homosexuality) and others feel that the baby may learn to be gay. Most physicians agree that all babies are a combination of both homosexual and heterosexual genetic qualities, but the physicians do not agree that how you live later in life is a combination of experience (what you have lived), what you are made of (genetics), and what you think (psychology). They do not agree to the amount of these three forces.

As a baby grows, some are more aggressive, temperamental, or practically any other emotional description and physicians do not agree why the baby has those characteristics. Few physicians will say these emotional traits are all because of the genes. Most will admit they just do not know.

One personality trait is that some babies are more effeminate than others who are more masculine. A male baby may be more effeminate, but that does not mean he will be gay. A female baby may be more aggressive and masculine, but that does not mean she will be gay. Doctors agree that both masculine and effeminate characteristics are in both male and female babies.

That a female baby grows and she likes masculine games and is termed "tomboy" and a male baby grows and is effeminate and is termed "sissy" does not necessarily mean the baby will be gay. However, these terms could be an indicator, but it is not a very strong indicator since the way we behave is more a learned response to our environment. In other words, we are taught to be either masculine or effeminate, but there are many masculine girls and effeminate boys that continue their growth as heterosexuals. Newer definitions such as aggression is both an effeminate and masculine characteristic, and the older terminologies do not apply. Most physicians today agree that a prenatal child starts to develop and acquires other characteristics through physiological inheritance or through social responsiveness.

Other personality characteristics such as jealousy, honesty, and being conservative are also caught in time and place and the definitions of masculine and effeminate are subject to those interpretations. Doctors have told us most babies go through similar personality changes at certain ages; the "terrible twos", "the aggressive threes", etc. Most babies seem programmed as to their behavior through similar stages of behavior, and there is a direct link between behavior and natural child physical developmental skills.

One of these phases is "sexual identity", when children learn the differences between boys and girls. It is a natural curiosity phase through which most children develop without much difficulty. It's "playing doctor". Most physicians believe this happens anywhere from four to six years old. Others believe it happens earlier. Some babies, and physicians do not really know why, carry emotions, either consciously or sub-consciously, into later development. When a child develops through the period of "sexual identity" could be another indicator, but the theory lacks scientific research.

Another phase of child development is preadolescence, a period around nine to ten when a child has the emotional and physical possibility of reproducing but without the knowledge, or a false knowledge, of how. During preadolescence when the desires are ripe, sex may be introduced, but our American society is not ready. The sexual drive cries out without much of a way to satisfy it.

Into adolescence at the approximate age of eight to 11, the child has learned a very strong line of values which are good or bad, and guides personal values and behavior according to what has been learned from those around the child. In a state of rebellion against the control figures, the child may even repeat sexual acts of his/her own sexual curiosity from pure sexual rebellion or experimentation. To a few, these sexual acts may continue and be conscious.

A researcher's study involving 17,000 girls from ages 3 to 12 indicated that 48.3 percent black girls and 14.7 percent white girls at age 8 began physical development of breasts and pubic hair. Blacks experienced menstruation at 12.16 years and whites at 12.88 years average. [2] The maturation process seems to have started earlier than we commonly believe.

Some will argue that a gay person is someone who will allow same sex gay activity on him/herself or perform same sex acts upon someone else. However, the person may be doing gay acts, but may not personally consider being gay. "God, was I drunk." "I needed the money." These are acts of experimentation or desperation, and the person may or may not be gay.

According to a research center, the female experimentation with the same sex was more likely to happen after the age of 18. [3] 40% of gay men stated that they had same sex experiences before they were 18. Social values of the permissiveness of the male in the United States may account for their earlier experience.

Some other people are not aware of their true sexuality until they are older. Many lesbians do not realize they are gay until they have children. Many gay men are fathers. Some heterosexuals will claim they are bisexual, preferring both men and women or both with the same desires, and although their sexual activity may have been with both sexes, they really prefer one sex over the other, sex meaning different motivations to individual personalities. Others claim no preference except for the physical pleasure of having sex. Heterosexuals prefer the opposite sex to themselves.

So, the basic question of "What is a gay person?" must include a repetitive answer of "... a person who considers him/herself gay" and does not include those people who do not consider themselves gay although they may engage in gay sexual activity.

If you can forgive the cliche of "a person is what a person does", we can see that some who have gay activities do not consider themselves gay. Another question emerges.

WHAT KINDS OF GAYS ARE THERE?

One answer is that there are as many types of gays as there are types of people, all being individual in the way they have developed, as individual as the experiences they have had, and as similar as everyone who has had the same experiences.

A second cliche of "gays and straights are all alike" is equally false. It is true that gays and some heterosexuals have similar experiences and there may be a similar response, but there are unique judgments and experiences that happen in a gay person's life. Most gay men will not have the experience of being a father. To say that gays and straights are all alike is to say that all Americans are alike.

There are general stereotypes that most people accept of the gay person. There are the swishy drag queens that camp, the transvestites that want to be accepted as women, the lesbian truck driver, the bookworm, the straight looking male or female whose sexual interests are assumed to be in the opposite sex. There are very masculine females and very effeminate males, and masculine males and effeminate females. The stereotypes are only limited to our personal experience.

Some of the general stereotypes are noted only by their sexual activity and place. There are the tea dance types, the public toilet types, the book store types, bar types and many more. However, all of these stereotypes are extremes, and there are often gross generalities.

Television likes to focus on the most extreme; the leather bound, handcuffed, motorcycle driver who is gay or the limp wristed drag queen. The new century brings both male gays and lesbians where characteristics more closely match counter-parts in the heterosexual society, but also the opinions of many of the heterosexual as to how a stereotypical gay person acts. Today, many gays prefer to demonstrate and advertise that they are openly gay, and many gays prefer to fade into the background of just being another person not identifying sexual preference. There is not a right or wrong to the description of person a gay wants to project even if he/she is projecting something he/she is not; mainly straight, so long as the individual gay person is aware of what he/she is doing and why he's doing it.

GAY EXTREMES

In a country as large as the United States, there are bound to be many extremes in gay people and the gay lifestyle, some which other people both gay and straight can tolerate and handle, others which they cannot tolerate and may not be able to understand. Just because a person is gay does not mean that he/she must approve of every other gay person. From one extreme of the happily devoted lover to the other extreme of the pedophile mass murderer with all degrees in between.

There are as many strange desires in the gay world as there are in the straight world, the lifestyle of the majority of the others consenting or not consenting to any sexual action that we can imagine. Most gay men do not enjoy pain, but some do. Most gay men are not pedophiles, but some are. Lesbian sexual activity may include many unusual combinations, some of which other lesbians can accept and some of which they do not accept. Most gay men do not prefer straight men who are married to women, lesbians do not prefer married women, but there will always be someone who will break the deck.

The more sophisticated heterosexuals tend to look at gays in pairs, "the two girls ..." or "the two guys...". Most straights reason from their own perspective of being paired, and their exposure to gays has often been from the couple who have moved into the neighborhood, or maybe the new guy in the office and his friend.

The less sophisticated heterosexual tends to look at gays as singular people; "the old faggot", "the queer", "the girl across the street". That type of response from a straight man is from his own experience even if he has become suburban and adopted his married way of life. Since heterosexuals find out about homosexuality today at the same time that gay men and lesbians learn about it, the subject is common knowledge, a weapon to the straight kid, a dagger to the gay kid.

"Coming out of the closet" is a terminology that has been around for the past 20 years, ever since being homosexual was, to a degree, acceptable as a personality development rather than a mental imbalance. In the years before, a person could express his or her real desires, but with a fear of what the listener would evaluate. Until then, the married heterosexual male or female that desired the same sex was called bisexual because he/she had sex relations with the opposite sex. The function was there even if the emotions were not.

A major difference in the behavior of gay men and lesbians is how they react to what is available to them at specific times in history. Large cities have always had groups of gay men and lesbians, although society frowned severely upon their lifestyles of not conforming to the standards. Many gay men were married to women meeting limited sexual obligations, as well as lesbians were married to men and bore them children. There was always a double standard of the man being allowed to sexually cheat on his wife. Divorce seemed to have a greater social value in the older social order, and a "proper" man or woman seldom considered divorce. There was a very limited selection of the straight-married with children lifestyle. Certainly the Bohemian lifestyle did not appeal to the socially minded, but some gay males and lesbians found freedom in the movement.

Today, a straight, married man can have a same sex lover, but he is playing the old game of a respectable lifestyle with a mate and family and a sex toy on the side. He has decided he wants both his wife and his same sex lover. The senior citizens may even have children and grand-children, and some even remain married to the opposite sex, and often have tolerant wives. Many gay women have accepted the role of the divorced woman, and she still supports her children.

If a person decides he/she wants a gay life, and " comes out of the closet'", the person has decided to accept the possible loss of the family life of the heterosexual to adopt the lifestyle of the gay. The man of 50 with wife and family who decides he is gay and changes his life by divorcing or separating from his wife to live forever with his same sex sweetheart, may be creating a new dimension in our gay acceptance. The woman with three children who leaves her husband and decides she is gay is not a new story.

The difference in the lifestyles is that today the female is liberated to some degree to live as independently as she may want. Society has given different values to the divorced or single woman, and society has a different evaluation of the single male, gay or straight. As a society, we have started to learn that human relationships between two people don't always work out better than being alone.

WHO ARE TODAY'S GAYS?

Who are the gays today? How much money do they make? What are their characteristics? How can I tap the market? These are questions asked by many business people over the assumptions that we have made and research of the gay population and some wild guessing.

Gay people are better educated than the average. Gay people make more money than the average. Gay people travel and spend more money. But, gay people are not always happy.

There is tremendous difficulty in attempting to count the amount of gay people in the United States. To be counted as gay, you must confess your sexuality to the person taking the survey; perhaps many people won't. To be counted, you must realize you are gay; some don't yet. How many gays are there? That answer depends upon what study you believe.

It is difficult to compare one survey to another when the questions are asked a little differently in each study. A survey can be crafted to get almost any result the investigator desires. Surveys are always questioned as to their accuracy and to their procedure of gathering data.

The earliest studies from Freud theorized that about ten percent of the population was gay. A later study by Masters and Johnson estimated ten to 15 percent. A more recent study suggests that ten percent of the people in the metropolitan areas are gay, and about four percent in the rural areas. The National Opinion Research Center of the University of Chicago interviewed 3,432 people and concluded

9

that about ten percent of the males were gay and about 8.6 percent of the females were admitted homosexuals. [4] The face to face survey did not expose the closeted cases or the non-confessing answers, and the study was statistically reduced to 2.8 percent of the surveyed men and 1.4 percent of the females. This adjustment is probably the lowest percentage of any study.

Three recent surveys define the gay income and advancement with a little different results. Survey 1 [5] and Survey 2 [6] were very similar and a Survey 3 [7] supplied further clarification with additional questions:

	gays	straights
Survey 1 per capita income	$36,800	$12,287
Survey 2 household income	51,264	37,922 US average
Survey 3 household income	63,700	
individual	41,300	

Conclusion: Gays make larger yearly incomes than straights.

Survey 1 hold college degrees	59.6 %	18.%
Survey 2 college graduates	58.0%	21.%

Conclusion: Gays are better educated than the average straights.

Survey 1 professional and managerial positions 49.%   18.%
Conclusion: Gays have higher positions than straights.

Survey 1   gays are overseas travelers and have are more frequent flyers.

Survey 3   the gay is a white male of 36 who is employed after a college education, and lives in the urban area. [5] [6] [7]

We should question if these statistics also consider some of the other problems in securing answers from the gay community. Have older gays not accustomed to admitting they are gay been considered? Have people who move in and out of a gay lifestyle been considered? Have those who consider themselves bisexual, cross dressers, transvestites, and drag queens also been included? Have potential gays who have not admitted to themselves they are gay been considered? There are probably many gay people who do not live an active gay lifestyle, or who want to be reported.

In the years to come, we will better identify the gays and find there are probably many more than we can now survey accurately, but the time will be less threatening and there will be a greater acceptance of gays and the laws protecting us, and there will be a greater acceptance of homosexuality.

Gays can be found in every occupation, but the stigma of being gay still rests in the creative professions only because they tend to more liberal. Gays are more accepted in the creative occupations and, indeed, sometimes appear to dominate specific professions today. Gays often prefer to hire other gays, and they are not as easily accepted in a heterosexually dominated work force.

There are fewer gays in professions which demand a public, analytical observation of their lives, politicians or city employees, and acceptance is currently changing. Professions that still command the macho image, brick-layers, football players, mill workers, garbage collectors, those occupations that are heavily physically demanding will not attract as many gays or will attract gay men or women demanding the macho stereotype. Gays are in all professions but some do not announce that even in a marriage of a man to a woman, one may be gay, perhaps a compatible relationship often with much emphasis upon the children or upon physical things. Some gay women have married for financial security, but under today's mores, a female does not have to be dependent upon the male, and she may adopt children or select one of the many ways to have conception without a legal husband.

Since we have not yet advanced to legal equality with heterosexuals, the minority of gays will not make themselves obvious until it is to their advantage. Once we decide that Americans can accept each other as individuals rather than categorizing people into minority groups, gays will no longer hide. Gays will organize in groups feeling security within their own power of numbers. With the acceptance of a gay lifestyle, there will be more exposure of it, and smaller towns will accept gay organizations and the lifestyle, but not very rapidly. There will always be prejudice and hatred toward something that straight people do not understand, and it won't be cured in a generation.

There will always be those who for an undetermined amount of reasons like to associate themselves with the gay advance for acceptance. These are the "leaches" of gay life proclaiming gay acceptance because of personal rejection, financial advantage, security, boredom with their own lives, insecurity in their own emotional development, or whatever.

DO I HAVE GAY TENDENCIES?

You must decide what a tendency is. Usually it is a line somewhere between masculine and effeminate, a continuum of different actions that demonstrate themselves as either "more like a man" to "more like a woman". People are judged by others according to how they behave at a specific time in their social background.

The degree of masculinity/femininity is always caught by the values of the judges at a specific time in history. What was masculine in the early 1800's would not seem as masculine today. Men with wigs and lace handkerchiefs are rare today. A female basketball player today is acceptable as a woman's activity even though basketball was considered a man's activity. Science was a man's field; now it is shared by men and women. A woman President?

We are culturally trained to behave in a certain manner and, wanting acceptance and pleasure, babies react to being accepted and gaining pleasure by pleasing the person that gives it to the child. Male babies get blue blankets; girls get pink blankets. Boys get blocks; girls get dolls. As adults, we know we are conditioning our children to react and we are working away from some older stereotypes to establish newer ones. We will allow the boy baby to play with teddy bears, but we will shy away from the older baby boy playing with dolls. We still maintain a great many stereotypes that we apply to male behavior and to female behavior as two separate forms of behavior.

Since the child has been conditioned to please, conditioned to meet his/her parent's expectations as to what a boy or girl child should do, the child pleases for a positive parental response. In a large family, brothers and sisters take on the responsibility, perhaps grand-parents or other relatives, or the neighborhood. Each is relaying to the child how to behave, what interests to have, what kind of playing to do, and the adults are establishing boundaries of the child's masculinity/femininity, praising when they agree and denying when they don't agree. The parents are persuaded by their own experiences with children.

This process of the child attempting to please continues throughout his/her life lessening only when he/she becomes secure enough to rebel against those who demand. To some, the individual's personality and characteristics are established in the first few years of life, and he/she can not or will not change. A popular journalist, Cal Thomas reasons that gays have a "choice" of being gay, that psychologists have termed them so to avoid glandular disturbance, inheritance, or the scrambling of genes. [8] He quotes *Overcoming Homosexuality*, a 1980 book by Dr. Robert Kronemeyer that most people dispute today. Later articles imply that we can probably adjust to just about anything, but why should we. The American Psychological Association states that basic sexual orientation cannot be changed according to current scientific studies. A gay may be able to adjust or control his desires, but he can't change them.

We have heard many gays say that one of their earliest memories was being called "sissy" or confusion over the child's sexuality because of the way the child acts in relation to the way the comment maker feels the child should act. "She is going to be quite a tomboy."

It is true that some babies are more aggressive, more sensitive, less observant than other babies their own age, but there are many reasons, few of which would lead to the identification of the child's sexual orientation or that conclude that the baby would grow to be a homosexual.

Not to avoid the trite, there are many masculine and effeminate men and women who are heterosexuals and ten to 15 percent of men and women who are homosexual. We still feel that gays have a difficult time in adjusting to what they have learned. Imagine being an effeminate heterosexual male or a masculine heterosexual female.

A problem of our society is stereotyping gays as very effeminate young men, a "sissy", "swish", or "girl", and often the butt of people's humor, not only the humor from those of his own age. Girls should not be taught to beat-up on boys just because girls may be a bit larger and stronger at a specific age. Where is father's ego?

As adults today, it is perfectly socially acceptable for a man to help his wife with the dishes, do housework, join her in shopping and caring for the children, and for him to show affection not only to the child, but also to his wife. The masculine image has changed so that today's male image is a softer acting man.

The female image has changed even more drastically. She can now work outside the home; in fact, for financial reasons she probably has to work to aid the income of the family. She may eat in a restaurant alone, or even have a drink by herself without being identified as a prostitute. She can travel, make decisions, and hold many of the jobs that once belonged exclusively to men. She is not as yet equal to a man, but she is approaching his status very rapidly.

Thank God these stereotypes are changing not only for the straights, but also for the gays. Television and the news are headlining the gays not so much as drag queens and lesbian truck drivers, but as humans, undistinguishable from those with other sexual desires. It took the motion picture industry 12 years into the AIDS crisis to produce a motion picture about AIDS after years of hiding the personal activities and lives of its actors and actresses as well as so many other creative people.

The gays are also establishing new images of themselves. The gay Olympics, women in politics and business, gays who have come out of the closet breaking down the physical stereotypes that were held a short time ago. Gays declaring themselves in fields where they are respected. The gay marches are sending out messages to the straight world that there are many different types and kinds of gays with all extremes of personalities and differences.

The line from masculine to effeminate is a constantly changing line, and it will continue to change into the next century. Perhaps we will get to a point where we won't consider the sexuality of the individual, but we will judge by their individual personalities and their abilities

DO GAYS SEXUALLY ABUSE CHILDREN?

Statistically, heterosexuals are responsible for about 90 to 98 percent of child sexual abuse cases, if we consider a child as someone under the age of 16. The majority are heterosexual advances, but homosexual cases seem to make more popular emotional responses to readers. There are few gay pedophiles of very young children. Our laws make 16, 18 or 21 years old the age of maturity and legal status which is a questionable assumption.

Many children under 18 marry, have children, and rear families. Is a married boy of 17 wed to a girl of 16 a child abuser? Our laws say "no". Are two boys masturbating together considered abusing each other? Are two girls "practicing" being an adult with each other considered lesbians? The laws concerning maturity and majority need a great deal of explanation. Few if any give an accurate accounting of the degree of child abuse and incest in America. We need new definitions of maturity and majority, new guidelines as to child abuse and incest, and new laws for those who engage. Child abuse and incest are much greater than what we think, but the results of trauma to the child may or may not be as horrible as we are led to believe.

Take the example of a 14 year old boy going through puberty and making himself available to any older gay man who is willing to pay for his sexual services. The sensation to the young boy feels good. He has set himself up for this service. He pockets the money. He may not be gay. Is the older man a child abuser? Under current law, he is. Actually, the 14 year old has propositioned the older man. The kid grows up straight and forgets the incident. The older man goes to jail.

A gay child at the age of seven seduced his father, and the father allowed the behavior. The father is guilty of incest, but has he committed child abuse? Is the father a pedophile?

In experimental adolescence, there are probably many more incidents of same sex sexuality than what we want to know, and the kids grow up not tainted by the experiences. Is "playing doctor" a game of sexual stimulation to the child? Of course. It is also curiosity.

For the gay teen, the years of experimentation and puberty are hell. The teen has to figure out what is happening to him/herself as well as meeting up to the community's rules which seem not to apply. He/she is caught in a struggle of values and often does not have the maturity or experience to even know how to behave, much less what to believe. Sometimes experimentation, particularly with older children, is misunderstood by others who may find out.

Some schools have developed programs to help the young person through some of these very difficult times, and the subject is a part of the curriculum of teaching, but the subject is often left untouched. This period in the gay boy or girl's adolescent life is the most difficult time because for some reason he or she does not fit into the value scale at school. Behavior problems, personality outbursts, excellent scholastic records, humor and a care-free attitude, all, both "good" and "bad" behavior can be indicators to adjustment problems.

In the more progressive schools and curriculums, the young person may be referred to a school psychologist or even a caring teacher, but the role of the interested person is not to expose the supposed problem to the parents who are as confused as the child, but psychologists are accepting the changing values. The young child who may have urges toward gay activity, but who has no knowledge of what these urges mean or what they can do, can often act impulsively and be misinterpreted, and too often stuck with labels of "queer".

The mature gay man or lesbian will never let him/herself be put into the position where the gay can be accused of sexually abusing children. For your own protection, avoid baby sitting. Avoid playgrounds. You never want to be put in the position where you may be accused of molesting a niece or nephew or friend. The mere accusation will label you GUILTY. Although many will disagree with this advice, there has been too much money and time spent proving a gay not guilty of child abuse, because the gay person trusted the parents, the child, the school, the community, or the changing of values.

The mature gay will never ever consider sexual relationships with children under the legal age, and if he/she does, the gay should be smart enough to get psychiatric help before he/she is led into trouble, or at least smart enough not to allow himself to get into situations where the gay may be challenged by his own lust. The situation is difficult for the eager juvenile may dominate the gay person's logic, and the gay may lose. Those that are labeled pedophiles are the most hated people of Americans in or out of jail. Get help before you get into trouble. Notice we hear often of homosexual pedophiles of men and little boys, but rarely hear of homosexual females and little girls. One major difference is that lesbians are searching more for understanding and a young girl has not yet developed that type of understanding to appeal to the lesbian. The young boys tend to be more interested in physical things, cars and boats, and more interested in playing the sexual games.

THE SEXUAL SENSATION

Although we hesitate to admit it, the sexual sensation feels good to the the person doing the action and to the person who is having the action done to him/her. The tension of the body, the manipulation of the parts, the friction of rubbing together create an inward feeling of desire, heat, passion and aggressiveness that most people will not feel at any other time in their lives. With the entire workings of two bodies in sexual harmony, the emotional release, and the climactic ending, there are few if any other physical emotional experiences that can compare. The sexual act within itself can be an ultimate physical and emotional experience.

But, if the same sexual act is forced upon a person, demanded to be performed, aggressively sought and conquered by a cruel, non-caring, demanding animal on the physical attack, the sexual act can be destructive, cruel, inhumane, evil, painful and destructive. The attack can leave the body bleeding, and the individual victim's mind incapable of logic, sequential thought, and filled with guilt. The act itself is an invasion of the worst kind, the invasion of another person's trust which is sacrificed and an invasion of their sanity for having so loosely placed confidence in someone else, and the loss of their own innocence as well as their own guilt of the event for allowing the incident to happen. In a study of male prison sex, the force of a prisoner's fingers or fist or some handle in his anus causing severe pain may leave lasting mental complications. [9]

There may be pain of love when one person is trying so greatly to satisfy the second that first experience pain has usually been self inflicted. The pain follows the desire to please. In rape, the inflicted pain is there but there is no desire to please. That is ripped from you. That is stolen. Prison rapes are usually long term prisoners who are usually straight and have gotten themselves in jail where the only sexual expression is to their own sex, and they re-act accordingly. Once released from jail, the x-convict continues heterosexuality. In prison, he was never gay but did some homosexual acts. But, there are homosexuals in prison also.

What we often call "losing innocence" is two people experimenting with the pleasures of the physical body and enjoying it, not withstanding the threat of the later consequences, perhaps even the punishment. "I can have sex, but I don't want to get pregnant." "I can have sex but I don't want anyone to find out." "You touch mine and I'll touch yours."

Let's not think that the total experience of having sex in the experimental period is a painful experience; it doesn't have to be.

When the person grows from childhood, the experience of having sex does not have to carry the scars of a first experience if it were a satisfactory, kind investigation of sex rather than a rape of innocence. Many people have enjoyed their initial investigations of sex without bruises, but these experiences are forgotten when the lustful, brutal, criminal rape dominates the subject.

Since the introduction and investigation of sex is often between children, any adult who has any self-respect should avoid all situations which could lead him into a compromising situation for which he can only blame himself. Stupidity is a reason for failure, but not a very good one.

BEING GAY ASIDE FROM SEXUALITY

Sexuality is only one aspect of our personality development, but it is very important because our sexuality affects so many of our decisions, directions, actions, and behavior. Effects of sexual development are often overlooked by many. It is not the sex act itself. That could be overlooked if there were not other ramifications of the act.

The reasoning process, the goals and directions, the inspiration and creativity, the comfort to the individual and the accomplishment of his/her goals are directly related to sexuality. Gays and straights do not differ only because of the act of sex with the same gender partner. They differ in expectations from their chosen mates, advancement, goals, and satisfactions.

They differ because of many of the complexities that each has with handling experiences, emotions, and values that have developed through his/her sexuality. The complications arise from a frustrated fundamental drive, one unclear and perhaps confusing to the gay individual, an emotional reaction that grows in the gay person unless he/she is able to discourage the emotional reaction which he/she is capable of doing by understanding its appetite and allowing him/herself to be gay.

Sigmund Freud studied frustrated sexuality and his writings have become the basis of modern day psychology, his approach to the hall to which all rooms leading from the hall could be reached only through going down the hall of sexuality. The complication is not the act itself; it is the complications that arise from it or the desire for it.

Freud wrote about the consequences of sexuality to the personality, and he was one of the first who publicized in writing the importance of sexuality to the development of the human being. He introduced the outspoken words of sexuality; certainly not sex. He was followed by psychiatrists and psychologists that took his inspiration of sexuality and applied it to many different theories of psychology. He was the genius who threw out a hand full of seeds to watch a forest grow.

Our American society can handle a little sexual deviation without much difficulty. We do now and no one seems to care much, except those with political ambitions. The sadistic-masochistic trend. The cross dressing complex. The bragging male ego displays. The girl that wants sex, afraid to agree, but wants raped to clear her conscience. These are controlled sexual deviations. These may become the emotional and sexual responses to the sexual development of the homosexual, the gay person's fantasy world.

It is difficult to recognize homosexuality in America without realizing it is difficult to tell the behavior of a homosexual from a heterosexual. Being gay is a natural behavior to the individual; not an insane state of being. It is not controlled by status, wealth, class, race, or religion, male or female, "good" or "bad". It is a natural occurrence of a part of our population, one just within the last 30 or more years has become obvious and public through the fight for equity. Being gay is not as obvious as being black or Oriental. It is a variation that is not chosen by the individual, but that does exist. Most important, it is a percentage of our population that must be protected against prejudice and bigotry. In this new age of minority rights and equal treatment, homosexuality, because it is not always obvious, has become the mysterious, unidentified devil.

Human beings think that anything that they do not understand is "bad". You can identify a black man by the color of his skin, tell an Oriental by the shape of his eyes, and you know what a Mexican looks like. But, you cannot identify a homosexual unless he/she tells you or behaves like one of the stereotypes which are rarely socially acceptable. Therefore, homosexuals are bad. Many hate things that are bad, particularly with those qualities that are not similar to their own. Homosexuals are different. Therefore, they are "bad" and should be eliminated or at least not considered as "real" people.

With a world where more than 50 percent are women, Caucasians are vastly outnumbered by blacks and Orientals, where the various Oriental dialects are spoken by far more people than speak English, where most of the work is agricultural, where masses cannot read or write, it is easy to be prejudiced against something many don't understand. Prejudice and bigotry say that we should learn to hate the things we are not, pass laws to prohibit others for being different, and limit the freedoms of those not exactly agreeing. That's not the kind of America we want.

IS BEING GAY MY PARENTS' FAULT?

Your parents probably reared you the best they could under their circumstances. If they gave you any degree of love and affection, attention and direction, be thankful to them. Praise them for what they have done well.

Most parents will question themselves attempting to lay blame on themselves for your being gay. You may blame someone else. "If only ..." The parents will carry a burden of guilt, and you have no right in building that burden unless you have specific scientific truth, and there is little proof to why you are gay. If you have the type of relationship with your parents that they realize you are gay, tell them that your being gay is not their fault. There is no fault.

You will have to face the fact that in our unsophisticated world, sometimes things just happen and it is no one's fault. Remember the expression of "Shit Happens"? But, it doesn't have to be "shit" by being gay unless you want to make it that way.

Life is not laid out in a plan. The unexplained happens. We have not yet answered all the questions of living and of life, and we probably never will. Accept the positive things that have been given to you and be thankful for them, and go on. The negative things will happen are negative only if you make them that way. Turn the negatives into positives. There is an old line from a once popular song, "you've got to accentuate the positive, eliminate the negative..." If homosexuality is negative, we must accept it and allow the individuals to live positive lives. We must accept the differences of the world because all of us are part of that difference. To a degree, we are all minorities of something, and we must learn to live together in harmony. We must do it. We must eliminate bias and prejudice and the effects of actions against others who are "different".

There have been many studies done in attempting to prove what causes a person to be homosexual, none of which are inclusive or exclusive. We do not know. Studies of identical twins show that one child may be gay, the other straight, but the greater chance is that both twins will be gay if one is. In two families of ten children, all ten can be straight in one, eight of the ten straight in the second. Most gay people have been raised with straight brothers and sisters, so singular children are not statistically different from those gays with brother and sisters.

Out of the parents' concern for their boy or girl being gay, the parents often rush the child to a psychiatrists hoping the doctor can change the child preferably into heterosexual like the parents. Sometimes the child's behavior changes, the child performs in a socially acceptable manner, but the inside feelings of the child have rarely been changed, and although he/she behaves straight, there is a craving inside the child that is not satisfied. Behavior can be modified, but there is more to the individual than just behavior.

Many psychiatrists accept a child or adult as being gay, and the parents must adjust to the changes. The study of human behavior is incomplete. There are no quick cures, few medical miracles. Accept yourself. Be true to yourself.

Some parents cannot accept a gay child or cannot accept that the child is not to blame. At the reasoning of the parents and the child cannot come to some type of mutually acceptable conclusion, it is probably better for the child to leave the family and community and accept being him/herself as being gay. Unfortunately, this action sometimes leads to loneliness. The parents should have concentrated on building positive self-esteem, values and direction, and the child away from the parent's influence should reflect these qualities.

Of all the many horror stories of child abuse, incest, psychological abuse, broken families, etc., they all break down to the point where the supposed victim finally decides to take control of his own life and stop blaming someone else. Even in true horror stories, there can be the conclusion of a happy person, but only if he/she sheds the baggage of victimization.

In the confusion of the physical body changing from that of a child into a preadolescent and the inability to communicate with parents, siblings or friends, the gay boy or girl realizing that no one understands him or her, an expression of the lack of love and understanding, will wish to be dead. Some are capable of committing suicide. Gay boys commit suicide at a rate of three times as much as lesbian girls but there are few statistics on how many attempted suicides have been committed by gay youths. [11]

The former U. S. Surgeon General Jocelyn Elders says that among children 15 to 24, in 1993, over 10,000 young people tried to commit suicide. Half, 5,000, succeeded. Some of the reasoning behind the suicides was the lack of family understanding, often the young person was gay. There is an increase in the amount of suicides of Latino gays and black gays of the younger people and we don't know the pressures of anti-gay attitudes that the youths have felt at school, in the home or on the streets.

Leaving the parents and the family unit is a natural progress of development and independence. It does not have to be a catastrophe. It can be a natural progression of living, the start of independence and guessed decision making. At 16 or 18, these demands are great. Leaving home doesn't have to hurt anyone including the parents.

Not long ago, women found marriage a convenient excuse to leave an undesirable family home life and create home lives of their own. Too often pregnant or run-away kids have left the family without knowing where they are going and what they are trying to find. Hopefully, the gay person knows what he/she hopes to find. It is not just momentary satisfaction or "kicks", but something with much more substance.

He/she leaves home as a loving family member who is off to college or off to a job and independence, but also as one who desires, maybe demands, the loving and support of his/her family. Don't burn bridges. You need your family and your family needs you. No crisis. No expressed hard feelings. (Don't worry as much for the young gay man or lesbian moving away from his/her family as for the gay son or daughter at 35 who has remained home under parental restrictions never to build an independent life.)

You do not blame your parents for you being gay. You do not blame yourself. You accept yourself and your parents and, maybe, hope they will accept you. Acceptance is the game. You better get used to it; you'll be doing it a lot in the gay world as well as in your community. There is a comfort in knowing yourself.

TOLERANCE

No where in our educational system does the teacher concentrate on tolerance, nor do the parents say much about tolerance except "share". We learn "selfishness". Some will argue that the basic state of man is to be selfish, to gather all to himself and his own reasoning rather than to compromise where he recognize someone else's superiority and gained wellbeing. If selfishness is the opposite of tolerance, selfishness may be a more primate instinct, but it is often difficult to support selfishness in a family situation. In fact, it is a stumbling block in human relations.

The compromise of selfishness, tolerance can be attributed to understanding and personal confidence, and probably there are many other personality attributes that are counter to the ego, the "all for me" approach. Selflessness is the opposite of selfishness, bigotry and intolerance. Parents, school teachers, maybe even the ministry do not know how to teach tolerance, but the child learns very early in life, a personality trait that he will hold and rarely change.

There are two basic parts to tolerance; my tolerance of allowing you to think and do as you wish, and your tolerance of me to do the same things. Between these two, the stronger drive is my tolerance of me doing what I want. If I want it, I will have it, often regardless of the cost. The egotistic, directional satisfaction of personally pleasing the desires of one person, me, are utmost in importance, everything else is secondary. I want what I want because I want it. It seems like circular reasoning, but there is no patience for anyone or anything that comes in the way of supplying the demand. I have complete tolerance for myself.

Should something block my getting what I want, I cannot allow that to happen without extreme frustration, which I do not like. Thus, I get angry at the other person who blocks me from getting what I want, and I have no tolerance for him/her and, thus, no respect for the other person. My lack of respect for the other person, the lack of tolerance, demands rebellion. I attack those ideas and actions that I do not understand with rebellious ideas and actions. If the deed is not for my personal pleasure or satisfaction, I will be against it.

Rebellious youth shows a lack of tolerance for something that does not immediately satisfy the individual. Fight against it. Adults do the same thing. If they do not understand an idea or action which does not directly affect them or their lives, they are against the idea or action. "If the person likes collecting dead animals, I'm against the person."

As a child, our tolerance is limited by our siblings or our parents, often children teaching children what responses gain action or what responses are ignored. If I cry, I get fed. If I am hungry and do not cry, I might not get fed. So, if I am hungry, I learn to cry and get fed and I'm no longer hungry. When I learn to speak and communicate like crying, the same procedure holds true. When I am hungry, I ask and get fed and I am no longer hungry. But, what happens if asking receives a negative answer? Confusion. Frustration for not getting what I want. Rebellion. Maybe through rebelling I can get satisfaction equal to my original demand. "If you won't love me, I'll make you hate me."

American society does not teach the ability to gracefully lose. Children and adults are constantly brought in competition of being tolerant to others and others being tolerant of us. We, as the American society have not yet adjusted to the fear of not being loved because we have failed at something, and yet we all hold failing in common so we recognize tolerance as a positive strong motivation. Can you imagine an application for employment that would ask you to list your accomplishments and to list your failures? Can you imagine hiring someone who has never failed? Yet, you can not imagine someone who has not failed.

The gay male or lesbian wants society to be tolerant of their way of life, the gay lifestyle, but often he/she is not tolerant of the straight lifestyle or even the gay lifestyles that some of their gay friends lead. It is not unusual for the gay man or lesbian to be ashamed of the nellie drag queen, the butch motorcycle driver, the sissy nellie screamers because he/she feels that these stereotypes are not typical of the gay scene as he/she would like it to be. The mother who beats her children, the run-away father, incest, etc., are not typical of the straight lifestyle. Which has the most tolerance?

CUIQUE SUUM - "TO EACH HIS OWN"

No one knows all the many directions of life that may bring happiness to the individual. We are born into a certain style of living and our parents have taught us their rules and regulations for happiness. We blindly follow hoping that by using their rules, we will obtain some similar type of happiness.

As we grow older, we realize that our parent's rules and regulations are not as stringent as we had imagined, our parents often breaking their own rules. We also realize that the way our parents live may not bring total happiness to them, and we learn that a loving relationship is a two way street, certainly not a given Utopia. We begin to see the flaws in our parents and in their relationship. Unfortunately, we have to compare our parents' relationship with our own limited knowledge. Again, we compare to our false idols, "Ozzie and Harriet", "My Three Sons", "The Partridge Family" and the many examples through novels and television. That's all we know, and we begin to realize that our family is not the perfect family. We know we are not the perfect children.

With a small degree of tolerance, we allow our parents (not that we could stop them) to be themselves, and we learn to respect the peculiarities of them and of our brothers and sisters and others around us. We find that to a limited degree, all people are a little bit different from each other, and this difference is not necessarily bad. We learn that people have things they like or dislike, and those things do not have to agree with what another person likes or dislikes.

The Latin "Cuique Suum - 'To each his own'" is a conclusion to the evaluation of others as well as it is a symbol to hide our own individualities. So long as these peculiarities are not a threat to someone, acceptance is easy for the young person. When they become a threat to the individual, these evaluation differences grow into biases, and the biases grow into prejudices.

From the time we are born, we are taught to be prejudiced by our family, siblings, and associates. Prejudice is a man-made factor; nothing innate or genetic, nothing without being taught. The song from "The King and I", "You've got to be carefully taught".

The gay person approaches "to each his own" with a great deal of defiance meaning "to each his own so long as they agree with me". That's self defeating. Each gay person must be tolerant of others who do not think along the same lines. The gays demand tolerance, but they often do not display it. A gay person in a straight group who tells jokes against the gay lifestyle to amuse is making fun of him/herself to please and be liked by his/her audience. Gay people can be very vicious toward people who think similarly about being gay if it will add to their advantage.

We dislike the person, particularly the politician, who acts against the ideas of the gay person, and give him the greatest insult to ourselves we can imagine: "He is probably gay himself". We take the male or female politician who votes against legislation which promotes a gay cause and term him "a closet queen" or "gay" or "dyke". When we suspect any gay activity on the part of the politician who votes against gay causes, we expose him/her for the hypocritical attitude, the "outing". We have swung the saying "to each his own" around to "to each his own if he agrees with me".

The phrase also has its limitations, and that is the reason that "so long as it doesn't hurt anyone" is often tacked on. "To each his own so long as it doesn't hurt anyone." If the liberal interpretation of "to each his own" could include animal brutality, human suffering, psychological pain, the phrase is useless for a happy life. The phrase becomes too narrow of an explanation with too many exceptions.

SHOULD I GIVE WAY TO MY FEELINGS?

We have imaginations and many times the fantasy of making up a story sees us through sleepless nights and empty days. There is nothing unhealthy about pretending or daydreaming so long as a person is aware of what is real and what is fantasy. You imagine in your dreams what you want to be, how you would like to be treated, and what you would like to happen. We've been many things in fantasy from rich kids, to priests, to hustlers. Fantasy is escape, and there is nothing wrong with escaping so long as you are aware that is what you are doing.

Most people remember their fantasies with a degree of respect usually realizing how and why they have felt certain ways and created themselves in stories about it. (My most common fantasy was that I wanted a relationship with an unsuccessful veterinarian and we had to keep all the animals. God knows how we would have lived and made an income. A detail.) The pleasant little imaginary escapes are harmless and often amusing to the private world of the individual.

In some people, these trips into non-reality can give indications of a much more serious mental state, problems that may not be legal, healthy or sane; an indication that would have to be acted upon before it came to any kind of reality, an unhealthy fantasy hiding masochism, where sexual satisfaction depends upon humiliation, suffering, and pain, or sadism, the aggressor. The harmless, pretend world becomes much more serious, particularly if the person allows the pretend world to start to be actualized. The fantasy world, when acted out, starts to become real, and the individual may lose control of what is actuality and what is fantasy, and of his/her behavior toward making the fantasy reality.

"I want to be held down and raped by the whole football team. I want them to call me names and humiliate me. I want them to beat me for what I've done wrong." This statement is hardly an innocent confession of desires, but contains many deeper problems of significant personality deficiencies. He/she needs psychological help, and fast.

Most straights like most gay men and lesbians do not allow themselves to vent much emotion to their darker desires. They hold their own minds and bodies in control of their thinking. They separate fantasy and reality.

We are, however, living in fantasy. Look at the fantasy in advertising as well as in the local bars both gay and straight. "He swaggers in with his skin tight Levis showing a bulge in his pants that is as large as his ten gallon hat." "She slinks in with a skin tight dress, the neck cut to the navel and slit up the side revealing her smooth buttocks." Harmless fantasy? To most people, yes.

You should be allowed to express your feelings, but also consider that your feelings may not be accepted by other people. Be careful in expressing too rapidly to a potential mate your innermost fantasies. If the listener does not accept the fantasy, the story teller expressing his/her emotions feels foolish, and foolishness often shadows rejection, and no one wants rejection. In the game of life, you learn to taylor your emotions to your audience, only allowing a portion of your feelings to seep out at one time until you have tested how your feelings will be accepted. It is trial and error.

Something has to be said for the person who lacks the ability to express his/her emotions as well as the opposite side, the person who gives his/her feelings too openly in a desperate attempt to have someone. God did not create uncomplicated people.

GOD AND GAYS

The Bible is one of the oldest philosophy books written hundreds of years ago which outlines the way people should live in harmony with one another. It was written by various people, and has contradictory theories on which we place various interpretations. It has been re-written, re-defined, translated and, semantically, the meaning of words have changed from period to period. The subjects of the Great Authors are various, but no writer mentions homosexuality directly.

Some religious believe they have the right to interpret the Bible in their own way, and they insist their interpretation is the only authentic and "right" belief. By twisting subject content, semantics, and interjecting their own interpretations of scripture, they are trying to prove homosexuality is against God's will. They misinterpret the Bible for their own desires.

In Genesis 1: 27-28 is stated that God created man and woman and told them to multiply. Most scholars interpret that man and woman are equal, and a goal is to reproduce. The statement says nothing about marriage, fidelity or infidelity, homosexuality, love, rape or any other human act. We must understand what is written, not what we interpret.

In the story of the men of Sodom, they were accused of treating their prisoners to sexual abuse; Genesis 19: 1-9. Later, Exaekiel in 16: 48-49 says that sodomites, the people of Sodom, were "... arrogant and abominable". Should we damn all arrogant people? "Abominable" usually translates "nasty, disgusting". Should we damn all nasty and disgusting people? Was his word "abominable" or "abnormal"?

Paul criticizes the idol worshippers for their sexual clan meeting of priestesses and eunuchs, self castrated male prostitutes, in Romans 2: 26-27. The subject is idol worshiping, the ridiculing of Pagans, not homosexual. He does talk of "males working shame with males, and receiving penalty for their error" but he is talking about the horror of venereal disease. Paul does refer to pedaerasty, meaning " to love boy" in First Corinthians 6: 9 and Timothy l: 10. At that time the man had a wife for producing an heir, and effeminate young boys for sex, often a substitute for disease ridden prostitutes. We cannot say that homosexuality did not exist during this period, and we cannot say that some people did not object to it. The Bible is not advocating homosexuality for everyone, nor is it denying that homosexuality exists. Paul warned of the consequence of disease in gays and straights. (Through modern research, we know that pedophiles are usually heterosexuals.) Recognition is not acceptance or rejection of an idea.

Perhaps the most often stated idea from the Bible concerning homosexuality is Leviticus 18: 22 and 20-13 where he says that "... man should not lie with a male as with a woman; it is an abomination" or "... it is abnormal". Again, "abomination" means "nasty and disgusting". "Abnormal" means "not normal." If something is not normal, it is not necessarily wrong or bad or against the will of God. Left handed people, blue eyed, red heads, physical defects, stutters, and overweight are not the average, not the normal, but hardly abnormal. Should we damn all people who are not typical? The term does not mean "insane". Sodomy can be abnormal sex with the opposite sex or animals. Nothing has been said specifically about homosexuality. Gays are not requesting a hundred percent homosexual world. [11]

Jesus said nothing about homosexuality. His profits said nothing. Even the Bible says little. If it were as large of a sin as some religions today want us to believe, don't you think these philosophers would have said something?

Why are some current religious philosophies so opposed to homosexuality? Do you believe religion is business? Is Catholicism not the oldest big business? Don't all religions want more members? Why are some religions against birth control when there are thousands of people starving? Why do other religions like to create conflicts within the congregation to gain attention to get pledges? Ask Jerry Falwell, Pat Robertson, James Kennedy, Jim and Tammy Bakker, Oliver North, and Billy Graham. There are some religions that want increased memberships, not philosophically, but monetarily. Are the religions that accept gays wrong?

There are gays within the Catholic Church. Until recently, they have tried to ignore them. The United Church of Christ, Unitarians, and Quakers permit ordination of practicing homosexuals. The Metropolitan Church is mostly gay. The Presbyterian Church ban any sexual relations outside of marriage, the Episcopal laws do not bar ordination of gays; and the gays can be non-celibate. The Central Conference of American Rabbis endorsed same-sex marriages in March of 1997. [12]

Who really cares about someone else's sex life? Who really cares if someone is gay? It is not a philosophic issue. Hatred of gays has made being gay purely a man made moral issue. Do you think God really cares if you are gay?

CAN I LIVE A STRAIGHT FACADE?

Yes, you can. You can live in a family tied to society where you are allowed certain duties, obligations, and responsibilities. You can live around people who do not really understand you as a real person, but do understand the family obligated, directed, and cultured person you have become. You can live a lie. The Victorians were noted for it. You can be ashamed of yourself, unclear as to who and what you are, fake happiness and probably be successful in fooling those around you.

Sooner or later (but, unfortunately, never with some), the problems of living an artificial life based upon what people want you to be rather than on what you are is going to explode. You will do more harm pretending to those who love you, although they don't know you, than you would if they knew and loved the more honest you. You are hiding under the false assumption that the real you is a "bad' you because you have not been taught to respect the real sensual you. You are ashamed, but not knowing of what you are ashamed.

When you learn there are more people who can love you than your birth family and siblings, when you realize you can love your parents and your brothers and sisters regardless of the "difference" in your life, when you understand there are other people with whom you can create a family of your own. It is a family probably more understanding of you, and one that cares just as intently about you, the real you. Then you have come into modern day living.

As a gay person, there is so much more out there in the larger world which can please you and make you feel part of living at this time in this century with these people who care and will help you, aid you, and allow you to flower to be the best person you possibly can be regardless if you are gay. You will also become the happiest person you possibly can if you don't fall into one of the traps. Above all, you will become the most honest person you possibly can to the person who means most to you ... yourself.

You must decide if you want to take the chance of being responsible for yourself and being honest to yourself and your sexuality and the complexities that develop around your sexuality. You must decide if this is what you want.

THE REALIZATION OF BEING GAY

Growing from a baby into a preteen involves one of the most mysterious and misunderstood periods of our lives. This period is a time of the most dramatic growth of sexuality, a period of rebellion, and the desire for personal growth and independence. It is a painful experience of self-analysis.

Many gay men and lesbians will argue they knew they were gay ever since they can remember. They easily admitted they were "different", and they wanted to open the closet door.

Others, particularly those who have tried to conform to what parents expected and have failed to fill the parent's expectations, are often hesitant about adopting a new lifestyle, ideas of fantasies of which they know nothing and of which their greatest influence, the family, knows nothing. Some have denied being gay to themselves and, maybe, they want to face a decision later. The young person may be in a state of confusion without knowing which way to turn.

There is comfort in the family's established values and ideas. Young people have learned the rules of the family and have adjusted to that lifestyle. But, their ideas, fantasy and desires are different from what they find at home. As their world stretches from the home to the community to the city to the county, they pull away from the specific family values to guess at the values they would like to establish for themselves.

GAY LANGUAGE

The words that many gays use is not really a language different from American English, but there are certain terms that are used that may have a different meaning than what most people expect. To the uninitiated, gay talk can sound like a foreign language.

In American English there are jargons, slang, and colloquialisms. Jargons are words that are associated to professions; "hand me the monkey" meaning "monkey wrench". Slang is using words that are associated to age group; "he looks cool" meaning "nice". Colloquialisms are words that are common to a particular region of the country; such as "he has his druthers" which means "he would rather do this or that" typical of some forms of speech in South Carolina. The gay talk is a form of slang.

Much of the change in definitions was born from the necessity to be clearly understood from one gay person to a second without the true meaning of the conversation being overheard by straights. 'She came over last night and spent the night." He's talking about a male calling him 'she'. Gay people seem to have a difficulty with pronouns, purposefully misusing the genders when talking about the same sex to hide the meaning of the conversation from being overheard by someone straight. "She said ..." may mean "he said ..." Some gays use the slang just for "camp", to act amusingly like a female.

Today, to hide a conversation is less necessary, nor is the campy slang. Gays still have difficulties with definitions and continue to have difficulty with pronouns. They kiddingly say "she" for "he". To state just a few: "butch" meaning "masculine", "fem" meaning "effeminate", "rough trade": meaning "a masculine, physically permissive person that may have sex with you but may also beat you up", "drag" meaning "impersonation of gender", and hundreds more.

Judy Grahm, 20 years ago gave a listing of terms that had meaning at the time because the words were introduced to all but specifically related to the gay person. The words have become signposts of discrimination and hate today depending upon how the word is used and by whom. "Dyke, queer, fairy, faggot, purple pansy, bull-dike, lesbian, camp, gay, butch, and femme". These are recognizable words to most pre-teenagers today. Many terms are used against the homosexual putting his sexual desires as the major aspect of his personality.

There is also a new kind of printed slang or abbreviations made popular through the many publications which seems to have lost all vowels; "NYB lkng 4 GWM who luv 2 wear L" meaning "A New York City black man looking for a gay, white male who loves to wear leather," I think.

WHERE CAN I FIND SEX?

Without doubt, sex is only one part of being gay and, although it is an important part, it is not exclusive. When you develop into adolescence, your sexuality awakens making sex seem very important to both gays and straights.

It is not unusual that you will try some experimenting with your brothers or cousins or friends. You'll attempt experimentation with the opposite sex, but the beginner usually ends in failure and frustration. The gay male often "is suppose to initiate sex perfectly before he knows what sex is." [1] You'll try experimenting with your friends in over-night camp-outs or afternoons alone at home, some fantasy that may be actualized. What your parents never told you is that sex feels good and is fun. Along with having a good time, you realize you are breaking family rules.

If gay, you may venture away from your friends making yourself available to anyone who will give you a sexual thrill, mutual masturbation and eventually to oral sucking. You'll first go to those places that you have heard have reputations for having sex, perhaps the local park toilet or the local gay bar. If you are not 18, you'll hang around until you meet someone, often an older prey who will invite you for a ride or a beer at his house. If you accept, he will try to get you sexually aroused by talking about sex with women, and he will eventually sexually approach you.

Hanging around these outside corners are other boys your own age looking for experimentation or knowledgeable enough that they know what to do particularly for money. These are hustlers, usually too young to legally drink, and often allowing the men to fondle them for money.

Picking up hitch-hikers used to be a popular way for the men to take advantage of the adolescent boys. The car stops. The boy gets in. The man may be fondling himself. He talks about girls and, compliments the hitch-hiker on his build. He pulls off the road or goes to his motel or house, perhaps a beer, and his purpose is obvious. Hitch-hiking has become too dangerous for the driver and the passenger.

Bus stations were once notorious for an older man to be masturbating in a booth and a young boy stiffened by emotion to put his penis through a hole in the wall, a "glory hole" for the aggressor to fondle or sodomize.

Movie theaters were places to make yourself available. By sitting the second seat from the isle, someone would sit on the isle seat, fondle himself, tap his knee to yours or wait for a sexy part of the film to see if you would fondle yourself, and he would reach over. Movie bathrooms were particularly notorious.

If you were old enough to drive, you may have hit a roadside park where in the men's room would be someone exposing himself, or perhaps you would be waiting in a booth making yourself available to him.

At another time Boy Scout camps and camp-outs would be experimentation spots for the Scouts as well as the Scoutmasters. You can guess who were the most popular Scoutmasters for the gay kids.

All of these techniques were for gay men to meet someone for the purpose of a homosexual encounter. Many of the actions involve public exposure and procuring juveniles, and the action too often developed into embarrassment and jail terms, the consequence of sexual lust.

Young lesbians had similar sexually arousing experiences, but the experiences seem not to be as purely physical as with the teasing young boys. Girls often got crushes on other girls, particularly counselors, and the young girls often sought companionship, understanding, a 'buddy" relationship rather than hard core physicalism. There could be some contact with back-rubbing or hair combing, but there was little obvious, overt action from the aggressor. Women physical education teachers, Scout counselors, specific teachers were very much aware of the girl's physical development, but most were hesitant. Gay relationships with females often started with friends of the same age group.

Modern cruising techniques have changed little except the young people today are much aware of what is happening in the bathrooms, more alert of the truth behind graffiti, more conscious of how to get something for what they want to give away. They have computer games and telephone sex lines, and they recognize the "dirty old man" down the block.

As you know, anyone over the age of 18 attempting to have some kind of sexual experience with a person under 18 is against most state laws, and everyone, the active one or the passive one having a sexual release is equally guilty and can be arrested. It is a dangerous game and cost you or your family humiliations and expense. Dealing with the years of a boy during experimentation until he becomes a legal adult has put many gay men in jail.

The adolescent girls of years ago often had the first gay experience with a gay older woman, a school teacher or Sunday school teacher, or perhaps, a girl friend of her own age. Females have their gay sexual experience usually much later than males and often after 18. Again, the young girl is not necessarily a lesbian; she is simply experimenting. If she continues with frequent same-sex relationships, she must then examine her sexuality.

These are not gay commitments because the relationship is only sexual. They are simply gay experiences. Having a gay experience does not make you gay; it is usually just forgotten for the heterosexual.

However, if the young boy or girl continues to frequent places where homosexuals are known to be, regardless if it is for hustling money or pure physical kicks, he/she better look at their own sexual appetites. Even if he/she may state attachment to a person of the opposite sex, the person may be acting as a homosexual.

Today with a more educated society, you can read about homosexuality, read homosexual themes in books or magazines, or biographies of homosexuals in every walk of life which are available at many libraries. If you do read these books or articles at the library, you are not necessarily a gay man or lesbian.

Some schools have clubs for young people to meet others who feel they are gay. You can always phone a gay hot-line listed in the yellow pages for any information and the operator is trained to make the answers the least embarrassing to you. Be honest. Don't lie about your age. They will not ask your full name or address.

Many schools have programs in the curriculum that includes homosexuality in the study of behavior and many of these excellent films answer questions that many young adolescents have.

Unfortunately, many schools prefer to keep their heads in the sand. Most school counselors will, however, direct a student to reading information and maintain the student's confidence.

In his period of the complications of being HIV Positive and the tremendous amount of reading material there is available concerning the danger of contacting AIDS from sexual contact, the young gay male or lesbian is left with a tremendous amount of frustration; common sense yelling to stay away and the physical body calling out to be satisfied. Everyone must be educated with the knowledge concerning AIDS and all must know the penalty of ignorance. Not getting the warning from the national government to the state, local and community organizations, the churches and schools is completely un-excusable.

The real problem comes with middle America's not understanding homosexuality and not understanding that one sexual experience does not determine the child's sexuality. The young person must also be aware of what he/she is doing and if it is going to leave an impression on his/her personality.

IS IT NORMAL TO MASTURBATE?

Remember when you were a small child of six or seven years old you finally realized that your school teacher or nun went to the bathroom just like you do? To you, the new finding may have been truly amazing.

You'll find that the human body is beautifully designed and both the male and the female bodies have desires to be physically and emotionally satisfied, a desire not unlike getting hungry if you need food. When you start to become a sexual person, pre-adolescence, you'll find the body cries out to express itself. You are simply maturing.

Masturbation is a natural physical exercise that teases your sexual feelings and feels good. Most animals, including human beings, do it. Masturbating with your friends is not an unusual activity and it will not make you gay. Young boys often have contests to see who can urinate the greatest distance. Masturbation and urination contests are similar; most kids do it but they are not to talk about it.

What is really important is what the young adolescent is thinking during masturbation. Is he the Indian chief, the guy on the white horse, the hero of the football team, the greatest movie star, the best dancer? The child has a hero, but what qualities of that hero are important to the child? Having a same sex hero is not homosexuality; it's an extension of individual dreams and desires. Heroes fade as did Santa Claus and the Easter Rabbit.

Although some readers may feel that it is incidental to discuss masturbation, the awareness of your own sexuality is an early indicator or your demands, often starting with the thoughts and desires that have led to the first orgasm. You gain control of your sexuality as you satisfy and control sex.

It is not unusual in talking with a mature gay man or lesbian that they remember a freedom of their sexual drive toward the same sex as early as pre-adolescence, and this is common behavior. Most children are just establishing the qualities of the heroes they will try to emulate; a percentage will find a sexual fascination with their own sex. Remember looking through "National Geographic", medical books, or dad's magazines to see naked breasts or a penis?

The solitary activity of masturbation is in itself unimportant unless distorted, but the maturity is necessary in sexual development. Of much more importance is what is going through the child's mind, the collection of his/her desires played out in fantasy, and what this means to the child's mental and physical growth. How has it or will it affect him/her?

Once a person has accepted the fact that he/she is gay, masturbation still continues, but it is still physical satisfaction of the body, but the mind, the fantasy, the illusion of someone or something becomes more clear. The physical body becomes more physically satisfied if the person obtains a partner or another dream.

As an adult and having not obtained that partner of the imagination, masturbation satisfies the physical desire and allows the person to indulge in imagination, but an imagination with a basis of his/her goals, lust, diversions, and desires. There is direction.

With the threat of AIDS, many gays find that masturbation meets their physical desires even though it does not satisfy their emotional desires, and they are willing to compromise. Dirty films, sexy books, pornographic literature, and toys have become the substitute stimulant to expressing this basic, human function during masturbation.

WHY DON'T THESE FEELINGS GO AWAY?

There is a natural pre-adolescent, earlier than a 15 percent of Caucasian girls and nearly half of black girls by the time they are eight years old, a time when boys are attracted to boys and girls are attracted to girls. Each are learning a pattern of behavior of which society approves. Each has accepted the parent's values and the values of those around them. Girls like girls because they are showing behavior to other girls and that's acceptance. Boys demonstrate to other boys and that's acceptance.

Then the period of sexuality moves in. The child starts to become a sexual being. The parents are frustrated watching their baby turn into a sexual being, an adolescent. Girls physically mature at 11 to 14; boys follow a year or two later. During this transition girls of the same age as boys become interested in the boys, but the boys will have little to do with them because the boys are maturing more slowly.

A couple of years later, most girls are sexually interested in boys and society yells "Not yet", and boys become sexually interested in girls and society yells "Don't get caught". Not all girls and boys through adolescence develop strong desires, although the teenagers have been taught that in order to get approval, they must play the game.

Adolescence is the period when the children take a longer look at their parents to find they are not perfect. They have problems. They argue. They make the child follow seemingly unreasonable rules. The parents don't give the child respect for his/her knowledge. The child develops street smarts. The parents lie or say nothing. In fact, the parent's activities are boring to the child, yet the parents still control. The child wants to control, and rebels. (We've probably never been as smart in our lives as when we were fifteen and knew all that was worth knowing. The older we get, the brighter our parents become and the more stupid we seem to become.)

It is sometime along this maturing process, the rebellion within the family unit, the struggle of maturing sexuality, that the child questions his/her own sexuality. Many psychologists say it started years earlier. Whatever theory, the outcome is that some adolescents, both male and female, are gay. The cause is not absolute; the result is.

The gay boy or lesbian is besieged with many questions and few answers, many of which he/she is unable to understand, most of which the parents cannot understand, and brothers, sisters, and friends offer no answer. Even science seems not to understand. Religion denies it. It is difficult to accept an answer of "It happens".

HOW DO I KNOW I'M GAY?

The answer is not going to satisfy you very much; you'll understand the answer as you grow older. The most honest answer is "... you'll know." The realization does not come in a moment, but it is a conscious, gradual self-realization of your sexual desires and pleasures as well as your emotional make-up.

To some, the realization of being gay may come very early in life. 83% of gay men reported having homosexual fantasy before the age of 13. [2] This amazing study should be done of lesbians. Also, how many seemingly straight men have had homosexual fantasies?

To others, the realization comes later in life often after the person has not had a satisfactory relationship with the opposite sex. Others have had satisfactory relationships with the opposite sex and found that something was missing. It was an association that could not be complete, and there was still a desire to be around and involved with the same sex.

No one can make you gay. A sex act or an emotional relationship does not instantaneously change you from a heterosexual to a homosexual if the directions has not been implanted. The emotional and psychological framework must be built before any kind of acceptance of your own being and worth can be established. The actual sex act happens long after you have developed the traits that underlie your being, your personality and make up. Perhaps the sexual act can be the culmination of this previous thinking, but it is seldom the beginning.

It may be very confusing to you challenging many of the ideas you have been taught. You will feel alone, and you'll fight with your own emotions concerning the things of which you have been thinking or dreaming. You'll be confused and, usually, ashamed of yourself. You'll feel alone, misunderstood. Although there is no logical reason to feel ashamed, you will wonder as every child does, what will the next feelings hold? To most children, sex has been taught to be dirty, and now the child is having the feelings of being misunderstood, confused, and directionless.

OUT OF THE CLOSET

It is at this time, fighting yourself and wondering at your own destiny, that many young men and women decide on suicide, and that is a poor solution. For most, the experiences that he/she has had centered around the family and neighborhood and a very few people and a limited amount of experience. Suicide only proves the individual does not understand himself and his/her situation, and with such a vast world of so many people and experiences ahead, suicide is such a drastic, final end.

For the adults who contemplate suicide, the act shows a very low self value, self approval and an ignorance of the individual's worth as well as to his/her friends and loved ones. The broken hearted "...I'll make her pay; I'll commit suicide" makes only the victim pay.

A wiser approach is to read as much about the subject of homosexuality, of being a gay male or lesbian. Expose yourself to the knowledge of what being gay is all about and decide for yourself if this is the kind of lifestyle you want. Knowledge hurts nothing, but may help a great deal to understand yourself and your feelings.

Confide in someone older and wiser. For the young gay, this is difficult to do because the older and wiser people you know are your parents, and they are often too emotionally involved with what they expect from the child's life to point him/her in the right direction. How many horror stories are told of parents rushing their children off to psychiatrists to cure the child of homosexuality? Sometimes the psychiatrist can calm down the physical activity for a while.

Confide in your school counselor, your priest or rabbi, a favorite teacher, but not your best friend of your own age. Take the problems of how you are feeling to someone apart from your group of friends and problems. Call a hot line where you can remain anonymous. You may consult a psychologist with the understanding he/she will not reveal your secret to your parents. Above all other advice, get help. You may feel you can put these thoughts back in your mind, but they will come out again and again if you are gay, and they will fester into other problems. Get help.

The comment is always repeated of "Why would I chose to be gay if only ten to 15 percent of the population is gay and 85 to 90 percent is straight?"

Many would insist that if it were a choice, they would have chosen the heterosexual life over being gay because everyday life would be easier and the possibility of a mate more available. Perhaps this is the reasoning behind "I'm not gay by choice."

The most dangerous of the choices is the person who has very strong gay sensitivities, but prefers to live life as a heterosexual. Often, the person is rebelliously fighting his/her own feeling rather then adjusting to them. The refusal to admit your own identity often breaks out in hatred toward what caused the refusal. One direction of Act Up, a political gay group who exposes the gay tendencies of supposedly straight men who constantly vote against laws which are advantageous to gay, is the very act of exposing the person as gay, an "outing".

Once a person has decided that he/she would prefer the gay life and that other people will consider him/her gay, the term is "He/she came out of the closet", a realization that the individual considers him/herself gay. But the process of making this decision that may include revelations, actions or realizations, may take many months or even years.

Realization of being gay has been a popular trend of the nineties and, to a degree, a very popular catch-word. It holds the alure of being dangerous and exciting, sexy and addictive. Literature has long had gay characters, and eventually books about gays were written. Plays like "The Kiss of the Spider Woman" and "Tea and Sympathy" have been made into motion pictures, eventually to play on television. "Boys in the Band." "Birdcage." "In and Out." It took the motion picture industry close to 15 years after the AIDS epidemic to portray the homosexual as something more than a psychologically disarranged pervert and/or killer. Hollywood skirted the issues of their movie stars being gay; finally Rock Hudson joining the many who had died of AIDS. Then the film industry found they could make money off the gay exposure, and television jumped in with an ABC production of Ellen, who was coming out, and the actress Ellen DeGeneres who was personally coming out also. There were politicians who were running for office who admitted to being gay, and they sometimes won. Athletes confessed. Successful businessmen outed themselves. Even the Vice President of the United States, Al Gore, recognized in a public speech in 1997 that there were gay people. The "Gay '90's" became a trend.

It is probably more difficult for an older person to come out of the closet than it is for a younger person simply because the older person has established more ties, more friends and associates, more things. He/she may be attempting to share a life with someone else of the opposite sex and the husband and wife will have a newly formed relationship once the information is exposed.

Older people than teenagers do come to the realization they are gay, and by admitting they are gay to themselves if not to others allow a personal freedom and victory over themselves. There are many who will never allow themselves to understand the inward feelings, and they have to live not really knowing themselves. Some may know, but they wish to do nothing or say anything about it. These decisions are all choices of the individual.

With all of the exposure, the confessions, the novels, the movies, the television programs, the plays, the pornography, the internet, the personal confessions from statesmen, athletes, businessmen and the average Joe, one would think that the world is well informed of the presents of gays and the gay lifestyles. However, this information, not unlike fantasy, never touches a great percentage of the population. Many people will say they honestly do not know a gay man or lesbian, and they may be right. Many do not want to know a gay man or lesbian for social reasons and/or religious reasons.

Although the figures of ten to 15 percent of the population is gay, we do not know how many are hiding and that want to hide. They do not want to be outed. They want their own private world which may contain happiness to them as well as the confusions of being gay. They would rather live not knowing that a gay lifestyle exists, or they may profess to be gay only a portion of their lives. They probably won't admit any degree of homosexuality. There are in many towns, villages, and cities those that do not have or want the knowledge and sophistication of recognizing anything other than what they are. Thus, the gays flock to the bigger cities or within small groups within smaller communities.

There is a term that all gays hate, "faggot". It means a bundle of sticks that were thrown on the fire in burning witches and warlocks. In Quaker times, witches were often women who did not have a husband or produce children; warlocks were about ten percent of the group, men who would not go to war or reproduce. Both were thrown on the fire for their sins; the faggots. [3] [4] [5]

There are many who still believe in faggots, the "...abomination to mankind", and many supposedly Christians feel their responsibility to God is to get rid of them. The small towns of America that suspect only the local, swishy hairdresser or the owner of the flower shop as gay, still carry a hating attitude against anything which they personally are not. (Legal integration of blacks into Caucasian society implies a one way street, and neither way, although improved from previous years, has not been successful. It is less than 100 years since Hitler sought his "master race.") The parents of gays have found a most successful road to travel, the straight road, and they believe it is the "right" road.

In this age many young gay people will want to tell their parents, and in doing this, the newly admitted gay risks the possibility of the family not understanding and/or accepting the information, maybe even splitting the adolescent from the family. It is very difficult to explain a lifestyle to someone who has had little or no experience with the style. What the parents may know about the gay life may be dated 20 years earlier when there was a very different gay life.

Telling the parents is a very difficult decision, and you probably will be hurting them, making them wonder "What did I do wrong?" Do you really want to do that? Many parents, although they may not admit it to themselves, already know, or really don't want to know. Are you going to tell your parents every little event of your life?

There are some people who feel they must tell the world when they realize they are gay. Don't waste your time. Some people already know. Many do not care as long as you are happy. There are the vicious who will use the information against you. You may lose friends, and you will make new friends. Just go on living as happily and free as you can.

If a person is gay and admits it to himself, he/she can drop a lot of the socially acceptable lies he/she has been telling in an attempt to be liked by the heterosexual majority. No more made up dates, false awareness of the opposite sex, created stories of the broken heart, failed romances. There is a feeling of relief once you are honest with yourself, and this opens you to a more confused world, but a world in which you are not alone.

Perhaps embarrassing to admit, there are some people who will want to identify with being gay to satisfy their own complexes. If being gay gains attention, they will say they are gay. If they can satisfy a desire to make money by wearing the hat of being gay, they will go to that extreme. They are "gay by convenience", their own convenience.

AM I BISEXUAL?

Science has taught us to analyze a substance, we must break it down into parts and analyze each part, and then put it back together to create a whole. We do this by classifying each similar set of parts. For example, we categorize boys from girls because of their sexual differences. We can also separate brown dogs from black dogs because of their colors. It would be unscientific to separate brown dogs as being girls and black dogs as being boys. It would be unscientific to say that sexual differences differentiate brown dogs from black dogs.

Most gays will accept a category of bisexual meaning a person who does not differentiate between having sexual relationships with a man or a woman, and the term implies that the person goes continually back and forth between the two sexes. I question that category as not very prominent in gay life. True, considering a lifetime, a man or a woman may be attracted physically to the opposite sex or to the same sex, but certainly with preference over a larger period of time than the one night stand.

There is a level of sexual activity that we title bisexual for the activity when an individual may be having sexual relationships with men and with women in an attempt to satisfy making a decision on his/her preference. It is possible for a person to have physical sex with both sexes, but he/she has a preference of one. A man may have sex with the guy next door and return home to have sex with his wife, but he prefers one. Convenience may not allow him to have the one he really wants at a particular time, so he may take the second choice. His sexual instincts are toward one sex or the other, although he may function with both sexes.

The group that clusters together to confirm their individuality may call themselves bisexuals, but they are just swinging between two cultures of homosexuals and heterosexuals. The so called bisexuals have no specific social significance except they have not matured to decide what they really are.

There is no difficulty with the interpretation of bisexual being the person who has had heterosexual sex, eventually to try homosexual sex or the person who has had homosexual sex to eventually experience heterosexual sex. The switches may appear at different experiences in a person's life, but this is not the common definition or concept of bisexuality.

So called bisexuals are using just one of the qualities of the sub-culture, sex, and they are identifying themselves by that alone. But, sex is not an end in itself; it is a means to a greater, mature means of loving, a meaningful relationship with another person, homosexual or heterosexual. What they term as bisexual is having the means of getting to this relationship through the act of having sex as their goal.

Sex is not the goal, although it may seem like it is in the adolescent period. The goal is finding something greater than the sexual response which we call love. Sex is only the device that is used to get to the greater goal. Love involves a mental and physical relationship, caring, understanding, patience and a whole list of attributes that are much greater than the sex act. Involvement in a group of people either homosexual or heterosexual in lifestyle with inter-relationships leads often to acceptance, although specific involvement does not guarantee acceptance.

A straight conclusion cliche is "Let the gay guy have sex with one good woman ..." or "One good man will cure her ..." and implies homosexuality will be over. Not true. Many gay men and lesbians have had sex with the opposite gender, and it has not fulfilled them because their search is beyond the physical sex, and sex is a means. The many gays with children are not confessing to being bisexual. Some heterosexuals have experimented with same sex relationships and found it lacking in what is demanded. Some people have experimented with gays and found that to their likings. All people prefer either male or female; there's no other choice.

Although a person may have bisexual relationships in his/her lifetime, a constant flip-flopping in his or her bed is disturbing, and it indicates the opportunistic, hedonistic personality. There are not too many of them.

There are many gay men and lesbians who have never had a sexual relationship with the opposite sex, and it does not mean their lives are lacking. There just may be no opportunity or desire and their lives are filled being gay. The opposite is true. A heterosexual woman may have no desire for a relationship with another woman. There can be gay celibate men and women and straight celibate men and women.

The person who desires only sex as the end objective of a relationship is immature and headed to disaster. Older gay men and lesbians will verify that a mere sexual encounter with no future dreams is usually empty.

Many of the studies concerning homosexuality are relatively new, probably forward from the 1930's, although the literature of homosexuality is well dated in history. With any newer theories about human behavior, always be careful of the people who want to be authorities and those that tie on to the theory for personal benefit. There are a great deal of people who consider themselves bisexuals and fit themselves into the homosexual classification (category) not challenging the fact they can return to a more personally accepting, consenting, heterosexual category.

All people are impressed by status and authority, and certain types of personalities create themselves through education or experience in being the grand authority, and it is easier if the expertise is in a new field. Everyone has experiences, and it is the combination of many people's experiences to be a generality. Otherwise, the single act could just be an isolated event. Generalities, obviously, are not all inclusive.

Whenever there is practically any event or action involving human beings, there is someone who is trying to make money. (Some call it "selling a service".) Books are written, badges are made, posters are sold, advertising guarantees. Even magazines like "The Advocate", the "National Gay and Lesbian Newsmagazine" depend upon advertising from guest houses, cruises, to buying your life insurance if you are HIV Positive, gay flags, china and erotica. For some of these straight businesses, they advertise "gay friendly." Is a bisexual with his wife "gay friendly?"

CAN I LIVE WITHOUT SEX?

Yes, you can if you decide not to participate, but why would you want to? Sex as a means is a wonderful, emotional experience, a physical thrill, a part of being alive and living. Why would you want to eliminate it?

Priests, nuns, and some individuals have decided, or it has been decided for them, to live without the sexual response, and we are all aware of the anxieties, problems, and frustrations that has caused. We read it weekly in the newspaper.

The lack of sex does not imply that a person cannot go through periods of time without having sex. The unattached gay man or lesbian knows that, but the dreams and desires of the person are still there, hoping for tomorrow and the world of a relationship with someone that will fill those dreams. We are aware that many homosexual relationships do not work, probably a greater number than heterosexual relationships because of the lack of financial ties. So? The dreams and directions are within the individual. Even the person who lives alone without any significant person in view has similar dreams. Try again. Try again.

IS THERE A CURE FOR BEING GAY?

In the history of many religions, the act of attempting to reproduce without the logical possibility was a sin against the religion or God. Obviously, the religion wanted more followers, a larger flock to help the church. Some religions were against masturbation. Heterosexual sex carried the idea that the man would marry the woman, thus creating a family and more children, and the church would not prohibit having more children, new members of the church. Let us not fail to remember that religion has been and is big business. Man's function usually attempts to compliment the church.

Through our early history, homosexuality was the deviate and unnatural action which became a punishable sin particularly in the Victorian era. Sometime in our history of religion we had renued that sex was not just for procreation; sex was also enjoyable and felt good. But, don't let the church know you are enjoying sex. Sin was punishable by the church, and the church considered homosexuality a sin against the church, and it was punishable by death or long terms in prison. In the eighteenth and nineteenth centuries, castration and imprisonment were the methods of punishment for these sins.

In the early nineteenth century, medical doctors began to look for a physical reason that some of the population was homosexual although many had always known of homosexuality. All the new, scientific techniques to cure homosexuality began with the assumption that homosexuality was a "bad, degenerative evil" and a reflection of the devil. Bodies were drained of blood.

With a better understanding of the social ills in the early nineteenth century and an understanding that society and the environment are often responsible for the creation of unacceptable behavior, the study of social levels and people in the various levels became important. Psychiatrists and psychologists developed new theories including the social level had a great deal to do with homosexuality, often thought to be a disease of the poor. Physicians insisted on treating the problem as a disease.

Physicians were searching for a cure to the disease and went through some cruel and inhumane experiments for treatment. To list just a few, castration, hysterectomy and vasectomy for gay women and men, and lobotomy for lesbians was performed as late as 1951. Electrical and chemical shock therapy, nausea inducing drugs, sexual abstinence, primal therapy, vegetarianism, astrology and others were methods to find a cure. Although some gays may have stated they were cured, perhaps to avoid the method of the cure, no vital cure has ever been found.

Sigmund Freud in the 1920's felt that homosexuality in itself was not the problem, but that the frustrations and anxieties surrounding the personality characteristic formed and thwarted the emotional development of the individual. Freud was developing his theory that led to the adjusted homosexual lifestyle, the theory we currently hold to be the most desirable, and the current theory of most psychologist and psychiatrists. Actually, the problem became adjusting the individual to homosexuality and to life within the time and place.

Many interested in psychology are still debating degrees of stability and physicians are evaluating the extent of medical attention, but most approach homosexuality as a condition of the individual, a complex mixture of, perhaps, genetics, social influences, personality characteristics, and social acceptance. Most physicians feel that by admitting you are gay, the mere fact that you are more true to your personal emotions and living under less frustrations and anxieties that can manifest has made the individual gay person a happier, more sound and better adjusted individual.

Others will answer that you could have changed your direction by not becoming involved with gay people. Did you hunt out gays, or did they hunt you? You could have changed your direction, but could you have changed your emotions? You may have been able to live without a sex life, but would you enjoy that? You could have lived more honestly, or could you? Someone taught you to be gay. You are defying God's will. You are in partnership with the devil.

WILL I OUTGROW BEING GAY?

Probably not. The emotions will always be within you. You may outgrow some of the sexual desire, but you will substitute that sexual drive with such other expressions as creativity, security, comfort, things, prestige, responsibility, power, wealth and the thousands of other qualities that make both gays and heterosexuals do.

You may outgrow the physical, sexual desire that at one time seemed so strong, or you may become more skilled at controlling the desire, but your basic psychological make-up contains the seeds of being gay as well as the social behavior. You've reconditioned your thinking to the idea that sex is fun and that homosexuality is fun and enjoyable. Although you may become less active in having sex, you are still gay.

Being gay is only one part of life. There are many similarities and some differences in the activities and ways of thinking of the heterosexual life compared to the gay lifestyle.

The natural process of self realization, leaving home, finding a job, searching out friends, finding security of self and ideas, and constantly watching and contrasting the people you know and their ideas is a natural psychological development. It's part of maturity and should be part of the appreciation of being alive.

Who are we? We are individuals that have been born with certain physical characteristics, probably advantages and weaknesses. We are raised into a family, ideally the father, mother, brothers and sisters, into a specific socioeconomic class, and we behave according to the heterosexual rules of that class in that culture. We develop through similar psychological stages like all children. Somewhere in this development there is or was the not typical, someone who has the sexual and emotional preference for his/her own sex. When the person becomes responsible for his/her own choices attempting to be honest, the person may realizes he/she is gay. How the gay male or lesbian handles the information depends upon knowledge of the gay lifestyle, the problems and frustrations of day by day living.

ARE GAYS A THREAT TO HETEROSEXUALS?

Anyone can be a threat to another person if the second person interprets the first to be a threat. You are really asking "Do gays sexually desire heterosexuals?" or "Do heterosexuals feel that gays desire them?"

Start with the knowledge that there are many individuals of both genders and all different degrees of sexual attractiveness. People appeal to people. A heterosexual desires someone of the opposite gender; a homosexual desires someone of the same gender. But, there is also the "forbidden fruit"; the thrill of obtaining the unattainable.

There are probably some gay men or lesbians who desire a physical relationship with a heterosexual, but if the heterosexual is truly a heterosexual and has no sexual desire for his own sex, the relationship will not materialize. The physical relationship, "a throw in the hay", the one night stand will not be satisfying to either except maybe to establish a power base.

To a few gay people, the conquest of a heterosexual into submission is more interesting than the actual sexual conquest. Is the conquered person really a heterosexual except in the case of rape? "You cannot rape the willing."

Most gays are not even willing to attempt seduction of a straight unless they see tendencies in the straight that give him/her permission to continue. There is so much more to the gay lifestyle than just the momentary, sexual satisfaction that even attractive people of the opposite sex are off limits ... to most.

Some heterosexuals are afraid of homosexuals, but they are usually more afraid of their own personal desires than they are of being compromised or conquered. The homosexuals are no threat to the heterosexuals. Those who preach programs of hate against gays are often hiding behind their own guilt or ignorance or desires.

In the world of today, there are many heterosexuals who enjoy the company of gays. With our morality and our open opinions about our sexuality, many gay men and lesbians develop lasting friendships with heterosexuals and vice-versa. Where we lack binding ties is often through the hesitancy of the gay people and their awkward relationship to the heterosexual world, and that is improving. It is obvious in the bars: the mixed bars of gays and straights are enjoying popularity as opposed to the strictly gay male or lesbian bars. For years even gay men and lesbians seemed not to mix well, and most of those days are gone.

Ignorant straights are afraid of gays; stupid gays may desire straights. The truly heterosexual man or woman finds gays no threat to their sexual relationships.

Human relationships are built on a common theme of preferences. If you like a person because he/she likes the things that you like, you have a basis on which to build a friendship. A straight man sitting beside a gay man watching football have the common interest of football. If he has nothing in common with the person sitting beside him, they don't talk except for the original introduction. Your friends are very much like you, or they wouldn't be your friends.

You do have a right to your private side, a side which is no one's business but your own, a protective side of your own life or procedure. You do not want anyone to impose on that part of your life only because it is private, not because it will reveal you as some psychologically strange person. Private things are to be kept private and only your business. You don't have to expose everything. Your friends also have private lives that you have no business knowing about. You don't ask your mother about her sexual relations with your father; it's unimportant and none of your business. People reserve the right to have a private side of their lives, and there are limits to friendships and limits to the amount of knowledge you should know about your friends and your friends should know about you.

DO GAYS AND STRAIGHTS COMMUNICATE?

If two people, one gay and one straight, are talking about a subject in which both people have respect for the opinion of the other, attention is drawn from their sexuality and to the specific subject, and the gender of each makes no difference. However, how often are we in that involving subject matter?

Most of the everyday conversation from each individual is about his/her problems, reflecting his/her life and their friends. Married heterosexuals talk about the difficulties of being married, their mates, and their experiences of buying a house or paying the rent. Unmarried heterosexuals overuse the word "I" and married heterosexuals overuse the word "we". The gay male or lesbian can use the word "I", but "we" grows a suspicious awareness as a different attitude, and it takes time for the heterosexual to accept the "we" of a gay relationship. Much of the everyday trivia of conversation, the "What did you have for dinner?", "What television did you watch?", "Is your family coming down?" is interchangeable between gays and straights although certainly not very exciting for either. The conversations build friendships and caring, but they are mostly meaningless.

Both usually establish a conversation limit beyond which neither will tread as we do with most of our friends of either sex. You become aware of what questions you can ask and how far you can delve into personal conversations until you reach that limit.

The British never ask "What do you do for a living?" which implies "Where do you get your money?" Americans would and they would assume other things. If you answered "brain surgeon", "housewife", "bricklayer", or "poet", it would bring up other stereotype qualities of the employment and the personality of the person being asked.

I was amused to introduce a heterosexual man to a group of men when, in the conversation, the new man referred to "Tony" as his mate, and not only because I had made the introduction (I, a gay man) but the assumption made of the new man. "Tony and I ...", "We ...", "Tony was with me when ..." The listeners turned cold. The new man mentioned that Tony was his wife's nickname, and the interest of the group perked again.

You will meet people, both homosexual and heterosexual, most commonly at the work place, or the meeting after work which is usually more personal. You have in common the working situation, the physical lay out, the bosses, and maybe even the company goals. You share the knowledge of common pay, the advantage and disadvantages of working there, and getting to know and understand the people. The best advice would be to keep quiet about yourself, but that is practically non-human. A person says "a girl friend and I went to the movies last night ..." or "I was with this sailor ..." and she or he has revealed a direction, perhaps unconsciously.

THE DIFFERENCES

There is a vast difference between the communications of the straight person to the gay and the communication of the gay person to the straight because of the content of the message being exchanged.

This subject content does not interest each to the same degree. The lack of a common subject matter creates barriers which are difficult to adjust by each person.

If we are honest about the content of our conversation, we will have to admit that the content is mostly selfish, and we give a great deal more concern to our talking than our listening. In fact, we listen with interest in constant comparison to our own lives and experiences relating the content of the communications to ourselves, and we are a reflection of our experiences. Most adults talk about those things that directly relate to their world, what is happening in their relationships and activities. A straight man talks about his relationships with other people in his business, his wife, his children and their activities. The conversations are rarely universal subjects, matters of great importance. We often lack subject matter of high intellect. Last night's fight with the mate, the kid coming home too late from basketball, the chores of keeping house, and the relationships of the gays is not of great intellectual significance.

The gay person does the same thing. He/she talks about things that are directly related to the everyday events of their lives, the work-a-day world of gossip, laundry and trying to get along with someone of his own sex. There are probably no children. Certainly the straight is not interested in the gay's sex life except for the toleration of it being discussed. He does not re-interpret in his own specific terminology.

The gay person and the straight person, both speaking from their own private biases, have very little interest is listening to the other person speak. Casual conversation is not only the majority of conversation, it is the most significant to each individual, and the gay person and the straight person have difficulty in finding a subject of content that interests each. Talking to someone with very similar experiences, a straight man talking to a straight, a gay woman talking to another gay woman, has much more direct communicating and puts less strain on the conversation.

When the gay man or woman with a partner mimic the behavior of the straight person by adopting of terms rather than experiences, the communications between gay and straight fall apart. If a gay male refers to his "wife", or "marriage", or "she", the straight listener is confused and must translate to his own experience. Like it or not, the country is predominately straight, and the values of straight society are upon all gay people.

There are some people who feel that the American public is much more understanding and liberal than what has been described, and these are often gays who feel that the war for recognition has been successful, and the gays can now express themselves as they wish, in any manner and on any subject. This may be true in groups in larger, more sophisticated cities, but even there many people feel "why expose your laundry". The fighting gay will answer "It's not laundry ..." and we've all heard the follow-up. The point is that there are some gays who cannot put aside for very long their own banner of being gay, and they will interject it into everything, anything, and at any time. They're boring. Most of America is not that knowledgeable or caring about homosexuality, and the subject is rather meaningless to them. Even through the heartlands of small cities, towns, villages, and farms, many of which have gay people living in them, the general public doesn't really care very much, and certainly not discuss the topic. To many people, except the gays, homosexuality is a boring subject.

STRAIGHT SUPERIORITY

Straight superiority is a feeling that gay men and lesbians have when they are dominated by a heterosexual without the knowledge of how the straight feels about homosexuality. It"s the gay person's insecurity coming to the surface. It is someone who has been accepted as better than you without this person having the humanity to accept you or recognize you. It is the stereotype of marrying the boss' daughter, and his attitude toward you of "just not good enough". It may be his disguised insecurity, lack of knowledge or know-how or pure stupidity, but this person's superiority is played out in a bullishness that is degrading to gays. Although unintentional, although it may not be honest feelings, it exists as an attitude superiors often have against those seemingly inferiors.

It is ignored in public but obvious when it's your boss. These are not people to hate. They are people who need your sympathy; those playing the wrong cards of success. Threats to them will only turn them against you. There are some battles you can win directly. Sticking by the bull may be better than the red cape which draws anger. Sticking by does not mean walking in the bull's footsteps. The person may just never have been exposed to gay people; better than the introduction of "Oh, I used to know one".

The superior attitude does mean recognizing job superiority and position. Hopefully, it should mean that you have enough job security, contracts of discrimination procedures and fair employment laws, to be protected against this kind of boss. There is a thin line to walk between the bullish straight boss and the masses of workers who want his blood. Careful. You may someday be in the boss' position.

Straight superiority often looms when someone has found a "right" rule, a principle by which all people should live, something so great that it dominates any other person's ideas. The Born-Again-Christian attitude and the stereotype message proclaiming heterosexuality as supreme are messages and destruction against someone who does not agree, and the conclusion to destroy him. When the Pilgrims took the Indians' land, when blacks were needed as cheap labor, when women should be having sons, when the church wanted more members regardless of the cost in human suffering, when man becomes the dominate gender are all signs of the "right" decisions. We rationalize the decisions to our own advantage.

Let us gays who have found more freedom in the larger cities not forget the stupidity, hatred, fear, anxiety, frustration, and pure pain of many of the minorities, and particularly the gay minority, in the small cities as well as the organized hatred of the larger cities. Show me a large city black community, and I'll show you a local Ku Klux Klan organization. Show me a library that limits what can be read, and I'll show you true threats to our freedoms. Show me bullish superiority, and I'll show you a weak and ignorant boss.

WHO IS AGAINST GAYS?

Whenever there is any minority there will always be the opposite side of the coin, those against the minorities. When the Italians settled in America, there were those against the Italians. When the blacks were freed from slavery, there were and are those against the Afro-Americans. Some people make a career out of being against everything that does not mirror themselves.

The arguments for being against any group are the same; the minority is less than equal, anti-God, against the American way of life, immoral and destructive and history teaches us that all the arguments against minorities are based on superstition, bigotry, and ignorance. It is predictable that there would be a group or many groups against the gays and the gay lifestyle.

It is amazing that the anti-gay groups hide under the banners of the Religious Right or Family Values implying they have the true word of God and that anyone who does not agree with them is misled, evil, and should be punished or eliminated. They are homophobes, actively against homosexuality.

Their procedure is to get into politics, religious groups, school boards, and any organization to present ideas, policies, rules and laws not allowing gays to have the rights as heterosexuals. Fortunately, the American legal system supports that all people are equal and have the right to express themselves if they do not hurt others. The Family Values groups interpret the Bible to meet their own values and discrimination.

Phyllis Schlafly of Illinois and her Eagle Forum are against the ERA and the NEA funding, abortion rights, AIDS education, sex education in the schools, daycare and family leave, and she claims 800,000 members.

Concerned Women of America proclaim a "pro-family" position which includes anti-gay attitudes. The group claims 800 American chapters with 600,000 members.

Many of these groups start locally such as the Oregon and Idaho Citizens Alliances and the Colorado for Family Values group and include the Christian Coalition, and they will probably continue to increase. Most are hidden behind positive sounding titles such as The Christian march of men in Washington, D.C. in the fall of 1997, a seemingly un-political agenda with political influence.

The American Family Association is against pornography, profanity, and the liberal media as well as being against abortion, the freedom of the National Endowment to the Arts, and homosexuality. They claim 640 chapters with 600,000 members.

Notice all these groups are anti-something hiding under terms like "Christian" and "family". I know of no gay man or lesbian that is anti-religious and/or against the family structure. The titles sound positive even though the messages are of bigotry and ignorance. The membership numbers are impressive, if they are accurate. As with any minority bias, the group against personal freedom, the slick interpretations, their influence and their power should be carefully watched by all.

These and other groups with the "right answers" should draw the attention of gay communities because they can easily influence the laws under which we live. They infiltrate into communities of the gay lifestyle often disrupting marches, parades, demonstrations and rallies, an effort to push their own values of "right".

There are some religious groups that are against homosexuality, although an increasing number of religions are including gays in their organization. The Metropolitan Community Church, a predominately gay religious group, has caught the attention of other religions. The accusation of cover-ups of gay Catholic priests have drawn publicity. The gay community is a source of members, and religions may bend rules to get members.

The gay influence is carried into other fields. President Clinton's "don't ask; don't tell" program for the military has been supported by the Military Justice Fund at the 1993 General Conference, a military office for the purpose of gays knowing their legal rights (202 328 32470). The theory was President Clinton's compromise, many expressing failure of the procedure, and failure of the theory.

The travel industry, particularly the International Gay Travel Association, has over 1,000 members and it is composed of "gay friendly" agents who book tours and trips for gay people. Some airlines offer special advantages to the gay travelers. Gay destinations advertise the gay lifestyle of the particular city. Even Disney World in Orlando, Florida, allowed a "gay day" with 15,000 known gay participants. The 1997 boycott of Disney World in Florida by the Baptist demonstrates the rebellion of some religious organizations

Businesses are adding "significant other" to their benefits and pro-gay advantages to their packages. "Gay friendly" has become a welcome sign. Even predominately straight bars are welcoming gays but not because of their sexual orientation. Money.

Although there are many who are opposed to the gay lifestyle or being gay, there is an increased awareness that it exists and it is not going to be closeted. The television show "Ellen" displayed the actresses' character and Ellen DeGeneres, the actress "coming out of the closet". From politics to entertainment to the worker on the line, business is become aware of the power and money of the gay minority. About time.

A FAG HAG

A fag hag is slang for a female who prefers to associate with gay men. Rarely is it a man who prefers lesbians. This woman feels amusement, comradeship, and safety in being around gay men who show her respect, courtesy, and companionship. Although the term seems degrading, many gay men enjoy the company of women, probably more than lesbians enjoy the company of straight men.

Often widowed or divorced, the fag hag enjoys the flattery of the gay men, the attention to her requests. She is often financially secure, and the gay men maintain a mother image type of respect for her without the girlfriend sexual obligation.

There are many heterosexual couples that enjoy the company of gay men and lesbians for the same reasons. Often, the couple is tied to a gay lifestyle through business. If you run a restaurant and have gay cooks and waiters, you'll be exposed to their lifestyle. If you are a book salesman, you'll be exposed. The straight couple accepts more than the sexuality of the gay man or lesbian. If not the business talent or smarts, they like the wit, charm, manners or stories of their friend's personality.

There is in practically every family the unusual "uncle" or "cousin", the flamboyant one who does so much in the arts, and the family is amused as well as concerned. The gay uncle or nephew/niece is maintained as a friend to preserve the family unit.

The single straight or the heterosexual couple may feel no repulsion of the gay friend; a truly straight man is not afraid of losing his virginity and the wife relates usually on a more effeminate level with their gay male friend. The gay and the straight man find many things other than sexuality on which to base their relationship. Why do women with gay hairdressers tell the stylist practically everything?

It is not unusual for a gay person to marry someone of the opposite sex. When the male and female responsibilities were quite different, each desiring what they had been taught to enjoy, a woman may marry to produce children, and a man could marry for the security of a home and way of life. As responsibilities became more similar, the acceptance of the singular person became less of a novelty, and some people accepted the person's lack of interest in the opposite sex.

It is not uncommon for a gay man to marry a woman. Usually, the man is older than his gay group, but younger than his wife, and he has a difficult time competing in the gay game of youth-to-youth. Sometimes, he is just bored with his lifestyle particularly growing older and having so many of his contemporaries dying. Marriage for an older gay man is usually to acquire a more secure way of life. A gay man marries an older, financially secure woman for social assets and personal companionship. These situations are sometimes business relationships that have the external appearance of a normal husband and wife lifestyle, but the major objectives are usually financial and for companionship. The wife is just as aware of the motivation, and obviously willing.

We are also more aware that marriage is a "changing" concept, the individuals still growing and accepting different parts of their personalities that they have not yet allowed to be exposed. One aspect could be the gay realization; a finding that has been un-exposed until after marriage. As a product, many mature gay men have children, but probably not as many as lesbians with children.

WHAT DO I DO SEXUALLY?

This is certainly not a discussion of sexual activities, positions, and procedures. Other books carry those details with pictures.

A sexual relationship develops with an understanding of what you will not do sexually with a partner who has expressed what he/she will not do and, if agreeable, you perform whatever options are left, and there can be many. In a committed relationship meaning one that is for sex and love, experimentation may take place on the "not do" items, but not without both consenting.

When you desire sex, you are desiring the natural biological function that it takes to reproduce, a sensual experience. According to a study done by Revlon, men get erotic pleasure from sight, women get more pleasure from touch and they ranked the senses from most to least as touch, sight, smell, taste and hearing. This is purely physical and means that it is without any emotion except pure lust.

You are probably looking for intimacy, a combination of mind and body, an emotion pleasant to both. Intimacy involves an assurance on your part that you are pleasing yourself and your partner, that you are working toward a committed relationship that is wanted by both. It can have profound meaning of emotional satisfaction that moves toward spirituality, a bonding of souls. Unfortunately, few meet a level of physical and emotional satisfaction that is spirituality.

We give attention to the animal level of the physical and often don't reach intimacy. Or we become selfish in our intimacy and don't think of the other person, and we no longer have intimacy. We satisfy the lowest level of desire, make a half attempt at the second level, and never reach commitment and spirituality.

Making the flesh work and the mind work through the body and into the soul is the goal of a committed relationship of mind and body; not just the physical orgasm. For most couples, the orgasm marks the end of the evening's activities.

Gay men and lesbians play with the same steps of emotion as do heterosexuals. Their failure rate is about the same. It doesn't take much logical thinking to be physically attracted by someone, but that could result in just raw sex. It takes more to be selfishly intimate, and another step to think of the other person's intimacy. Many physical relationship stop at this degree or go one step higher to commitment. "I've got to get to sleep because I have to work tomorrow morning", but it is an excuse. Complete satisfaction of the sexual experience includes spirituality. Few reach this step, either heterosexual or homosexual.

WILL BEING GAY AFFECT MY JOB?

If you are selecting your conquests from the people with whom you work, being gay can certainly affect the way you respond to the people around you. If you are gay and your boss is gay, it can be an advantage or a disadvantage depending upon how you play it. What sexuality does your boss' boss have?

If you brag to your straight work mates of your sexual conquests, your stunning appearance in drag, your roommate's body, your night life, they may be amused at your "difference", but they are not going to understand you. A gay man never gets roses at the office unless he works in a gay office. Your more sophisticated straight work mates may be tolerate of your behavior, and laugh at you behind your back. Your less tolerant will count the minutes you are in the bathroom, and they will tell you their opinion face to face.

The degree that being gay will affect your job is completely up to you, the amount of emphasis you place upon it, the amount you tell or do not tell. You are being paid to do a specific amount of work and to get along with the other employees who are paid to do a specific amount of work. Your effectiveness as an employee depends upon the way you handle yourself, and the way you do your job. That is what should impress your boss; is he/she doing the work?

But that is a business school objective; not a real life situation. As people, we like to be around those of our own kind and our own values. If a gay person is working in a straight office or plant, the gay is not around people who have all similar values. Unless a gay worker can find something in common with the job force, the gay will become the outsider.

Once you have established a rapport with your co-workers, they will put together bits and pieces. Your being gay probably won't be discussed at first, but they will begin to know. If it does matter to them, you are in for hell at work. Nothing is so vicious as someone with the "right" answer.

The gay man or lesbian with a gay or lesbian boss in a straight scene has a much more difficult line to walk. Does the boss admit he/she is gay? Are you competitive? A challenge? A buddy? Does the boss fear you will expose him/her? Are you willing to play the boss' game?

At the time of women's liberation from the sexually demanding male heterosexual bosses, many rebelled in vicious law suits proclaiming harassment. But, there are many who did not rebel and play the game and they may be in higher positions tomorrow. Regardless of the sexual harassment movement, they do what is better for themselves, and some even enjoyed the act. It is still possible to "... sleep your way to the top" in both gay and straight lifestyles. With women becoming bosses, the same values exist, and men employees are suing women bosses for sexual harassment.

The quantity and quality of your job demonstrates your validity to the company, and your personal life is unimportant to your employer, but what I would rather think and what is true may be miles apart. When dealing with people and their jobs, expect the unexpected.

We were once in a period where longevity to a company mattered, a guarantee of employment for as long as the company lasts. That has changed. The average employee will be with six to eight companies in his/her thirties. What seems to count most is the bottom line of profit. When you are 50 years old and more expensive, your boss is aware he can buy two for the price of one employee regardless of how much experience you've had. Keep networking.

There are many awkward situations for the gay man and/or lesbian in dealing with a same sex boss. Women have the tendency to excuse themselves in groups for the ladies' room and should the lesbian with a female boss join the group if the boss knows she is gay? If a gay male and his boss stand together at a urinal, is the gay male and/or the boss overly aware of the other person? When traveling together and sharing hotel rooms, is there a sensitivity on whose part? Does an accidental knee bump on an airline mean a pass from the gay employee? These incidental occurrences point up that the gay male or lesbian and, perhaps, the boss becomes super sensitive to the differences between their sexual motivations where the private moments are more vulnerable.

The gay male or lesbian who lives exclusively in a gay environment with gay friends learns how to handle the private and personal moments with his/her associates. But, the work place can be a threat to the gay who is not aware that he/she is in a straight situation. Many gays who have straight friends learn quickly how to relax in a straight situation.

Feeling comfortable in a straight situation is as important for the gay man or lesbian as it is for a heterosexual to feel comfortable among gays. For many gays who live exclusively in their gay society, they need training of how to be comfortable in a heterosexual mix. Particularly lesbians, the lack of being gregarious and the repeated female insecurity in the equal rights struggle often leave the gay female to fade into the background. The gay male learns aggressive behavior from his rearing, and he may become the center of attention. In an all lesbian situation, the more masculine lesbians seem to dominate and become more aggressive.

The gay male or lesbian who fakes his/her background with wild tales of heterosexual adventures usually falls into his/her own trap. An effective liar must be very intelligent to keep up with his/her own lies. Avoid painting a picture that is not you. At the same time, don' expose yourself (no pun intended) at the workplace. Just do not respond.

If a person is so crude to ask a direct question which, to you, is personal, use your wit to avoid the answer. A lesbian worker was being teased by a co-worker concerning not being married, and she responded "A spinster, yes. But not a virgin." There was nothing more to be said. "Why do you want to know?" usually quiets an investigation, as does "When I know, I'll tell you." When asked how much you paid for something, answer "considerable".

If you work at a larger office, business or plant where there may be a group of gay men or lesbians, the new gay employee should not run quickly to join that group. Become your own independent person. Remember that the gay group can become more vicious than the straight group because they are aware of your vulnerable spots.

In the work force the attitude of the employees is very important, and it is much easier to work at a job where there is a positive attitude, a pleasant work attitude, rather than constant complaining and bitching. As strong as a person may think he/she is, he takes the work attitude home. If you are living with someone, your negative attitude may not be fair to the other person.

Concerning work and the work place, notice that the job is becoming so technical that it can often be done through computers, and this does not necessitate having a work place away from the home. In the future, more jobs will depend upon productivity and the employee will be paid accordingly regardless of where he is physically located. There will be more employment and work places in private homes.

A third of your life, the work place often stimulates gay men and lesbians to leave an organized structure of having a boss, and they want to establish a business of their own. They want to be their own boss. Time, money, the lack of responsibilities of raising and paying for children, freedom of making decisions for which you are responsible are good attributes of a gay establishing his/her own business. Discipline and aggression must be considered. For the gay man or lesbian, avoid the "what difference does it make if I go to work" attitude and constantly fight "I can't do it". Even gays make their own beds.

BIASED?

Of course we are. We all have preferences. Our backgrounds have taught us to like and dislike various things from religions to races to behavior. The problem becomes what we do with our biases. How do we act out our biases.

Do gay men hate women? I have met only one gay man that completely disliked all women, and he had no communication with women; I doubt even with his own mother. The action of his extreme bias completely distorted his reasoning to where he was an unfunctional person, one hated by many, and he got some sadistic kick out of this self-inflicted punishment.

Most of our biases are not so severe. What we hold as a hate with a little education and experience soon becomes something with which we feel comfortable. We adjust to and often eventually like those things to which we were once biased.

Gay men like gay men; that is why they are gay. Lesbians like lesbians, but they also like straight women as gay men like straight men. Most gay men like lesbians as lesbians are often not as fond of gay men because of the unequal pressure making women second to men, a rather strange combination because of the common fight for the same rights. Straight men and straight women may like the individual gay male or lesbians, but he/she does not really "understand" the homosexual, which means he/she is tolerant only to a point. The gay person is tolerant only to a point also. Then, Stonewall.

I'm constantly amazed at how biased and prejudice some gay people are, but no more than the mass of society. The gay person wants the straight community to be tolerant and non-prejudicial toward the gays, but to what degree is the gay tolerant and non-prejudicial toward the heterosexual community? It should be a two way street, but it is not.

We have all heard gays make prejudicial statements toward blacks, Jews, and many other minorities including fag jokes or remarks. Many gays rebel when heterosexuals make fag remarks, but they don't seem to hear themselves making remarks against other minorities. Can I be sensitive only about gay jokes and not sensitive to other minorities? Do I march in only one parade?

SHOULD I LIE ABOUT MY SEXUALITY?

If I were asked 30 or 40 years ago if I were gay, I would have definitely responded "No" because being gay could easily cost your job, your supposed friends, and your way of life. Of course, it was a lie. We tried to clean up the lie by cute sayings like "I'm happy most of the time" or "Do you want me to show you?" as a way to avoid the truth, but the answer was still a lie.

Many gays feel this was a period of lies, and it was, but usually for self preservation. Few people supported homosexuality to the public. The gays were raised in fear and embarrassment for being gay. The gay people hid. The gay lifestyle hid in tacky alley bars and warehouse sections. There was a group, a very brave group, that yelled that if you do not stand up for being gay, the myths will continue about you and your lifestyle, and they were right. They often stood up. Stonewall was a rebellion of the drag queens against the straight police.

I did not want to be, nor did the time warrant, a sacrificial lamb. Perhaps it was small thinking, but I was concerned with my survival, my job, more so than the gay movement. I kept my sex life to myself rarely telling even my best gay friends. It was secrecy and a private lifestyle to be shared with practically no one. As I grew older and retired, I was free to admit my homosexuality because I was independent of the pressures of being gay. Did I lie? Yes. I wish I would have had the survival skills to take a more active part in the liberalizing of the gay movement.

Some of the young people who are willing, if not delighted, to expose their sexual desires to anyone who listens, their families, friends, bosses. That may not be so wise. The person may learn to regret his/her openness. Most people are not interested in your bathroom habits. Do you use your right hand or your left hand with bathroom tissue? Or, should they be. Many people are not interested in your sexual habits either. Why should your expose your habits? You may take the chance of regretting your confession.

Currently, many laws are based on the freedom of choice of the individual, but these laws are certainly not everywhere in the United States, nor do people obey the laws. Your boss may not be able to fire you because you marched in a gay parade, but he can find a reason or method to fire you. Business and government are not necessarily fair. Think of your chance before a jury; one hundred percent of the jury being heterosexual and you are accused of a gay crime.

The gay community has made many tremendous gains in individual rights that were previously given only to heterosexuals, but the clash is certainly not over. Our heterosexual community has many, eager homophobics. The north-western states, the south, and areas of the original colonies will take years to reach acceptance or understanding of homosexuality. In truth, I question if the heterosexual community will ever understand.

There is arrogance with many gays that they feel the rest of their community, town, county, or state should know about the gay lifestyle, and the prejudice against gays. The truth is that many places and people don't care about the gays, their struggles and their rights because many people know no outwardly gay people. They feel there is no need to know about gay people or the gay lifestyle if it does not affect their life, and maybe it will not be important to many. Because there are some gays who know the lifestyle, these gays often assume that all should know what they know. For the activist homosexual, the gay television themes are a bonus in educating the public about gays and their lifestyles. Although there may be gays in every larger city, many do not feel that educating their community is their responsibility. Others feel that it is their mission.

There is a significant difference between a heterosexual and a homosexual; a difference that is played out in each step of our growth from childhood to death. Science doesn't study this difference much; why deal with a smaller percentage of the population? It will, given time.

THE ADJUSTMENT TO BEING GAY

Developing at the same time of the late teens, decisions on college or career must be made. The gay person must make his play for independence from the family, a new set of values and opportunities that he/she must select from a list about which he knows little or nothing. Guess-work. Exposure. Learning. The gay and the straight must leave the family nest.

The gay male or lesbian must either adjust to the gay lifestyle, deny it, or rebel against it. How he/she adjusts sets the foundation of how successful and happy he/she will be in the following developments of personality. Accepting failures, mistakes, or poor or bad judgments is all part of adjusting not only to life but also to gay life. There must be constant self-analysis.

LEAVING HOME

Leaving home is not a day in your life when you walk out the front door, say good-bye to your family, brothers and sisters and friends, get on a bus and go away. That is the final event. But leaving home has taken hours and hours of questioning, days of wondering, pretending, expecting and a constant state of confusion. "What if ..." becomes the introduction to something that you cannot name, an adventure that is filled with decisions that you have made and real confusion as to where the adventure will take you. You'll someday look back and realize that even the specific day was one of the most important days of your life, a day when your life changed.

With the vocational interests of high school, the classes and directions that have been offered to you, the material you have read concerning being a nurse, or plumber, or lawyer, you have some idea of the direction you want to investigate. "I want to be a _____." Your choice of vocation probably has a list of requirements for obtaining the job. You'll have to meet those requirements. You have choices. Do you want to go to college? Do you want to go into the military service? Do you want to move away and get a job? Fortunately, if you realize you are gay, you do not have to get married. Although some marriages with one partner being gay have survived, the chance of success is limited.

HOW DO I GET STARTED?

If you decide you want to go to college, you have done all the applications, waded through the catalogs, read about so many places that your head swims, checked all the costs, and assumed you would attend for the next four years if you make it through the first term. You have questioned how smart you are, how difficult is college work, and the possibility of failure. You have the security of coming back home.

If you have decided you want to go to college, you have selected a friend from around your home, and you will become college room-mates. If you have not such a friend, the college will select someone for you. He/she will probably not be gay, but you'll be so busy the first quarter or semester that you'll have little time anyway.

If you are not living in a dormitory, you can get a copy of the local college paper or a gay college paper and take your chances on a roommate, or you can live alone in a rooming house. Avoid the college sorority rush and pledging no matter to what your mother may have belonged because you will find yourself into the same anti-liberal situation, the one you left at home. Above all, do not select a partner for life with which you will live. Disaster will strike because you are yet to get around, meet other people and ideas, and yet to know yourself. Allow this decision to come later once you've established your life.

If you go directly from high school to the work force, rent yourself a room temporarily until you meet someone with whom you can be roommates, not lovers. You'll have someone with whom you can pal-around, someone gay with whom you can share his/her confidences. Be careful of selecting the older man or woman who may just be smart enough to turn your head while you are going through an investigative age. Relationships are easy to fall into because almost everyone wants one; disastrous in which to get out.

Now you are independent and you realize you are gay. You've moved away from your family original home, found a place to live, and you may have a job or the obligations of college. There seems little reason to hold resentments of your family's limited understanding of your desire, so try to just forget the earlier bad times.

Getting a job may be difficult at first because you do not know the people, the town, or the opportunities. Your finances are probably low, so take about anything that will not hurt or obligate you. You'll change jobs many times until you find the job with the benefits that you want. The first job is usually one held by desperation and usually reflects your working experience in high school. "Well, I can always wait tables."

You will be meeting people that you may have for friends the rest of your life. These are people who do not like you for your money, position, fame or personal influence or being gay, but some will like you for yourself, and this is why you have been struggling. At this age, it is more than acceptance; it's a true interest in you.

There are pitfalls. Some supposed friends will be dishonest. Some will hurt you either knowingly or unknowingly. Some you will find are not very true friends. The only thing you may have in common is that you both are gay. Today, extend this invitation to both gay men and lesbians, as well as heterosexuals.

You were born into a given family and a given circumstance with specific values. You broke away. Now, with a roof over your head and a job, you can make your own choices as to friends. It's confusing, but it will be one of the happiest times of your life, but you won't appreciate it at the time it happens. We rarely do until it's passed.

DO I GO TO COLLEGE?

There was a time in our history that a young man would turn 16 and quit high school in order to work. A young lady's direction would be to have children. If she were as old as 20, unmarried and without children, she would be judged an old maid.

Time has shown us that these directions were limited and did not always lead to happy lives, but the fact that men had a certain amount of skills for which he was responsible, those usually involved in bringing in a living, and the woman had her responsibilities of keeping a clean household and rearing a family, separated the sexes into specific designated goals.

As we approach the twenty-first century, we have made tremendous strides toward equalizing the goals of men and women and, although not as yet complete, we seem to be striving toward the realization that women can do anything that men can do, and vice-versa except have a baby. This opens the fields of employment to everyone regardless of their sex.

It was not always that way. Ohio State University did not allow women in the Veterinary Medicine program some years ago because the three story building in which the school operated did not have a woman's john. Someone came up with the brilliant idea to make the third floor men's john into a ladies' room. Women could be admitted into the college. A woman becoming a medical doctor was the only female in previously all male biology courses. The situation has changed.

Leaving home and an early marriage and children should be avoided by gay men and lesbians because the marriage establishes a set of guidelines that may not be true to the individual's real desires. Although marriage may be a way to escape the original family confusion, the new family unit may bring other complications. Our 53 percent divorce rate is evidence.

The greatest amount of time and energy will probably be your job, and most of us have to work. Be sure that you select a vocation that is emotionally important to you as an individual, not one that someone else or the government has emphasized. Consider what is not needed now in our society, but what may be needed in five or ten years. The government awards money when they find a need for nurses; five years later there is an over surplus of nurses. In what are you really interested? What is your fantasy world? How can you make that world come true? "I just want to be rich and happy" is not a realistic answer. Don't we all.

The gay male or lesbian must realize that he/she will probably be working most of his life as probably will the heterosexual male and female. It is now common for the husband and wife to combine incomes, and also for single fathers and mothers to support their children without a mate. Most of America works, so select a job that you enjoy.

It is wise for a gay man or lesbian to have a job where the job benefits are maximum regardless of the hourly wage. Social security, job growth benefits, health insurance, and dental insurance are important to the single person regardless if he/she is gay. Job discrimination laws, equal pay for equal work, automatic advancement are elements of the larger companies. The gay employee benefits often shape the boss' approach and employee discussion. A unique job in a large company in a large city offers more security for the gay person.

THE JOB

Regardless if you go directly into employment after high school or to college during the next four years, the objective of your experience and your college education is still centered around the job. To Americans, the job is the singularly most important aspect and adventure of living, often coming before the family and, sometimes, worth dying for.

Employment has changed considerably since your parents hunted for a job. Some of the physical jobs are no longer needed by employers for they are done by machines. The emphasis of every company is making money; their objective may not include making the employees happy. If both things can be accomplished at the same time, making money and happy employees, fine. But with the invention of computers, less and less work is being done by hand, and more by machines.

The office as we know it today is going out of style quickly replaced by a representative office, perhaps only a machine that relays messages to the person responsible for getting that job done. We have measured a job in hours but we will soon measure a job by the production done, and you will not be paid by the hours, but by the production. Where you do the production, the office or your home, will be your own business. Of course, there will always be jobs of the assembly line, but even that is becoming computerized.

Work will take a great deal of your time. One study indicates the woman will work an average of 56 hours away from the home. The male will work an average of 61. [1] The single person then has the day-to-day responsibilities of laundry, housework, and the many other domestic chores.

As the worker and the college graduate search for jobs, salary or hourly wage should not be the major consideration particularly for the gay person. It would be wise for you to be very familiar with the policies of the job you are considering. Most of us operate out of necessity and don't investigate a company's views that may affect us until after we have taken the job. Hopefully, you select a job or find a job that has a liberal view toward sexual discrimination.

What happened in the Clarence Thomas prejudice case was to make America aware of the bias toward women and other minorities, and businesses began to adopt anti-bias policies much more rapidly than previously. Matthew Puleo of the National Gay and Lesbian Task Force's Work Project found that anti-discrimination policies have tripled since 1990.

In a study of 1,000 companies in the U.S., 200 responded and of those, 134 companies had written policies which specifically prohibit discrimination on the basis of sexual orientation, and the study was called the Wall Street Project. Can we assume the 800 businesses that did not respond did not have an anti-discrimination policy?

A study concluded that 635 companies said their company does not discriminate, 38% have policies in writing, 34% have management training in diversity, and 6% include training in gay and lesbian issues. [2] There are eight states (California, Connecticut, Hawaii, Massachusetts, Minnesota, New Jersey, Vermont and Wisconsin) that forbid anti-gay discrimination in employment. But, there are always ways around rules.

Ed Mickens' book titled *The 100 Best Companies for Gay Men and Lesbians* outlines the many advantages of some more advanced and liberal large companies in the United States, but these are mostly for the professional managerial employee. [3]

It may seem like tremendous success for the gay movement, but it is barely a scratch on the business level. We must not forget that 23 states have sodomy laws on their books. [4]

Laws and rules do not change human behavior, and the behavior that gays have to fight is that straights do not know their lifestyles and, therefore, do not understand gay people, what makes them tick and how important they are to society. The gay person is wiser to get employment with a company that has at least considered an alternate way of living.

It is a slow, gradual change of attitudes which is not accelerated by quick laws, but is accomplished by proof of gay contribution and happiness. It takes time but many feel the time has come. Anti-discrimination is moving into a lot of businesses, but, unfortunately, many gays will be fired from their jobs regardless of the charges, because they are homosexual. You must admire the individuals that fight bias and prejudice.

The benefits from the employment package may be many, but should include medical health insurance even if you have to pay a percentage. Some plans include dental insurance. All kinds of other incentives may be offered including absences for sick days, protection of significant others, benefits for children, etc. Roughly, you can estimate that a good employment package lifts your weekly income, although it is not in cash, approximately one third. That benefit may not be important to you while you are young and healthy, but it someday may.

SHOULD I JOIN THE MILITARY?

The military offers many advantages to the older adolescent; particularly the advantage of moving away from home and, perhaps moving from a family in conflict. It promises to teach discipline and behavior patterns as well as the ability to secure an education and a profession, and it pays well offering medical and dental services as well as PX advantages, housing and even death benefits. The military life is a neat package gathering most of those things together and guaranteeing them to the majority of American citizens, but not to gays.

Prior to President Clinton, there was a great deal of drafting anti-discrimination guidelines and rules and those laws that would supposedly grant freedom from prejudice of all kinds. The military was particularly appealing to American blacks, but not without prejudice.

Some progress was made.

Riding on the anti-discrimination theme, the newly elected President Clinton promised the gay community that he would lift the ban on gay men and lesbians that had the sanction of the Pentagon, and he tried. But, it was a much larger fight than he expected, one that melted down to "don"t ask; don"t tell", a disappointment for the gay community, and a very thin veil for those who opposed the ban on gays. According to a "Newsweek" poll, 56 percent of Americans disapproved of President Clinton's performance on the gays-in-the-military issue.

President Reagan did not know what the word "gay" meant aside from his studio hairdresser. President Bush had heard the word, but didn't know how to pronounce it.

President Clinton recognized the word and its meaning. Clinton said, "I am the first president who ever took on this issue. Is that a sign of weakness? It may be a sign of madness ... but it is not a sign of weakness." Some gays will argue that at least it was a start for anti-discrimination of gays in the military.

There was a six month action delay agreement in which a decision would be made, and the legal appeals began to pile up. Keith Meinhold with 12 years service was reinstated. Perry Watkins with 16 years of service was reinstated, as was Joe Zuniga. Lesbians like Margarethe Cammermeyer and Tonya Domi fought the gay prejudice of the military. Many of the appeals favored the "don't ask; don't tell" theory, but we will never know how many of the gay military were kicked out for other surface, false reasons. The military anti-gay theory had been acted upon for years often under other regulations. The truth is that the person was released from the military service because he was gay.

Although it may be a start to anti-discrimination in the military, the "don't ask; don't tell" idea is similar to "continue to live a lie" and that is questionable progress. The whole gay movement is tied to "be proud of who and what you are".

In October of 1997, Vice President Al Gore praised the Ellen television character for exposing Americans to understand sexual orientation "in a more open light". The next month President Clinton attended a dinner benefiting the Human Rights Campaign, a 17 year old, 200,000 member political gay organization and stated "if we are ever going to build one America, then all Americans - including you and those you represent - have got to be a part of it."[5]

Undoubtedly surprising to President Clinton and specifically to more liberal minded Americans are the masses of people which are anti-gay, and these are often the backers of the upcoming Family Values movement that are gaining force. These various groups are holding prejudices of all kinds, against women, blacks, Jews, and anything different from what they are. (Remember that Hitler supported a "master race", and many supported him.)

To the young gay man or lesbian, avoid the military as a career choice. The time is awkward and probably incompatible with what you believe. There are few gay related military organizations, none sanctioned by the military. Being gay, you are left in the power and at the discretion of heterosexual values that do not want your participation. You can look forward to years of fighting for gay goals and rights, perhaps only to be dismissed on some other charge at the end of a long career.

For the gay men and lesbians who are in the military, and there are many, walk cautiously. You have to decide if being in the military is worth walking the tight-rope which you have made your career. Particularly lesbians who have had to fight the gender bias and the glass ceiling to job discrimination, it is going to be a very bumpy, awkward walk. You must think now while your mind is clear "what if _____?" Even in the fall of 1997, the military admitted to "...looking into" the sexual harassment charges of some military ranks from the women under their command.

Few in the gay movement are really for equal representation in everything, a ten to 15 percent gay representation in jury service, judges, church groups, etc., but they are for the principle of the door being open to gays, not the door slammed because they are gay.

For the activist, the military is the next battle front. The gay community will not be satisfied with President Clinton's policy for very long, and the unity of the gay vote is becoming increasingly strong. However, the religious right is also becoming more strong and vocal. A clash is imminent.

There is the built-in consequence to the job of being in the military. The job is to protect the United States, and that could mean sacrificing your life. "The fear of killing rather than the fear of being killed was the most common cause of battle fatigue in World War II."[6]

NOW WHAT HAPPENS?

You have your education, the break away from home, a place to live, a job, and you're gay. What's next?

You'll find that you are drifting further away from your original family home. Those every other week visits from work or college are getting further apart. It dwindles to once or twice a year. The letters home get fewer; there is less that you can tell your family. If you have come out to your family, you don't want to bore them with the details because they probably wouldn't understand or appreciate anyway.

You are concerned with the facts of your brothers and sisters and friends. "Who's getting married? When is the first nephew? Is everyone healthy?" You understand that the family is not that much concerned with your real life. If you have not come out to your family, information such as "Who are you dating? When can we meet him/her? Are you serious?" will continue to irritate you. If you lie to them and create a false identity, you'll begin to confuse yourself and drift further apart.

Your newly created family of gay friends becomes more important to you, perhaps losing yourself in the details of relationships and activities. You spend more time with them. You've sorted out those that seem not to please you as much and built those friendships you like.

You become centered around your job or career because that allows you the financial freedom to be around your friends. You start to make friends at your job. You avoid the heterosexual advances, or play them to your advantage in socializing only when you want. You look for advancement, more money, a higher position.

You begin to realize the drudgery and repetition of everyday living, the fact that laundry has to be done, the room cleaned, the clothes ironed, shopping for groceries, and sending birthday cards. You realize that a lot of living is tiresome if not down right boring. You take a second job to help the finances or you indulge in just another beer. You begin to feel that the whole world knows your life and lifestyle, and you do not care. You are waiting for Mr. or Ms. Right to get you away from such an uninteresting way of living. You review your life over again searching for your own self worth.

What you probably have not done is to look at yourself closely enough and determine what you can do to improve yourself. You are satisfied with yourself so far, but you've traveled only a portion of the trip. The next step is to look at yourself for the future.

A MIRROR

This is not about the gay person who preens for hours at her hair or make-up, or the guy who catches himself in the mirror and sucks in his stomach or constantly combs his hair, the posing for masculinity at too many bars. This is about really looking into yourself.

Too often we do not really look into ourselves, our personality, and how we translate to other people. All want to be liked, but few really do much to make themselves liked. Many dismiss criticism by saying "That's the way I am." Wrong. "That's the way you have made yourself." Take a look.

You must never ask a friend to tell you what in his/her opinion is wrong with you, because if he/she is honest and tells you, you will probably no longer be friends. You have to do it yourself. Look at yourself. Listen to you talk and react. Listen to what you say and how you say it. Look inside you. How do you like you? You have to like yourself before someone else will like you.

There are some men who do not like women, particularly lesbians. Some women don't like gay men. Some lesbians don't like men particularly gay men, and there are some gay men and lesbians who don't like anything.

Role playing is demonstrated in the gay bars which, at this time, are male dominated. A drag queen comes in and moves to other drag queens sitting at the bar. The leather stud comes in and sits down from others in leather. A group of four or five lesbians come in and huddle and talk among themselves too rarely moving out of the group to talk with anyone else. The lesbians tend not to be out-going and aggressive in the conversational grouping as gay men. Is this just a throw-back to our previous training? Is the security of a group that necessary? Are we afraid of what? Look how we behave day-by-day.

Gay men and lesbians are a strange combination based mainly on the fact that each like the persons of his/her own sex. The role of being a gay male and the role of being a lesbian are very different. Perhaps a better combination would be the gay male and the straight male, the lesbian with another woman, but history shows that this combination has severe limitation. The lesbian is often afraid or not interested in the gay man; the gay man hesitant for moving into the lesbian's space.

Gays are strange beings in that they play games with the straight world as well as among themselves. They have a desire to be natural, but it is difficult for them. They really want to be friendly, but sometimes they don't know how. They become defensive. They don't look at themselves very often.

Look at yourself in a mirror. Yes, you do care.

APPEARANCE

Sometimes you have to play the appearance game rather than the comfort game. Of course, a suit or a dress is not as comfortable as a sweat shirt and Levis, but it may be necessary. (Not a dress for you, Bill.) Comfortable clothes are for the privacy of your home and you can wear them to your local bar or to the grocery store. You don't have to live in them.

Sometimes, you have to play the appearance game, to look as conventional in your clothing as the majority. Levis and a tee shirt are not appropriate attire for most interviews. Skin tight clothes are equally inappropriate. A business suit may be necessary. Lesbians, you may have to wear a dress. Gay guys, stay out of the dress; it's not appropriate to all occasions. If you are in public at a concert, at the theatre or dinner at a nice restaurant, you don't have to advertise you are gay by what you wear. The difference in accepting yourself as gay is that you are aware of playing the game of expectations, but you still know who you are. You don't have to wear the symbolic clothes or the scarlet A. You can be a little versatile, and a little more interesting. The gay male does not have to fit himself with a ruffled shirt and skin tight pants, nor should the lesbian always wear bib-overalls.

The stereotypes of the effeminate gay male and the bull lesbian are still with us, particularly in less sophisticated areas. The way a gay male looks and the way a lesbian dresses is becoming less of an indicator of their sexual preference. In fact, some straights will "out gay dress" any gay person. Television popularizes the stereotypes. The general straight public is practically becoming conditioned to not being surprised by what people wear, but there are gay stereotypes. Gay men and women in athletics, politics and film are conforming to a standard that is simply appropriate clothing, not gay or straight. Being appropriate does not necessarily mean that it is bad or inappropriate to the gay.

There is something very nice about entering a bar of beautiful, well dressed women and handsome, groomed men even though it may be a gay bar. It shows a certain amount of being aware on the part of the gays; of being able to conform when it is relatively unimportant, of not carrying the gay rights banner to every event.

Be careful of the rationalization of "natural"; as God made it. Can you imagine the true Tarzan living in the jungle for 20 years, fighting animals. eating raw meats, bathing in lakes without his nails or hair cut. His breath and body odor alone must have been enough to kill the wild beasts.

AVOID STRESS

Most people consider stress as a mental problem, one that cannot be physically and specifically located in the body except for somewhere in the brain. Stress can affect the physical body in its many physical outlets as nervousness, anger and rising blood pressure to other mental processes as imagination, frustration and anxiety. If stress is not in itself physical, it is a function of the mind that directly affects the physical as well as the functions of the the mind that are currently not considered physical. Regardless, stress exists and it can be controlled through brain altering relaxants.

Stress is the taking of an idea or impulse or physical reaction and elaborating it to such an extent that it becomes out of proportion to its actual importance. It is taking that one reaction easily solved in a healthy mind and blowing it up to an extreme where it becomes all important, and reacting to it as all important through our physical body and mind. The fact you missed the bus last night is not going to end your world.

The extreme example is paying the light bill as the most important, dynamic, colossal event of the world. It is a common occurrence pulled to the extreme of reasoning. The singular problem breeds to other mental and physical problems. "I have a headache. My back hurts. My stomach is upset. My mind is slipping." No one has said that the mind is logical. Maybe it just reacts.

"I can't pay the light bill because I don't make enough money. I'll quit my job. I'll give up the apartment. Where will I live? How can I go on without having a job and a place to live?" The projections and rationalizations continue until a large mound of problems of life and living have been formed, the rationalization and extreme of not paying that damn light bill.

Certainly not to this example's extreme, but we constantly put ourselves into stressful situations and experiences, and most of them we solve with little problem. However, there are certain times when a minor event is thrown out of its significant content and pushed to the extreme. The office joke used to be "he has a short fuse today". Anxiety is high. Stress level is high.

One solution has always been to have a drink and forget about it. That only prolongs the decision or enlarges the problem, or kills the drinker. Popping an anxiety relaxer pill is also not meeting the problem. Avoidance doesn't work.

We all learn little tricks we play on ourselves to get us through a difficult time. "When I am solving the world's greatest problem, I take a walk alone. I go by the ocean to see what a small grain of sand I am compared to the whole beach. I run the dog. I sleep off my problem."

The gay man or lesbian finds that the most stressful times are in his/her relationships to other people. Although you may like to say "Can we talk about it tomorrow…" you cannot. "I said this… You said that…" doesn't work. The communication may be cleared through time.

When you see the possibility of a stressful situation, don't be afraid to run and not face it immediately and, perhaps, it may go away. The Indians said to meet your attacker face on, but there are few alive Indians to admit it. There is no dishonor in running away from your problems at that time. Get your stress level down and go back to the battle field. Think of all the good and bad decisions you've made under stressful situations. That's not very encouraging.

CAN I SPEAK PROPER ENGLISH AND SMILE?

There is no greater social indicator of your intelligence, education, and background than the way you speak, your grammar, and the level of English which you speak. Open your mouth and say something, and you have surfaced your background. What you say and how you say it from that mouth can be to your advantage or it can play against you.

We know that proper English is learned, and we learn English as children from our school, our friends, and our family. If our parents were not so fortunate to have schooling that emphasized proper English, we have probably picked up some English which is not considered as proper, and although the language may communicate the message's meaning, the language of the message tells something about the education of the person giving the message. If my grammar is so poor that you imply I have little education, you may be right. But, why do I have to expose a limited education when I can speak properly and be understood by all educational levels of society, and to those who do not speak properly, and still get my message across?

George Bernard Shaw's "Pygmalion" teaches the low class person how to speak and act and raises her level in society. Most people are as equal or better educated than the generation before them as most make more money than the generation before. You probably have a better job than your mother or father. Have you advanced?

There is a combination of three which go together; education, money, and social position. Our implications are that that these three in combination will bring happiness, but we have learned that is not necessarily true. None-the-less, having education, money and social position does not hurt the person. They are positive American values.

There are a thousand exceptions; the stupid kid that inherits a fortune, the village idiot who is the king's son, the farm boy who is brilliant and discovers a new medicine. In American life, not as much in British life, the three qualities are aids to financial advancing, social acceptance, and happiness.

The insecurity of gays has certainly placed a large emphasis upon education, money and social position. The three qualities become steps to get from where you were to where you want to be. They are all aspects of making you a better person, better than even your parents.

Speak without all the "uhs", "you knows", and "mans", the meaningless garbage of English that does not communicate. To speak with dirty words or swearing does hide the message of the communication. To constantly talk means you are having hearing problems or you have not learned to listen. Are you afraid to speak in public?

There is a time when you are first away from your birth family that you take a new friend home, and you feel a little ashamed of your family. You'll outgrow that feeling as your experience grows and you realize that there are many others who are initially ashamed of their family only to understand and appreciate them more as you mature. Remember how non-intelligent your family was when you were 16, and since then they have gotten smarter and wiser? You've just grown.

Another aspect of growing which is a carry-over from your birth background that may not have been quite as proper as you wished is simple manners. It is strange that in a great educational system as the United States, few schools, if any, teach manners. They are learned like language and the way we speak. We don't put a great value on manners because Americans tend to put the largest emphasis upon acquiring money, but it may be necessary to have manners even if you are a popular, wealthy singer. Proper manners cannot harm you; poor manners can show your limitations.

All of these characteristics of proper English, the ability to speak well, and the use of manners are socially derived attributes that anyone can lean. Part of maturing and looking into the mirror is to pin-point those characteristics of you that can be improved, and it is up to you to improve them. If you could not add, wouldn't you learn to add?

It may be wise for you to know some older people who speak proper English with unobstructed speech and who are mannerly. Just watch, listen and compare their actions to your own actions. Mimic them. You can learn a lot from them; and they are willing to teach if you make them aware that you want to learn.

The standard excuse is "that's the way I am" and that is a person who is not growing. "I pick my nose. That's the way I am." There is a responsibility of the person who cares enough about himself that he/she is willing to do something about it.

A pet peeve is people with rotten teeth that will do nothing about them. The excuse is usually money, but they can go through many dollars without ever considering to spend a few cleaning up their mouths. Since the mouth and, thus, the teeth is where the ideas come from, anyone who is listening to you is looking directly at your mouth, and a set of rotten teeth is not the most pleasant view. Again, "that's the way I am" is fighting " that's the way you allow yourself to be".

If you are conscious of putting your hand in front of your mouth when you laugh, of holding your head down when you smile, of even looking into a mirror and not smiling, check your teeth. You don't need the Hollywood version of choppers, but your mouth should be fresh, clean and inviting. Is it?

DO I HAVE A SENSE OF HUMOR?

Humor and attitude go hand in hand. You must have a certain amount of maturity to look at something supposedly humorous and find that it is actually laughable. If you have the maturity and lack the attitude to find it funny at the time, the joke will lack the humor, and you will react accordingly. At least, be pleasant enough to smile.

Can you teach humor? It is possible to teach the qualities of humor such as timing, appropriateness, pacing and content, but even controlling those qualities does not create the ability to make someone laugh. You can get positive reactions from your audience even without them laughing. Humor is not only joke telling. It is often a way of telling something that makes you, the humorist, seem human.

Our greatest source of humor is the ability to laugh at ourselves, but not as individuals, as a group of people who have so many things in common, the human race. People continue to make the same mistakes. We've all entered a room with our zipper down. We have all misunderstood and said the wrong thing. We all have misused or misunderstood a word. Our basic concept of humor is the universality of the subject matter.

We laugh at ethnic humor because we have stereotyped the characters with many attributes that we assume they have. "The big ma-ma said…" and we have drawn an image in our minds. "The moron was walking…" Another image. "The Catholic priest was serving communion and…" We form a framework of the characters involved before we have ever heard the circumstance.

We find the direct attack on another person humorous because of the aggression of the joke teller. "You are so ugly that…" may offend, but give the line a character as "My mother-in-law is so ugly that…" and we accept the character.

We like people who put humor into their own terms and make fun of themselves because we have all laughed at ourselves realizing how stupid or awkward or inappropriate we have behaved. "I was so dumb in school that…" Since we have all had similar experiences, we like to play in the common framework of relating to these experiences. We like the person who tells the story because he does stupid things like we all do.

Humor in the social situation can also be an alibi or a crutch to a conversation that you would rather avoid. We have all met the joker that never reveals a serious side of himself assuming he is pleasing everyone with his stories. We bore very quickly of him. There are always the Good Time Charlies that are never serious, hiding behind their humor. There is also the person that feels that if something is good, more is better. "I have ten jokes to tell you." He starts, and his audience falls asleep.

Some people look at the amusing side of life as the realistic side of life. "Just pay taxes and die." Seldom does anyone look at life as a total joke, the subject is serious, but the person prefers his philosophy of living to have humor. Newspapers and television present too many serious subjects from famine to forest fires, from floods to frustration, for everything to be light-hearted.

Have you met someone who could not "lighten up", be happy, maybe silly, maybe irreverent about a topic? Is he strained, afraid of not being accepted for making a mistake of not pleasing his audience, and appearing human? Is he stretching to find and relay the humor? The lack of humor, not allowing the freedom to laugh, makes the person too serious and not much fun.

DO I KNOW MY OWN EMOTIONS?

Going through puberty, the physical body changing from a child's growing body, developing sexuality, and into adolescence is a natural process of a healthy body, an evolution of growing. There are times of confusion and questioning.

Somehow in this wonderful growth through puberty, there is an amazing time clock established on a 28-day cycle that affects the physical rhythm of the body getting ready for reproduction and we call it the menstruation cycle. Both men and women go through this physical, measurable cycle although most men are unaware of the emotional swings, and the changes directly affect the emotions of their own behavior. Heterosexuals and homosexuals develop the same way.

During this 28 day cycle, there are times when the physical body and its health and development affect the energy level and emotions of the person. The time for the female to receive the male sperm is around the fourteenth day after the menstrual flow, thus the scientific basis of the Catholic rhythm system. These are the days the sexy couple should avoid if they do not want children and use the days before and after to enjoy the intercourse. The fourteenth day is only the mean, a way to mark the highest degree between two extremes, and many females are not average.

The influx of emotions and their responses happen in a reasonably predictable frequency and the emotions, highs and lows, can be charted. A male's emotional 28 days can also be charted, although few men ever do it. We all know there are some days for both men and women when your thinking seems to be more clear, your attitude is more positive, your direction is better defined, and the reason may be something that is happening within the unique structure of the body.

You probably know yourself a lot better than what you may realize although hasty ideas or decisions can be affected by the physiological body. The old expression of "I'll sleep on it" prior to making a decision may have some scientific reality. The phrase avoids making a hasty decision that may be a novelty and when the new idea wears thin, practicality steps in.

Out with the old yellow pad. Write down your emotions and desires. Go over the list for a long period of time. No hasty decisions. Get to know yourself. Many have described the personality as a flowing stream, ever changing, and there are certain rocks, ideas or desires, that are constant. Get in touch with yourself, your physical self as well as your mental self. What makes you tick? What is the rhythm of your ticking?

The gay movement in the United States is part of a much larger movement, the anti-discrimination movement and a recognition of minorities. From the ownership of slaves forward in history, the American philosophy of democracy has been that all people are equal; some may want to take it back to the formations of religions, the earliest teachings. All races are equal. All religions are equal. Women are equal to men. The old are equal to the young. If these concepts are not true, we know of no document that scientifically proves the superiority of one group over another, although there have been many writings attempting to prove superiority.

The government of the U. S. has been attempting to put these equalities into the laws that govern this country. Our goals are that the United States is against discrimination of any person who has charac-teristics over which he/she has no control; the sex, the color of skin, the social or financial level of his/her family, the nationality, the hand-icapped, etc. It is a very idealistic goal; one that takes constant tuning of our laws. Although it may not work completely or even fairly, the goal creates the Democratic stew of laws governing our country.

Our work is not complete, but look how far we have advanced; freedom of religion, freedom of choice, freedom from hunger, freedom of acquiring an education, etc. The goals are that all of these ideas should apply to all individuals equally.

Within the last 50 years, refinements in preserving these freedoms have taken place. Although there is still black prejudice, we are working toward social equality. Although there is still bias against females, we are working toward equality of education and equal employment and wages with males. There are many more unresolved issues. But, we are advancing toward our goals.

Let's not forget how far we have come. There was once Irish prejudice, anti-Italian bias, segregated schools, resentment of Jews and their religion, no understanding of Oriental religions, religious wars, etc.

The gay man or lesbian must realize he/she is part of a minority called "gay" and is a part of other American minorities. One night club entertainer described herself as "a Jewish, Afro-American, middle aged dyke with no money". The gay minority is more than based upon sexuality which changes the values of gays, but sexuality being a pretty basic drive to most people. But, we are still minorities by what many people feel is our choice, and we evaluate our choice by the quality of the social values in the society in which we have placed ourselves.

The majority of America does not fully understand the gay minority. A "Newsweek" poll indicates that 56 percent of Americans surveyed said they have no gay friends or acquaintances.

Advice to the gay man or lesbian: Get to a gay community, a society that understands you and values you.

WHERE DO GAYS LIVE?

That is pretty much like "Where do elephants sit? Anyplace they want to". With ten to 15 percent of the population being gay, they really can live anywhere they want, but there are some laws and other pressures in which the laws against being homosexual are more strict than other places. A distribution population study indicates that 9% of gays are in larger cities; 3% left in small towns.

It is not unusual for a gay person to remain at home or in his own home town or city. He/she has the security of the family and friends. Many move to the nearest larger city usually for job opportunities, and they are often close enough to their home town to maintain their family and friends, yet far enough away to give the gay person some anonymity and the opportunity to meet other gay people. Others leap across the continent to gain anonymity.

There are gay people and a gay culture in every city or larger town in the United States and the world. The amount of freedom they have to actively socialize with other gays depends upon how liberal the community may be, how tied to the activities of the town, how much tolerance the individual needs, and how demanding the town is of the conventional lifestyle.

It may be possible to generalize and say that gay people move from their rural homes to large cities, but so do heterosexual. The difference may be that heterosexual return to less populated straight areas with their families, and gay people seldom return for good.

In some countries, the gay person is not allowed a gay social structure of acceptance and society, and homosexual activity is either not recognized or against the law. Individuals cling to individuals or gay activity continues without any or much comment.

In the United States, there are few larger cities or even moderately sized towns that do not have their local gay section, but they can be as dangerous as the city park, to public bathrooms, to a bar frequented by gays. The gay bar is where many gays meet new people. There are many alternatives to meeting new people at gay bars.

There must be caution given to all gay men and lesbians that the bar is not the only place where gays can meet. Bars are out to make money and they seldom care who spends it. In a gay bar most of the people are probably gay, but that is not always true. The only thing you may have in common with the person sitting beside you is that he/she is gay, but maybe not. There are few requirements to get into a bar except either the money for a drink or the ability to get someone to buy you a drink. Little else. Too many people have spent their entire lives saying that are waiting for Mr. or Ms. Right in a bar. It can be a trap. The alcohol can be another trap.

Younger people today have found alternatives to the gay meeting places of the past. Events and activities they attend open other ways to meet gay people. Social clubs, religions like the Metropolitan Church, special events such as the Gay Olympics bring gays together. There are cruise ship tours, traveling, beaches and all kinds of events that encourage gays meeting gays, many that do not include the dependence upon alcohol with the new, health conscious generation.

Another trap for the gay going to the large cities is that he/she often does not make straight friends in the new place. No one wants to live a 100 percent homosexual lifestyle without the contact from the 85 to 90 percent of the other people of the cities, America, or the world. Some fall into the trap of working at a gay place, going only to gay events with only gay friends, and their lives need more.

It is time to preach that being gay is only a part of your life, although it is a part that directly affects your behavior, your interests, your goals and ambitions. It is the stuff that dreams are made of, but it can dominate you. You can become so involved that you cannot see aside from the gay lifestyle.

All people like to cling together in groups that have something in common. In a group of similar people, the individual feels secure. He/she creates a family of friends, people with whom he/she wants to share common experiences. Blacks stick with blacks. Jews cluster. Young families make friends with other young families. It is no wonder that gays prefer to be around other gays. But, each group must know that there is something outside of their special interest group.

The gay community is particularly exciting, often creative and artistic, today composed of both men and women intermixing with unique and foreign languages and a marvelous ability to laugh at themselves as well as each other. Generally, the gay community has money and they spend it on their own amusements of dinners, parties, homes, cars, all the lavish things that anyone probably wants. It can be a fabulous, extravagant, fulfilling lifestyle.

Something must be said for the thousands of gay men and lesbians that are not part of the "in" or "daily flow" of gay life, people who live reasonably happy and content with their lives although they are not in the full swing of the gay social set. Many are older and, surprise, have found many other things to occupy their time except for a lover. Many have other obligations and are leading their lives the way they want to. Not everyone who is gay should be "outed" or "come out of the closet" as long as the gay person is aware of what is there.

With the current threat of becoming HIV positive, the gay values of live day-by-day seem not to have curtailed the fun spirit. It has intensified having a good time with reservations on sexual activities. The gays take more risks in business and gamble more and appear to be living a rather panicked pace, but they are extremely aware of their health. They may appear to live a carefree lifestyle, but there is a sense of caution and fear under that shrill laughter. The gay lifestyle attracts liberal heterosexuals to join them because they seem to be having a wonderful time.

Go into any artistic community of any larger city and find an area filled with hair dressing saloons, art galleries, antique stores, specialty shops. Follow the local swish into a bar and it will probably be a gay bar, and you will find a gay crowd. But, don't let that alone be your guide. There are many gay men and lesbians in the more mundane business offices, sales rooms, libraries and warehouses than what most people realize.

The liberal, gay places in America are constantly changing and they will continue to change depending upon the laws of the community; laws which protect their way of life from fear of prejudice, bigotry, and bias. Today, some of the most liberal areas are Coconut Grove of Miami, Polk Street of San Francisco, Fire Island, Provincetown, special sections of Hollywood, Los Angeles, Chicago and New York City, but cities constantly change and the gay areas change. Once the Village of New York seemed very gay; today it is not as much. Every large city has its special area, and they are not difficult to find.

Most medium sized cities have gay sections, but these are usually not so flamboyantly advertised. Medium and smaller sized cities like Oklahoma City, Columbus, Ohio, Detroit, Michigan and the list is endless have gay sections often in the lesser expensive parts of the town and often sharing the street space with rowdy straight bars, topless bars and adult movie houses. Only the rural, family oriented, off the main path, little towns seem to lack gay neighborhoods, but there are gays there. Try a local straight hotel bar, the sportsman bar.

Various states have gotten reputations among the gays of their laws being lenient enough to allow gays a certain amount of freedom. Perhaps the most progressive is California. According to the U. S. Census, 1990, 25 percent of the nation's 154,130 self-identified gay or lesbian couple households live in California. Vacation spots like Florida and New York, masculine states like Texas and Arizona and Nevada all have gay bars. The coastal states seem to have more, but they have a more dense population. The traditional South like Tennessee, Arkansas, and Georgia seem to have fewer, although maybe they are better hidden than states like Washington and Oregon that have stricter laws.

There are many books that show the locations and give descriptions of the shops, bars, and businesses that are gay or gay friendly in all countries of the world. Get a copy of "Gayfellow Pages." Each gay area publishes newspapers and small magazines advertising their spots of entertainment and their activities. Most gay bars have free magazine racks of local publications. Most cities have gay hotlines for details of events or to know what's happening where in the city. Even some libraries carry everything from local newspapers to the "Advocate", probably the most popular of gay news magazines.

Remember also that you are not stuck to one large city. There are many which offer many different directions and you may want to investigate several and you may end up living in a few. We are a mobile society and our employment or our sense of adventure may take us to many different places. Where is it written that we have to settle in one place?

DRAG

There is a gay form of humor that gay males often use that is partially historical based on a period when conversation had to hide gender between two gays in a public place for fear of being overheard. The "she said ..." meaning "he said ..." It makes the males sound like they are talking about women when they are really talking about men, or they have reference to a make-believe woman. The gays call it "camping"; gay males talking as if they are females. "As he came over to me with his muscles, what's a poor girl to do?" is campy, gay talk.

In accord with the conversation, pretending to wear or really wearing ear rings, a necklace, a female wig, pretending to be female is a form of humor; "drag humor". The gay male is not trying to hide behind some other created personality, but merely having verbal and visual amusement with a few female traits expressing his being gay. He is not impersonating; he is simply hinting at impersonating by being obviously effeminate and "girlie" which usually is not himself and amuses his friends. Although probably crude, this is just one form of humor based upon the homosexual stereotypes that is harmless to the gay person, but often devastating to the straight that overhears the conversation. The humor is silly and usually meaningless.

There is a current movement of gay men desiring not to hide under historical precedence that dislike the effeminate role that American gay males have been stereotyped into. They actively rebel against gay slang and campy conversations by being more direct and, thus, masculine in their selections of ideas, actions and words for their conversations. They attempt to phrase and present ideas much more vocally similar to the heterosexual's stereotype. Sometimes, the too-deep voice, the pattern of swearing, the masculine approach gives the gay person away because he overly plays his concepts of being a "real man".

There is also a serious side to gender identification. In the gay male during adolescence when the person has accepted his being gay, there is a small percentage that hide the surface by acting and dressing in the comical directions like a woman. Built upon the fragile personality of the young male, a move toward hiding true feelings and insecurity, the young gay man applies a persona of being a woman, often a mimic of being outspoken, clever, conversational, and too witty, his real personality hidden behind false hair, a dress, chic and class, false eye-lashes, powder and make-up, a disguise that fools few except the very gullible.

In this attire, the gay male can fool few including himself. He lip-syncs to a popular tune with all the female movements and attention he can draw to himself, perhaps herself. In a way, he is compensating for the attention he did not receive as a gay male. He is creating an illusion of himself wanting approval from the outside world which he can get by pretending to be a she.

He is usually only in his late high school years or early twenties when he moves away from his birth home to the big city where he meets similar copies of his newly found identity. They live in rooming houses or hotels on a hand-to-mouth, month-to-month basis, staying up most of the evening and night and waking around dusk the next day to prepare for the night's substitute personality. They get into many clubs free, perform for $30 to $100 a night a few nights a week. Liquor and drugs are available to them for little or nothing. They spend their money on mascara, startling clothes, high heels, and jewelry. They are popular whores because of their youth and too carefree for medical care. They have often been rejected by their birth families, and have reinvented themselves into an outrageous personality of which the audience approves. They adopt names like Brigitte Buttercup, Helava Lay, Miss Brasilia, Hellin DeSac, Miss Steak, and Flame.

If the lifestyle of the drag does not kill him with the drugs, liquor and wild behavior, he grows older and takes a routine employment only making occasional appearances in costume at the gay clubs. Straight people find him amusing which satisfies his ego and buys him a drink even though gays feel he has established a reputation for being the stereotype homosexual. He appears on the streets of larger cities in the early evenings and he is often photographed as the "typical homo" although the percentage of his type is minimal.

Lesbians have less difficulty with these impersonations because the current dress fads for females acquire many of the styles that were once exclusively male. The vogue and her style make her desire to appear more masculine, more acceptable to the time. A woman can wear slacks, a tie, a suit, and coveralls hiding her sexual identity, and she can be fashionable. Lesbians often don't wear make-up and some prefer the rougher "un-ladylike" crude language. The night club opportunities are not as available for the lesbian and those with theatrically aggressive desires usually turn toward low comedy and maintain a lesbian identity and pun on adjustment jokes. Both the drag queens and the butch lesbians are extremes. Those whose sexual desires are indistinguishable from anyone else, wear clothing like the average person.

The deeper into rural America, the more masculine the women are because of their responsibilities to a more difficult lifestyle. City women can imply anything from street hooker to elegant wealth. Rural women have to get a specific job done, a job that often requires physical labor and long hours that their grandfathers had once done.

Americans love to be entertained; they take little concern for why they are being entertained. Many performers walk before the public allowing their real personalities to accompany them, and their created personalities dominate their behavior to amuse the audience.

There can also be a very serious and medical problem to those men who want to change to women, or those women who want to change to men. A man saying "I feel like I'm trapped in a man's body" is revealing some serious problems of gender identification, and special psychological examinations and physiological operations are available under very strict supervision. But, this is an extreme.

Strange combinations of heterosexual men and drags, homosexual men and emotionally cold women, cross-dressers and their wives and husbands make up a part of our population. Some men like to wear women's panties. Our situations often affect our behavior;

a physically horny male prisoner may attack another male in desperation although the act is not part of his ordinary character. Others can abstain. What makes the difference? We do not know. Because of many reasons the mind may suggest many things to the sensual body, and we have yet to investigate most. Sodomy. Rape. Beastiality. Sadism.

WHEN WILL I FIND A MEANINGFUL RELATIONSHIP?

There can be no precise time when you will find someone with whom you can establish a meaningful relationship except when you are personally ready for it. The gay person dreams of some kind of relationship with a person of the same sex from the time he/she recognizes him/herself as being gay. Remember your first encounter and you were hopelessly, passionately, intensely in love? The partner was to solve all your problems, and you were sure the love affair would last forever. It didn't' work. You were not ready. You needed time to mature.

When you become more mature, and it takes a lifetime of working on and understanding yourself, you may find someone with whom you can create a compassionate understanding of your worth and value as well as his/her worth and value, and you decide to join forces, to work as two separate halves toward the same goals. It should not be blind love where you refuse to admit your partner's limitations, but a mature acceptance not only of your partner's limitations, but also your own. Your friend will have to agree.

You will go through periods of time where you are experimental and a potential partner, an attempt to find Mr. or Ms. Right, if you match your maturity to his/her maturity, a meaningful relationship may be accomplished. It takes experimentation and time. When you fail, and you will often, it takes the ability to pick yourself up and continue the search.

A meaningful relationship is not an end in itself. It is the recognition of two people working toward continual growth and understanding of each other.

There are some ideas which a person can use to see if the potential mate is suitable to you:

1. Learn to talk. This is the process of finding communications easy without held back barriers. You must get to know the other person, the good things and the bad. Talk about sexuality, love making, goals,

ambitions and desires. The conversations must flow easily and honestly even if you don't show yourself in the best light. Communications means both people are talking and listening, but not both talking at once.

2. Listen and evaluate. Most people can understand where there may be problems in a meaningful relationship, and they assume what the problems are from the other person, but people hear what they want to hear rather than what is said. If the problem manifests itself later, it should be no surprise. Most people hear; few listen. How does what you listen to fit into your life? Can you live with that?

3. Don't insist upon acceptance. Don't say things just because you want the other person to like you. Don't try to make yourself look good if it is not true. Be honest. Expose your biases. Tell your weaknesses and your strengths.

4. Don't break off your friendships with others. You have designed a group of friends that have become your family, and they need you as much as you need them. If some potential mate cannot accept your family, you may have a difficult time accepting him/her. Don't be pulled away from your family to be boxed into a corner forced to make a decision.

5. Have free time away from the potential mate to evaluate what he/she has said and what it means to you. Think from his/her perspective of "Why does this person want me?"

6. Take your time. The greatest financial decision you will probably make is buying a house. The greatest emotional decision you will probably make is selecting a meaningful relationship. Fortunately, the emotions heal much more rapidly than does the wallet. It is much easier to not go into a relationship than it is to go into a relationship and have to get out of it. There may be other houses to buy. There may also be a better meaningful relationship.

These are only ideas to direct you toward making a logical decision. We are all aware that what we think is a meaningful relationship is not necessarily a logical decision. There is something called lust or love, something way beyond the physical aspects or logic. There is the awful reality that there may be many meaningful relationships. The other person adds to you and you add to the other person at a time in both of your lives when you are idealistic and romantic enough to think that a meaningful relationship will last forever.

WHEN WILL I FIND THE PERFECT MR. OR MS. RIGHT?

Probably never. There is no such thing as perfection and only liars will say that living with someone is 100 percent wonderful. There are going to be problems. How you resolve those problems, if you do, determines your desires and maturity.

Remember that going into a relationship with a person of the same sex reflects directly upon how you and your lover act out what you think was the relationship among your original family. Your family, friends and your experience are all you know about the family, and you want to have a different kind of gay, family relationship.

Are you mature enough to enter a lover relationship? Are you going into a relationship to make up for deficiencies that you have? Is your lover going into the family relationship for deficiencies he/she has?

Years ago marriages were established as a "matter of convenience". She was pregnant and the family did not want the social stigma of her not being married and having a bastard. He was wealthy and "you can love a rich one as well as a poor one". She may not get another chance; "losers can't be choosers". He can continue to play. "Do the 'right' thing by her." Even as we approach the twenty-first century, many gays find lovers for similar reasons. He has his own apartment and furniture. "Two can live cheaper than one." "Everybody is doing it." She can keep me in "...the style in which I would like to become accustomed". "He's great sex."

The gay relationships usually have the advantage of not being so legally complicated to dissolve, that you can just walk out. Is that an advantage or a disadvantage? Breaking a long term commitment with a house, business, social friends and all make dissolving a gay relationship more complex. Heterosexual marriages are usually more legally complex and often with the additional complications of children.

Today as we move toward greater acceptance of same sex marriages, we must also consider the complexity of resolving these marriages in some kind of legal divorce. Palimony? Premarital contracts? Unchangeable right-of-survivorship? A lawyer's dream. What are the problems if a dog, cat or children are involved?

There are, of course, some same sex understandings that do work, but they should be idealized. Usually over time, the two people have worked out their individualized roles. They have either compromised their disagreement or have learned to tolerate it. Compromise is a major word. But, this is the process of maturing.

We admire the same sex couple who have been together 40 years. We never say "That must have been 40 boring years." Have you ever noticed how similar lovers that have been together for a long period of time look? Too often, like each other.

I do not mean "sour grapes" on same sex marriages. I do mean to show how rare they are, often in small town communities where there is little gay competition, but to point out that longevity is not necessarily a prerequisite for gay relationships, and happiness is not assured by longevity. Nor is acceptance.

A small town in Iowa had a middle aged, gay male, wealthy lawyer and his 22 year old lover. They traveled extensively and their lavish home was the scene of opulent parties, mostly heterosexuals. Since they seemed to have many straight friends and their parties were well attended, their homosexuality was accepted. Right? Wrong. They were merely tolerated. There are many homes to which they have never and will never be invited, although the people of these homes eagerly await their invitations from "the gay couple" on the hill. Although there are many of the heterosexual trappings, they are still gay.

In years past, lesbians seemed to have longer lasting relationships than gay men. Lesbians were less mobile, a single gay woman did not move as rapidly to a larger city. Fewer women were employed and the earnings, compared to a man, were much less. They were probably less adventuresome. Careers were less available and the stereotype of being a wife and mother was socially acceptable as was an "old maid" or "spinster" in the community in which she was born.

The modern woman, gay or straight, has proven that most of these once accepted modes of social acceptance are no longer true. The modern woman can be whatever she wants if she is willing to make the sacrifices, probably exceptions being a sperm donor or a male model. She has become a dynamic force in our working society. A lesbian does not have to hide behind outdated ideas of what a woman should be. In fact, she is open to mold the kind of woman she wants to be without much of a rigid stereotype. Society accepts single parent families, a woman without children, and husbands, lovers, and slowly, lesbians.

The problems involved in establishing a relationship with the same sex are not too different from the heterosexual relationships. Each gay individual must ask him/herself "How mature am I?", and it seems an unanswerable question for many because the person is answering only through his/her personal experience of his own personality. He/she cannot judge himself through non-biased eyes. He guesses at what he wants from the relationship for himself.

Most people establish a relationship on what they know about the potential mate and their personal attitude toward what he/she wants in relation to what the person can bring into the relationship. There are some basic questions which must be answered honestly:

1. Do I know myself?
2. What am I doing about those pieces of my personality which I would like to see improved?
3. Am I considering a relationship because my potential mate can do things that I cannot do?
4. Will my potential mate solve my problems?
5. Why am I considering him/her for a potential mate?

A gay relationship that has the opportunity to succeed is based on similarities of their emotional backgrounds and often similarities of their financial background, status, values, and ethics. In rare cases the differences in the two personalities can work in a relationship, but the relationship is usually doomed to failure. A 60-year-old woman who is in love with a 16-year-old is headed for rough water. A medical doctor who is in love with a dishwasher, an environmentalist that loves a hunter, a religious activist in love with an atheist are close to the waterfalls. If the only thing two people have in common is that they are both same sex gays, crisis is around the corner.

Perhaps this is the reason that long term, same sex couples begin to resemble one another. They are building other similarities of their association. Two real estate ladies. Two out-doors men. Two body builders. When the opposite is true in the long term, same sex couples, the hairdresser and the construction worker, the athlete and the drag queen, you can be sure that other similarities exist in their role playing and those similarities or preferences are very strong.

We must compliment same sex relationships that enjoy maturity, sincerity and direction, often a deep understanding of each self and an honest direction in aiding the other person. Their relationship will be envied by many and it should be, but they will admit that it has not been all roses, and the relationship is constantly challenged while each person has to work toward their mutual goal. A relationship between two people is constantly demanding, but it can be accomplished.

There are more same sex relationships that have fallen into complaisance. The individuals are satisfied with the status quo. They are no longer building the relationship that has fallen, but they are willing to allow it to ride because it is convenient and comfortable and with little hassle.

There is another aspect of same sex relationships; one that gets little attention. It is the ability to step apart from it or the ability to be alone and love it and appreciate the relationship that you no longer have or want, but that you are glad you did have. It is not as dramatic as having a mate, but it is satisfying and often a pleasure. It is the period when a person has fully looked at him/herself and concluded that he/she will keep looking but is satisfied with life. Opportunity knocks many times; it depends when you open the door. Some don't want to open the door. The gays are not all suffering with broken hearts or tragic situations, but some prefer to be alone.

THE MEANINGFUL RELATIONSHIP

We are now being allowed to include "the meaningful relationship" or "significant other" in newspapers, magazines, and television. Aside from the obituaries which add "…a companion for ___ years," little more is said of the relationship between these two people. Were they friends? Brothers? Platonic buddies? No. They were lovers. They were sleeping together and probably doing a lot more things together. The printed page tries to be discreet. The public knows.

We honor a relationship between two people of the same sex that lasts over a great period of time, particularly if they have lived together which implies the sharing of their lives. We understand by the amount of time that the relationship between the two has been happy. How long does a successful relationship last? 30 years? 40 years? What a wonderful conclusion of ending life after having shared it so long with someone.

Of course, we realize that any two people living so closely together have had the complexities of life that have not made every road smooth. There are many bumpy roads. There are problems, misunderstanding. There are confusions with both partners. There is indecision, questioning, and solving. In spite of the bumpy road, it has been a good trip. More power to them.

The gay relationship that is a lasting understanding is what practically all gay men and lesbians want, but it is not an easy acquisition. It takes time, energy, maturity, and work. Some gays are not willing to go to the trouble. Their dreams become fogged, and although they realize they are gay, they are not sure of how to grab hold of that dream to make it reality.

A more common story is the gay male who is with a series of three or four potential lovers over his lifetime each lasting three or four years or less, and either he or his friends have reached barriers that they could not resolve. The barriers split them.

The cause of male misunderstanding is often in dealing with monogamy. There are many gay male couples who have not remained monogamous, but their relationship has continued. Even not being monogamous some have been able to continue their emotional relationship with each other, and some couples will argue that not being held to a monogamous relationship has helped the two. We hear the stories of the three-somes, the "night out with the boys". A monogamous relationship is not a prerequisite to all male, gay understandings.

Lesbians have a higher record for a lasting relationship. It is not unusual to find two gay women with an emotional understanding that has lasted years. Part of this is probably the role of the woman in yesterday's society. Will the length of the relationships change with the increased independence and wealth of the American woman? Most lesbians demand a monogamous relationship. A non-monogamous partner often breaks the relationship's trust.

There is also a trend for the gay man to continue to allow himself to become emotionally involved with someone else after the loss of a lover, perhaps by death or by a lack of understanding. Often lesbians, being more monogamous, adjust to being single once they have lost a lover of many years. As so many heterosexual widowers do not remarry, many gay woman do not take another partner after the main mate has gone.

If you consider that the first 20 years of life are a learning process, the next ten are the hunt for a mate, the next 30 or 40 are with the mate, and the last ten or 20 are without the person, the same sex relationship is important to many, and it should be respected by all, as

sincerely as the husband-wife bond, the brother-sister bond, the child
to the parents.

MONEY AND HAPPINESS

There is a great tendency to be modest and say "no" to the
question of wanting money, but that is not practical. A more valid
answer would be "It can make misery so much more comfortable".
Money in itself is not bad. What we do with it, and how we
evaluate it, and what it does to our personalities could have bad
effects, but that is not the fault of money; it is more the influence we
can buy for money. Cash in itself is a convenience. If you were to buy
a house that costs dollars compared to five cows and 50 chickens, it is
easier to carry around the paper than it is the cows and chickens.

Money depends upon the amount of money and your needs and
the costs of your needs. If a dollar a day can feed a baby in Haiti, you
will be willing to give. If a dollar a day is a part of the congressman's
bar tip, you certainly will not contribute. The only value to money is
for use. If you can buy the basic necessities of living, food, shelter and
health, then you will want a certain amount of whatever is comparable
to pay the other bills. If it takes 20 dollars a day for giving you some
things on which to live, you may even dip into that money to afford
something that you want, not need, at that time, like an alcoholic
drink, cigarette, crack or a chance on the lottery.

We live in a world where we strive for money because the money
buys us the physical things we want; the chair, car, travel tickets,
luxury items and it satisfies the expenses of habits. Again, it is not the
money but, it is what the money can buy. "Money is not the root of all
evil"; what money can buy, our demands and greed, are the evils.
Money is simply the way to get there. Of course, not everything can
be bought with money, but many things can.

Some people will do practically anything for money, from lying to
stealing, cheating to murder. Obtaining the money is one factor; what
has to be done to obtain it is another set of values. Can people be
bought? Probably. It depends upon the price. The desire for what
money can buy may be so great that having the money justifies
whatever the person does for the money.

The gay lifestyle operates upon money. Owning a gay bar is not a
philanthropic enterprise; they are out for profit. If no wages were to be

paid in any company tomorrow, how many employees do you think would show up for work?

The gay man or lesbian is just as concerned about money as the majority of Americans because he/she has a more liberal environment. The rules and regulations include a common association with street hustlers, prostitutes, and those that break honesty values to hide in a sub-group minority, a group that is more understanding of drugs and abusive substances. The liberal gay group is more accepting of non-traditional behavior, a little more street wise than most straights. Since their values are liberal, they more easily accept the thief, burglar, prostitute or hustler.

Too often, the gay man or lesbian is an easy mark for a street wise attractive kid. Cash disappears, jewelry disappears, the car is gone, and so is he. "I better not call the police because they'll know I'm gay." Enough said. Often the gay man or lesbian does not have the personal family or the original family to "fall back on" in a time of financial emergency. The person probably took a wild risk without a solid backup. There are probably as many gay men and lesbians that commit crimes as the rest of society.

Does the source of the money make any difference to the gay person? Probably not much to most Americans. We had a President whose family money came from boot-legging, and no one seemed to care. All gays know people who have made their money if not illegally, let's say questionably. But, if you are British ... Somehow, as in the straight lifestyle, we can absorb the young bride or groom waiting for the older one to die. No one would deny someone picking up the bill and paying it with money inherited from an aunt who ran a Chicago whore house.

There is also the falsehood that money brings unhappiness, a statement usually made by people who have little if any money. Although it may not bring happiness, it affords some of the pleasures of making one comfortable during misery. It is less comfortable to be poor and miserable.

The amount of family money many gays and straights would like you to believe is their family inheritance is unbelievable. In Miami with a heavy Cuban population, if you believe all the stories of Latin families' land wealth in Cuba, it would be twice as large as the United States.

THE GAY COUPLE DOWN THE STREET

In every suburban sprawl with moderately priced houses and eager, hard working people who have dreamed of their own home, there are homemakers, mostly heterosexuals. Then a gay couple moves into the neighborhood.

We are to a point of sophistication where America feels it can recognize the gay couple, two people of the same sex sharing the same house. (God help the poor heterosexual of the same sex in a roommate situation because the neighbors may assume they are gay and it will be the scandal of the neighborhood.) Being liberal, the neighborhood accepts them like other "married" people, and the neighbors try to treat them accordingly.

What the neighbors expect is what they have been taught; there's somebody wild in the neighborhood. Somebody is flamboyant, weird, dressed in women's clothing, adoring Judy Garland and trying to be like her, someone who lisps, likes women's make-up or dying his hair, or wearing leather pants and a harness for a shirt. There are two people who are tragically sad and physiological lonely men or women of desperation, unhappy, alienated, marginal and destined for tragedy. These people party all night, drink too much, yell and scream at all hours, bring home strangers, and indulge in "strange" sex. These gays will molest your children, and you better be careful.

This view of the homosexual lifestyle slices across these concepts when the neighborhood realizes that most homosexual couples, both gay males and lesbians, are relatively quiet people, home folks that may live together for many years without a neighborhood drama, people that have jobs and responsibilities, obligations, and directions and those that work eight to five with Sundays for washing the dog and the cars and looking forward to vacations and, eventually, retirement, and when they die. They are content and thankful for their relationship as well as the community.

THE GAY NEST BUILDERS

Birds have built nests for thousands of years and most biologists believe that the desire and drive to build a nest is inherent, maybe genetic. Each kind of bird builds a different kind of nest; one that specifically meets the bird's demands.

People differ little from the birds. We are raised in our family nest.

When we fly from our family, or when we are pushed out of the nest, we have a strong desire to build our own nest, the way we want it, sometimes close to our family's design; rarely directly opposite of the design, but always with improvements.

As people, we start out in our organized family nest, to progress to college room or a job room, to a shared apartment, to our own apartment either living alone or with roommates, maybe a lover, to our own first house, to a couple of different rented and bought nests, eventually to our last one. We leave the nest to get food, a job, or for our own flights of fancy or entertainment, but out basic security is our nest. There, we feel safe and secure.

As different kinds of birds build different kinds of nests, people build different kinds of security reflected in their room, apartment or house. All people, heterosexual or homosexual, desire the security of their nest, and they treat it accordingly being surrounded by the things they like, their games and amusements, their personal remembrances. Each is a little different.

There is no one way for a gay person to build a nest, each as individualistic as the person. Some swamp their room with Marlyn Monroe posters, others search out junk stores and readily accept hand-me-downs, some are spotlessly clean and others not so, eclectic, more modern. Many are filled with the physical fitness machines, the computers, books, a stereo system, personal photographs, naked figurines, prints and paintings, whatever the person wants. Over the years, the location of the nests may change and the stuff in the nests change but, it is security for the gay male or lesbian.

An old decorator told me that the person starting out buying furniture should always buy two matching French Provincial chairs with arms from a good furniture store. They can be used in any setting of any period and in any room for your entire life. A second choice was a Parson's table. Think of the amount of furniture you've gone through in a lifetime. Where does it go?

A different kind of security, aside from the nest and its furnishings, financial security; the money that all people worry about. A wealthy person never says he has too much money; someone talking about a wealthy person may say the wealthy person has too much money. Wealth implies success and those whose money is limited will say it is not important. We use money to buy things, and all people like things.

Gay people have a very definite advantage over the married heterosexuals with children, the advantage of being able to spend their earned money mainly on themselves and their selfish desires. With a husband and wife working, their social value of a respectable apartment or home and the cost of raising and educating children presents a financial struggle for many parents. Today, many women work in jobs aside from the home because of financial advantages. There is still something negative about the working wife and a stay-at-home husband, the reversal of the past roles.

A same sex couple or roommates without children allow the two people to have a double income which is more spendable income. That's the reason gay men and lesbians eat out more, travel more, buy bigger and more expensive cars, and have larger houses than their heterosexual counterparts.

It is amusing that a gay couple's apartment or house must always have two or more bedrooms. One is usually very comfortable and reasonably plush. The other is often office like, but always containing a bed. Who do we think we are fooling?

The independent gay person has the opportunity to gamble in business, investments or even across the card table. The heterosexual husband and wife expecting children can not gamble as much. When businesses or investments are successful, it allows the gay man or lesbian more independence in gambling. "Nothing ventured is nothing gained", and the gay person has an advantage to venture money.

The secret to saving money is very simple; save ten percent in a separate account of whatever you make, and you will eventually become a financially successful person. Everyone knows the line, but few actually do it.

The independence of gays force them into being self-centered, and there is not as much necessity to invest in life insurance, death insurance, health insurance, and all the securities that the heterosexual family demands. Many will argue that this is not wise for the gays to ignore such important things, but youth is indestructible. Many gays operate from emergency to emergency. (I'm not attempting to sell insurance of any kind, although it sounds like a pitch.)

We find that the world of the gays and the world of the counterpart heterosexuals is very different when you are young with the gays interested in home furnishing and, traveling, investing, self-improvement and social interests and the heterosexuals interests of marrying, having children, protecting them on limited means. No wonder communication and friendships between the gays and straights is difficult at this time, as it will continue to be.

Buying a home is probably the largest investment an individual will make during his/her lifetime. A 30 year mortgage used to take half a lifetime to pay off. Today, financing and refinancing is a business game, one played between what a person can afford and the finance and interest charges written on the income tax form for write-offs. The investment in real estate as a home seems to be secure, one that helps to satisfy the nest building instinct.

What makes a piece of property valuable is established by the values of a majority of the buyers, the heterosexuals. Close to schools, near a shopping mall, a community of similar priced homes, a yard for the kids to play, the location of a church, parks and playgrounds.

The older houses had small bathrooms because it was not proper to discuss bathroom habits, God forbid anyone being comfortable in the bathroom. There were many small bedrooms, a goal that each child should have his own room. The neighbors were similar with blue collar husbands and wives and three or four children, a professional neighborhood of two or three children. There were similar values of joining the PTA or Boy Scouts, Little League, or the Brownies.

These communities were established to advance the comfort and security of the heterosexual family. Even the older people of the community had been through the same straight up-bringing, and their grandchildren could visit in a similar and familiar value scale.

Into this community move two gay men or two lesbians living together. There is a mistrust in the community because these people are "different". Each wants to help with Little League or the Girl Scouts. Caution. The couple wants to be active in the religion that demands traditional values of the straight community. Caution. The kids want to sell things and knock on their home door on Halloween. Caution. The gay guys or lesbians give parties or have people over who are "different".

Of course there are neighborhoods that are not to this extreme, neighborhoods that will be more tolerant, until something in the community happens, and then there is the attack on the "different" people. It could be the spinster or the straight bachelor, the widow or,

God forbid, the Catholic priest. The community is tolerant of the "different" people, but they do talk, the gossip grows, and action often follows gossip.

A 60 year old gay man has nieces and nephews now grown with their own children, and he tells them he never wants to be alone with any of the children. He's vulnerable to any story the children make up, vulnerable to be guilty of the neighborhood's imagination. He's protecting himself.

What other suitable living locations are there for the gay man or lesbian or the gay couple to live? There are many that you may not have considered.

Most large cities have an area in which many gay people live and often work. It is usually termed as an artsy-crafty community containing gay centers of activity and bars. An older section of town or an ethnic section, the Victorian Village, Russian Hill, German Village is more liberal than the newer suburban family, child rearing, sections.

Unfortunately, the homes in these more gay accepting neighborhoods are more expensive than the market value of the houses in other neighborhoods because the neighborhoods are more exciting to more lenient straights and gays to single people. The outskirts of these identifiable sections may not be as expensive, less liberal, but within a couple of blocks of the action.

If you are interested in opening a shop or office In a growing artsy-crafty community, consider living above the commercial space. Living above the shop has been done for years. With modern working conditions of the demands of computers, in-house working space may be important to you and your business, and your location may be close to your clients. The upstairs apartment and the store downstairs has some advantages, and there may be more advantages in the future modern work places.

Consider renting in a large apartment building where gays already live. The amount of gays living there and the amount of units protects your anonymity. Don't dismiss renting. It allows mobility. Some people believe that all we do in life is rent, even if we own the property. After we die, the property goes on so even if we have bought it, we are really still renting for our lifetime.

You may want to consider a large condominium building where some gays live. Avoid the small condominium where a few unapproving negative voices can swing the vote to make your life miserable.

There are also many warehouse districts, some close to the financial and business districts, that are less desirable for the husband, wife and children. Although usually rougher, you can often get a lot of cheaper square footage for the dollar. After all, you don't have to keep up with the Joneses.

There is also something to be said for a country lifestyle where you are seemingly separated from your neighbor, even a place of expansive forests or farms. Most are centered around a small village, and these villages are not only small in size, the people know practically everything that happens, or they may create what they do not hear. The gay stands out, known to all. Although we like to think the country is becoming more sophisticated, many of these people have never associated with gays nor do they want to. You won't be ignored.

It may read as though I'm trying to separate the gay community from the straight community, but that is not entirely true. As a gay man, I must be aware of the prejudices that are held in an attempt to make my life as happy and as least complicated as possible.

If you are a Baptist, I would warn you of moving into a Mormon community. You are legally allowed to buy or rent practically any place you want to go. Point yourself in a direction that will cause you the least amount of complications and allow you the most fun.

SHOULD I MIMIC A STRAIGHT LIFESTYLE?

Most heterosexuals want a mate, a home, a family, kids, one or two cars, nice furnishings, a successful job that is personally satisfying, a social group that is entertaining, time to travel, financial security and a secure day by day living with hopes and desires for the future. We are taught that these things will bring us the desired, elusive state of mind called "happiness".

People know that acquiring the things of happiness does not always bring happiness. Acquiring the emotional aspects does not secure happiness. Working hard with a comfortable life style does not always bring the desired results. There is disappointment, discouragement, lack of contentment, emptiness, anxiety and frustration in everyday living.

Many children are aware of their parent's faults. Sometimes as gays grow older they are not aware of the problems of their parent's lives, the family in which they were raised and their values formed. Often the parents tried to hide the frustration and lack of fulfillment in their own lives, certainly not to burden the child. Many divorced parents handed their problems to the children in detail.

A bride walking down the aisle to meet the awaiting groom is not aware of their life ahead, the troubles in the future and the desperate search to make some kind of sense out of the future. Is it just a rose colored flash of the moment? With a 53 percent divorce rate, single parents, runaway kids, disease and eventually death, the moment could be painted in deep, somber colors.

The gay person wants many of the same things that idealize the straight desires, but he/she differ from the heterosexual in the selection of a mate of the same sex, usually in having his/her own children, in fitting into the pattern at work and his socialization with neighbors and straight friends.

Sometimes the gay couple fake the heterosexual lifestyle. They live in the comfortable house in the suburbs, have the dog, participate in the community, have dreams and desires, a network of friends, security, and they are still not happy. What went wrong? Probably nothing, except the gay couple took off the rose colored glasses.

There is risk in a gay couple attempting to demand their own lifestyle in a heterosexual community. It is risky because the heterosexual community does not hold the same values of the gay couple or even the single gay man or lesbian and sometimes the straight can not relate to the gay world. Pretense, lack of confidence, and bigotry surround them.

If a black family were to move into a white neighborhood, the black family would feel a similar wedge although they have a similar family direction. A gay person or couple living in a heterosexual community, regardless of how sophisticated and worldly always will be reminded they are gay. This is not right; it is just the way it is. Yes, there is ignorance and prejudice.

As a gay person or couple, you may have moved into the center of a community that is basically ignorant of your lifestyle. It is not that you cannot be accepted as yourself, that you are not worthy. It is that you are different even if you do not consider yourself different. What is this compelling need that you must be liked by everyone in the community, gay or straight?

At least the black family is obviously different; maybe the gay couple is also. It is not going to happen that you are liked by everyone. If a black man were to marry a white woman and they moved into a black community, the woman would have adjustment problems with the blacks. If they moved into a white community, the black man would have problems with the white community. Why do gays feel they can integrate a heterosexual community without problems? It may be perfectly legal and fair, but there will be problems.

A CROSS DRESSER

A cross dresser is a male who likes to dress in female attire, or a female that prefers male attire. They may or may not be sexually gay, but they prefer the physical attire of the opposite sex. A drag queen is usually not a cross dresser, does not wear the opposite sex's clothes for sexual stimulation.

Throughout history, society has made the responsibilities of the male more dominant and different from the responsibilities of the female. If a female were dominant, a characteristic often displayed in lesbians, and she wanted into what was called "a man's world", she had to pose the pretense by dressing and acting like a man. Although we have had cross dressers throughout history, the obvious distinction is between the Victorian man and the Victorian woman.

The Victorian woman was educated to play the piano, read, raise the children, cook and clean, and be socially acceptable to the rules of society and to her husband. She attempted to dress appropriately and fashionably, and be dependent upon her husband. She had little knowledge of finance except for her own household budget. She could not vote, and knew little of men's business.

The Victorian man was dominate in all matters concerning money. He defended his wife and family in war. He made the political decisions. His voice was heard in the courts. There were in Victorian times gay men who would cross dress as women, but there were few because the female's role was so inferior to that of the male, and there were few advantages to gender switching from male to female.

Earlier than the Civil War in American history, the woman dressed as a man and was accepted as a soldier. Many were not lesbians, but accompanied their husbands or lovers to battle in male soldier's uniforms, and were accepted as men. Some lesbians and gay men have led their entire lives as cross dressers. The lesbians cross dressing as men took wives whom never realized their husbands were female. The gay men dressed as women usually didn't marry.

Unfortunately, today's lesbian has a double threat of minority status; being a lesbian and fighting the inferior status of being a woman in changing discriminations. The gay male has to adjust to his homosexuality.

Today, the modern drag is stretching his identity usually for the purpose of humor, but there are still some whose identity is so closely tied to the opposite sex, they prefer a medical gender switch which can be accomplished. Many cross-dressers are still not identified in our society, and probably won't be identified.

There are also heterosexual men and women who are cross dressers, but they maintain their true identity in every day life aside from an occasional get-together or party. The men may wear as everyday clothing a token of the opposite sex's attire, the most common being the female panties. The heterosexual who cross dresses is usually displaying a line of masculinity or effeminate behavior which contains current taboos.

Presenting drag is much different than cross dressing. Many straight men use cross dressing to receive a type of sexual satisfaction from the wearing of the opposite gender's clothing. The drag queen, usually gay, acquires a whole new personality and behavior; the cross dresser may only manifest the behavior or mannerisms of the opposite sex not interfering with his/her sexual desires.

What has happened in society is that there is not the necessity for the gay male or lesbian to fit into the heterosexual lifestyle. Women's liberation through education and employment status has brought the two sexes much closer together in responsibilities as in styles.

There is less serious cross dressing today than previously in our history because the role of the male and the female, particularly the female, has changed so drastically. Since the gay "lifestyle" is a choice, most gay men prefer acting male, and most lesbians prefer being female. Along the masculine and effeminate scale of today, most gay men prefer the masculinity of the male; most lesbians prefer the effeminate of the female, even though we may not portray them that way in movies and television. In entertainment at the bars, male or female go-go dancers have replaced some of the drag queen's stage acts.

AM I SELF-DESTRUCTIVE?

We are all self-destructive to the degree of what we think or how we act affects our health. It is impossible to live in a vacuum of completely free, constantly healthy, risk free lifestyle. That would certainly not be very interesting. We take chances every day, but most of these chances are free of extremes.

In the heterosexual lifestyle, the "do's" and the "don'ts" are more precisely laid out through a history of experience and constant research of what we should and should not do. These are concepts that do change, but that are slow to change. We were taught that we should not have more than, as an example, two glasses of wine a day or we would become an alcoholic. We stayed under this rule, breaking it from time to time often to find disastrous results the next morning. Was the hang-over from the extra glass of wine or from what we have been taught would happen if we had the extra wine? Probably a combination of both.

The homosexual lifestyle is not as patterned allowing for many degrees of diversity and, bluntly, the lifestyle is more dangerous because it allows exposure to the extremes and the acceptance of the extremes. The many temptations ranging from the taking of drugs through lying and infidelity are more obvious in the gay lifestyle and more accepted because the people are under less strict observation.

Once a gay man or lesbian has established him/herself in a mature gay community, and once he/she has accepted being gay, the person establishes values reflective of his background. There are liberal and conservative gay men and lesbians. "Yes, Virginia. There are also Republicans and Democrats." Since the social rules have not been so obviously put forth, there is more room for experimentation, and that leads to more excess.

Remember a major problem of the homosexual is low self-esteem, a problem with which he/she can deal, but a constant, nagging inadequacy that he/she must constantly keep in mind with attempts to boost self-esteem. No wonder there is low self-esteem. The gay person is constantly reminded that he/she is not like the rest of the population, an inferior species.

Once a person has linked to a gay family of friends, he/she begins to build self-esteem. Success on the job helps. A warm relationship with a partner may help. Self-awareness helps more than anything.

Living with the word "pride" helps a lot.

The gay man or lesbian without a significant person has the most difficult time building self-esteem because there is no one there to constantly enhance his/her ego. (Others may say that he/she has an easier time being alone because there is no one there to constantly deflate his/her ego…a poor partner.) The single gay male or lesbian can lead a life of self-indulgence and/or extremes apart from the firmly established rules and regulations of the heterosexual lifestyle, and often apart from the gay lifestyle. He/she can become self-absorbed and selfish.

The single gay male or lesbian may have more difficulty in growing older than the same-sex couple relationship. One major advantage of being a couple is that you have someone to talk with through each part of your life. There is someone there.

The single gay man or lesbian reaches the time of retirement and is unable to find traveling companions. He/she may have financial success and unable to find or unwilling to compromise financial security to buy the companionship. As he/she approaches growing older, the once beautiful youthful body melts. Friends are dying by natural attrition. Younger friends are dying of AIDS. The person is left having mostly completed a successful business life with time on his side, and unable to enjoy the later period of life. He is particularly vulnerable to self-destruction through living a dangerous lifestyle. He/she may smoke too much, drink too much, gamble too much or take a lot more serious chances in life.

ARE DRUGS CONTROLLING MY LIFE?

We live in an age where television is the major educational tool to teach us a way of life aside from our birth family influences. Where dreams were once made of motion picture stars and their romantic adventures, many of which were simply lies, we have turned to the personalities of television and stories in which the stars perform. We mimic the story lines and fantasize about the actors and actresses.

One very obvious direction of television is the reliance upon drugs or products of one kind or another to solve our personal problems. June Allison using a false teeth cream probably hurts no one. Candice Bergan selling Sprint phones implies if she likes the phone service and you like her, you'll like the telephone company. And who advertises

Depends? Harmless? Perhaps. There was once a singer in Florida that let her feelings about gays be known to the public.

What we know about the television idols as what we knew about the motion picture stars has given us some emotions that may buck directly against what we have been taught in our family values. "So-and-so had five husbands", and we at one time had a term for a woman who married five times. "He/she was drunk and got arrested." "He was caught selling coke. She was high." "I don't worry about drugs. I just use them on the weekends, or the weekdays when I have problems, or to make the time go faster, or to lift my spirits, or to have a good time, or to wake up or go to sleep."

We remain a pill-dropping society; taking pills as vitamins and supplements to enrich our lives, and pills to ease any pain, and pills to make us feel good, and pills to divert the blues. Pop. Pop. Pop.

The argument that this pill is legal and this one is not is not a valid parallel in this country where everything from an aspirin to murder can be obtained for the right price. There is no large city in the United States where illegal drugs cannot be obtained, and the smaller cities become pharmacy outlets for anything desired. We are not winning the war against illegal drugs; we're not even playing the same game.

What this has done is that we are losing the ability to cope with our own problems and emotions without the crutch of drugs. We take drugs not to cure the disease, but to eliminate the symptoms. We cannot cope with our problems, and we are often so drugged that we don't even know what the problems are. We walk in an artificial daze from one situation to another.

It is not my place to say that drugs of any kind are bad, legal or illegal. That's your decision. But, when a person loses himself to popping pills rather than seeing and coping with his/her problems, there should be an obvious solution. The behavior of popping the pills can easily kill the person. Can the problem kill?

Gay men and lesbians are particularly prone to the pill popping game having more than average frustration in early life, turning gay, and the difficulty of maturing as a single or as a couple. "There are no children to worry about. What difference does it make? Poor me. I'll pop a pill." When the chips really get down, "She doesn't love me. I'll show her. I'll kill myself and she'll be sorry."

No one was sorry. She had dominated her system with mood

changing, artificial pills, many dangerous in combinations which could cause death, and she died of the lack of knowing how dependent she was on pills. A senseless death.

The same can be said for the alcoholic. You'll never change him/her by reasoning or by nagging. That is often one of the things he/she wants to escape, the realization that he/she drinks too much. It usually takes a crisis before a compromise, the death of a loved one or personal physical problems. Some people won't admit their problems even at a crisis level.

There is no tolerance for the "do this, don't do that" approach. All have heard the "It's my body and my life and I'm going to live it the way I want" approach. To a degree the philosophy is understandable. But, you don't run naked in mine fields, or play in the streets in heavy traffic, or walk in bad sections with lots of jewelry. That is just common sense. You don't pop pills until you no longer know who you are. You live in this world at this time. Pill popping is not living in this world.

COURAGE AND PATIENCE

Courage is the ability to look toward tomorrow without carrying the disappointing baggage of the negative things that have happened today. Patience is the ability to wait with a positive attitude until something good happens. They are closely linked.

Both depend upon attitude. The ability to develop a positive attitude toward your dreams of happiness is within you, yet it seems easier to complain. It is easier to think of the things you want rather than what you have. Other people relate to complaining and looking at the negatives of living rather than the positives. We all know a person who has never been physically well a day in his/her life, the cartoon character that walks around with a black cloud over his head. Whatever complaint you have, the other person can double it. It is compensation to hear someone less fortunate than you. But, it is dull conversation.

The events of life do not necessarily occur at the time we want them. You were desperately in love at 16 and wanted the house, baby, and husband and, you may not have been ready, or you were escaping from your family. It is difficult to experience a meaningful relationship at 16 when you have so few years making you a meaningful person. It is easy to have sexual relationships, but there is a great difference between sex and love. As you grow older and wiser, you'll realize that sex is only one aspect of love and that a lifetime involvement with another person encompasses much more than sexual feelings.

So many of the qualities that make a successful relationship take time for you to understand and realize what they mean. Many are abstract, like faith, courage, motivation, and compromise, but they are the basic characteristics of who you are. You must wait for some of these things to happen; you must wait to grow up before you make these decisions. Patience.

The gay man or lesbian does not have to face the pressure of the clock ticking; get a husband or wife and have children before she can no longer produce. It does not take mature bodies and minds to have a sexual relationship with someone else. When you are young, use the word "love" very hesitantly. It just may be lust. Very few gay relationships remain several years later. Lesbians have a much longer same sex relationship record than gay men. Of course, no one can reason beyond what they know or have experienced; the fun of maturing being gaining the knowledge and the experience.

The real art of loving is for people with knowledge of themselves, and a genuine loving of themselves and their values combined with finding a partner of similar description. It opens the doors of compromise and true loving. At a young age, your job is to know yourself and like yourself. As you mature, that develops into allowing you to be loving, and only then can someone love you and have it returned. Youth is not the epitome of loving even though it may be the most productive time of sex.

SHOULD I HAVE CHILDREN?

We know that homosexual parents or parent does not make his/her child homosexual even if a great deal of the public does not think so. We know that 96 percent of pedophiles are heterosexual, even if the public won't accept it. Homosexuals having children today are bound to experience a great deal of bad and biased information from the other children and/or their parents.

The first question a potential gay parent must ask himself is "Why do I want a child?" followed by "Is it fair to the child?" If the purpose of wanting a child is to cement the relationship between you and your lover, forget it. If the purpose of having a child is to fit better into the heterosexual community, forget it.

However, if the desire for a child is not selfishly motivated and you are willing to take the responsibility of rearing a child, and if you can afford it, you may want to investigate the legal complications of an adoption agency. If you want the child by artificial insemination or the several other alternatives, carefully consider the complexities of each. Most states are hesitant about a gay person or a gay couple adopting; some outright refuse adopting to gays. This is a very big conclusion, one that should be in the workings for many months before a decision is made.

Again, we cannot forget our history. Prior to much scientific information, children were conceived and welcomed but rarely planned. They happened. Some were not even welcomed, particularly in the Depression. It was expected that a woman's obligation was to have children and they did, with or without a legal husband. Often women thought of having a child in order to get a husband. We know women conceive at different times and it is not as regulated as we once thought. Regardless, some children were planned and wanted not particularly scientifically or with accuracy. Mostly, children happened.

It was necessary, particularly in the rural times of our history, to have a child or plenty of children to help with the obligations and work of the farm. We know that the parents hoped the children would become literate, although many were not trained, and the children followed the parent's goals of happiness through repeating their lifestyle, but that has changed in today's world.

We know that children are a financial and emotional responsibility to the parents. The education, medical expenses, housing, and a million other things are expected of the parent or parents. We know that a child can "tie you down" and be so demanding that in order to be a good parent, you must sacrifice many things. We know that your gay lifestyle may not be practical to taking on the responsibilities of having a child. Rather than join two lovers together, a child may split them apart.

In our modern world, we have accepted the single mother. Scientifically, we know a great deal about how to have a child, but we really have not developed in how to raise a child. Not considering your selfish motivations, will a gay parent raising a child be able to give the child what he/she needs? What if you don't like the child? What if something happens to you?

The question is probably one of the most far reaching ideas the gay person can answer because it is not only affecting the gay's life, but also the child's life. There is currently more emphasis for gays to adopt, both gay men and lesbians, and these are usually couple relationships, although single straight men and single straight women are eligible for being adoptive parents.

Some gay men have considered donating their sperm to a surrogate mother, some lesbians have had children by surrogate fathers or been impregnated by close friends. Most gay people never allow themselves even the question, saying "no" immediately. We also must admit that giving birth to a child or fathering a child may not always be the desires of worthy parents. Some parents are simply rotten people and certainly awful parents not caring for their children.

Too often, the gay person buys a dog without ever asking the question of his/her responsibility to the dog. A dog to a child is a bizarre comparison, but you have seen many dog owners who are excellent masters. The dog may become a child substitute, but you have seen many stray dogs also.

As an indicator from "Newsweek", 65 percent of the Americans surveyed said same sex couples should not have the right to adopt children. For the gays that do adopt, the records are outstanding for the quality of time, attention, and energy in raising a normal, healthy and happy child either gay or straight. The child may be headed toward a tremendous amount of discrimination.

In the gay lifestyle, many of the gays with children have had the children before they had identified their own sexuality, and the parent was caught with an adolescent body of 14 or 15 demanding to reproduce, a wait by society until 16, 17 or 18, and a rush into parenthood before the parents knew who they were. Many gays with children have been excellent parents, particularly lesbians who at one time because they were female were always given the children in a divorce.

Today when a man may be given the children in a divorce, there are many single men raising children, and there are many gay men that would like to raise children. The married man or woman that comes out later in life may have already raised his/her children. Many divorced gay men have supported their children that the straight woman has reared. Many fathers have ignored their children as part of a previous moral conduct, a convenience to the fathers.

Even if single mothers are accepted, same sex couples with children are less acceptable, the laws against gay men and lesbians adopting children are more strict or have been interpreted more strictly. Even today in modern divorce cases, the woman may not get the children if she is gay and he is heterosexual. Is having a child and taking care of a child the rest of your life really what you want to do? Why?

There are many ways in which the gay person can get involved with children other than personally having and/or owning one, although you can never own a child. From Scouts, to Little League, through church groups to organized play-grounds, the gay person can be a model to other parents as well as the child. But, the gay person must protect him/herself against the old stigma.

The religious conservative right yelling for "family values" is confusing to the gays. Most gay people will support the school system through paying taxes all of their lives without ever using it. They will help with school projects if asked. They will support the community at practically any costs. They will back their family and their family's kids beyond their own comfort. The gays are usually giving and caring people, and they become non-conformist only when they are pushed into non-conformity. There are no other minorities that support family values more than the American gays. Although the gays may not play the traditional value of marriage of the opposite sex, they have deep seated family values in every community.

SHOULD I GAMBLE?

All know the cliche that life is a gamble and if you mean by gambling that you are taking a chance, it certainly is. We never know when we are going to get hit by a beer truck and the whole game is over. We gamble to beat the odds that we know are stacked against us. To some gambling is a compulsion, an addiction to prove superiority. To others, it is just a game where the person can maintain him/herself with the loss of the investments. We all end up dead, losing the game of life.

Sometimes people gamble for money implying that the money will solve many of their problems. Money seems to complicate the problems. Proportionately, there are just as many wealthy people who commit suicide as poor people.

The gay man or lesbian often has excess money with which he or she can gamble, and it does not affect his/her way of life and because of this additional income and lesser financial responsibilities, gay people gamble more than straights.

There are gay people who will not gamble with anything other than money. A broken love affair means they are out of the game. They have lost all and vow never to gamble again. The fear of gambling in a love affair would mean that they have the chance of losing, and they are afraid to take the chance. They can lead solitary lonely lives and, if they don't know how to deal with loneliness, they can be miserable. Many older gay men and lesbians who have built an amount of financial security and are fearful of losing the security, do not gamble.

Card gambling is a matter of chance; life gambling in realizing why you have lost and the ability to improve that skill and get back into the game. It is, again, knowing yourself. You can probably live as well without gambling, but will it be as much fun?

Some gays gamble with every person they meet. They do foolish things that will lead them into problems with themselves or even the law. You don't take a stranger home while you are wearing a lot of jewelry, and you don't let her borrow your car. Some win and some lose. The odds are with the person who has little to lose and he has experience. Don't play another person's game.

DO I HAVE MASCULINE DOMINANCE

In our society, girls and boys are reared differently; the boys are taught to be more aggressive, forceful, competitive and rougher than girls. The early introductions of boys to athletics shows the values that the fathers give to their sons. Those values are not good sportsmanship and learning to lose. They are to be better than the next guy, tougher than the competition, and win sometimes at practically any costs. Watch the bleachers at a Little League game and you'll see parents yelling at their kids to kill the competition; don't cry and get in there and fight. The boys respond to their fathers, more than to the mothers, because the fathers are models of what is appropriate behavior for the son.

The more passive boy child does not respond to his father's demands as rapidly and risks not getting positive feedback from the father, something he needs. The son has little permission to be feminine. Daughters, however, are encouraged to be more masculine like their fathers, and the daughters learn to idolize the father not unlike his wife idolizes him. Gay teen boys have three times the suicide rate as girls. [7]

It is easy and unfair to sit back and blame practically everything on family background. No parents can raise a family in perfect harmony without projecting ideas for the child's protection that may harm the child later in the child's life. The child learns trust, to obey, and leadership from the father. Not only the child's relationship to the father, but what the child realizes of his mother's relationship to the father raises confusion in the child's value scales.

Children were once raised in the theory that they should be "seen and not heard". America gave birth to the caring father; one who is companionable, tolerant, understanding, and sympathetic to his son or daughter. Today's fathers are much more sensitive to the demands and directions of the growing child, sometimes to the point of being rude to other adults. The parent interrupts the adult to listen to the child. Wait a minute. Manners must also be taught by the parents.

In the heterosexual lifestyle it is difficult for the aggressive, powerful, physical, masculine male to select a wife and not show trained masculinity. Athletes often do not make good husbands, and we all know publicized athletes who are accused of striking their wives. Statistics indicate the Marines have the most difficulty in adjusting to family life than any of the other military services. Marines have the highest divorce rate among the services. If size and strength are the best qualities of masculinity, the biggest and toughest husbands should make the best fathers. Somewhere the primitive urges of masculinity and dominance have to be reversed for a compatible family relationship.

Today, we are teaching little girls to be more competitive and aggressive. We are teaching them to reflect more of the masculine values to the degree that married women are rebelling against the dominating, physical attacks of husbands on wives. Strange that we don't hear much about husband physical abuse.

The homosexual lifestyle has less of the physical abusive relationships because the same sex genders are more evenly matched in their physiques. Many will argue the opposite saying the gay lifestyle is more physically abusive because there are few laws against the attacks of the same sex and the pair are more evenly matched. If you are in a physically or mentally abusive relationship, get out.

The gay relationship is not more masculine than the straight relationship. There are different degrees of masculinity and effeminate behavior or mental abuse, but the gay male learns to limit the display of physical dominance. Some will rightfully argue that the leather clad guys and the current emphasis upon the ego direction of body building are open announcements of the masculine male. It is disconcerting to listen to three gay leather clad jocks talking about baking a cake.

There is also the extreme of masculinity resulting in sadism and masochism, hurting someone or being hurt by someone. These are psychological problems involving more than just simple dominance. The president of the company likes to be spanked. These problems need professional help.

A SINGLE NEST BUILDER

Our society teaches us that someday we will meet someone, combine into a family, have children, live together the rest of our lives and eventually die together or join each other after death. We will be successful and happy through all these years.

Reality gives us another view. Sometimes we do not meet someone, we do not join into a family, or we join into an unhappy union from which we want divorced. We may not want children. We may be gay. We may die alone. There is no "happy hunting ground" where everything is fine, and we have been both successful and unsuccessful, both happy and unhappy. Life will not be one continual ball.

The single person, gay or straight, has a difficult life in our social structure and he/she does not fit into a pattern of family, children, rearing and making a living. It eases our mind to think that these rarities are minimal and we push them aside in our conventional lifestyle. Isn't it strange that we will accept a single parent who is divorced or widowed or just a single woman who has never married, but we hesitate to accept two women living together? We accept the never married career man, but question two straight men living together, the rare exception of the "The Odd Couple."

We have to recondition our thinking about the single man or woman, gay or straight. This period could be a time when he/she is taking on the responsibilities of being mature, learning to make personal and job related decisions, balancing the social world with the work world, planning and achieving new objectives, growing in independence and expanding. The single person may be very happy being single. He/she may want something more, but maybe he is satisfied with what he/she has, the solitude and independence of being alone.

Don't allow someone else to tell you how happy or unhappy you are. That is a decision that you must make yourself, and only you can evaluate it. Listen only to yourself, not to others. If you feel you are happy, you're happy. If you feel you are not happy, that's your decision, and you better do something about it.

The gay man or lesbian selects the single lifestyle because of the inability to find someone to share a life more meaningful than living alone. He follows his background experience of being raised by a mother and father. Sadly, many gays take partners just to have a mate, and they are not satisfied or unhappy. Many gay relationships are based on just complacency as are many straight marriages. People tolerate complacency, but there is no great lust to obtain it.

To be alone does not necessarily mean you are lonely, that you want anything more than just being alone. Flitting from one lover to another without finding someone of significance to you can be a long and desperate hunt, and it can be an interesting challenge. To some, the hunt is not worth the prize. If you can be happy alone, why do you need more?

Many gay men and lesbians live alone without an emotional, significant other relationship. It is a selfish but a satisfying life of eating what you want, doing what you want when you want, and of concentrating upon the self rather than a relationship. It can be a life of building friends, your own financial and emotional affairs, taking chances that affect only you, changing careers, and handling your own life. It does not have to be gay life lacking love, but the love objects are not permanent fixtures. Living alone can be respectable, as respectable as you want to be. It does not have the emotional heights or a sincere personal involvement, nor the emotional depths of disappointment.

Your lifestyle depends upon how you want to accept yourself. You do not have to present a false or untrue facade of being happy if you are not. You have to live to your expectations; not the expectations of others. Basically, you have to make yourself happy with the way you are living. It is responsibility to yourself. Once you are dead, and we all will be, who will care?

A GOURMET

The single nest builder always has the difficulty of outside people assuming that if you live alone, you are going to die of starvation. Aside from the fact you fit in well at odd numbers of dinner guests, the single person is not suppose to be able to fix a meal or eat adequately. Granted, the person living alone probably does not select foods that he/she does not personally desire, but that hardly means fudge and syrup three times a week. Particularly in this period of packaged foods, the individual eating alone can create a balanced, healthy meal and enjoy it.

However, there is nothing immoral about accepting the dinner invitations and playing to your friend's lack of understanding of your kitchen and cooking knowledge. "Oh, I didn't realize they sold meat that wasn't in a plastic bag to warm up on the stove." "What does broil mean?" Your ignorance will gain you a thousand points and several more dinner invitations.

Somewhere down the line, your friends are going to force you into the position of cooking for them, even if it is only to substantiate their belief that you have no talent with food except to eat it. There is a time when most con games have an end, and the joke player has to tell. But, don't give up too easily.

In order to protect your intellectual knowledge concerning food, start a collection of cookbooks and old "Gourmet" magazines. It doesn't make any difference how little you have paid for them or if they are old since you are going to admit that you have not read them. It just builds your anticipated appreciation of good food.

Collect at least a shelf of different size bottles and various herbs and spices, preferably strangely named and uncommon ones. You can buy out a complete shelf at a yard sale for a dollar. There is no reason you should know what they are.

Invite your guests to your place at a specific odd time, say 7:15. Odd time implies that you know what you are doing every minute. Have the table prepared and the food ready to go onto the table. Serve in very small amounts, just like your food is precious. Create your own table arrangement and order of serving (have the salad last before desert). Write it all down and have menu copies for your guests. If gay, have flowers for the table. If straight, arrange six golf balls.

MENU

APPETIZERS:

Real Onion Soup: Saute (boil in a cup of water) two cups of raw sliced and diced onions and add a package of Lipton's Onion Soup into the sauteed onions, and swear you did the whole thing from scratch. Add cheese on top, melt in microwave or broiler and serve. (Yield: 4 to 35 depending on the size of the bowl) or

Real Mushroom Soup: Saute (boil in a little water) more than two cups of fresh mushrooms cut into pieces and add a can of Cambell's Cream of Mushroom Soup into the mushrooms and serve with a piece of parsley on each bowl. You worked hours over the soup. (Yield: 4 to 10 pm).

ENTREE:

Don't forget your local Oriental carry-out. You can lie and tell your guests that you have done all the different dishes, but be sure to get rid of those white cartons in which they put the carry-out food. The primary rule: always empty the garbage before your guests arrive.

Buy your own tea, the one with the prettiest box. Serve tea hot.

SALAD:

Lettuce with any 29 cent seeds, vinegar and oil.

DESSERT:

Practically any liquor over vanilla ice cream tastes unique and a slice of a Mandarin Orange (from a can; hide it) soaked in any liquor over vanilla ice cream seems very special, or

An orange wrapped in a Burger King sandwich wrapper is also very impressive.

After you have gone through the whole gourmet evening of the soup, the entree, the salad, the dessert, tell your friends what you have done to fake that you are a gourmet of food. They'll love it, and you'll get another invitation.

THE MOST EXPENSIVE

The most expensive way to live is alone. America is not built for a one person, but it allows for two people with a marriage license or without license to live more economically than one; a per-head ratio that is amusing and costly to the single nest builder.

Builders do not construct half-bedroom apartments, plenty of room in which one person can sleep comfortably. Almost all bedrooms in America will hold the standard double bed, and you will never find the smaller sized singular bedroom as the only bedroom in an apartment, the smaller bedroom only comes with a major, larger bedroom in a two bedroom apartment.

Although the gay single nest builder will pay taxes for the education of children, he/she will not have children and is paying for something which he/she will never utilize. The public has decided to build a school for children and taxes you. The paid school board, all teachers and custodians salaries paid through real estate taxes of the gay person, has decided on a hot meals program, at the single tax payer's expense, and to redo the children's playground in the park. The children are raising money for the football team or Girl Scouts and asks the single for a donation. State supported colleges are paid for through tax money from the single tax payer's pocket. Who supports the college scholarships?

By not having a husband or wife, and by not having children, you as a single person cannot receive an income tax deductions or collect twelve deductions for the kids. A welfare mother can subtract for each additional child and a family can share accommodations of bathroom, bedrooms, and eating facilities, and a single person prefers not to share.

A single person eats small amounts; the savings in buying food is to buy in large quantities. Ten pounds of beef is cheaper per pound than a half of pound of beef. You cannot buy a half can of carrots. Thus, the single person eating alone spends more on food than the average of the individual member of a large family. Even the cost of cooking is more expensive. It takes four minutes each side for a steak for one person or for six people. You can't cook pasta sauce for one using much less gas and it certainly doesn't taste the same.

Churches, even though they may not be your own religion, are tax exempt meaning single you are paying the expenses that couples do and the church doesn't. If you have a religion as a singular person, why should you have to pay for everyone else who attends the other religions? You pay at your religion. Why should you pay for the rest?

Many years ago there was a New England woman who refused to pay taxes on anything involved with war and she subtracted on her income tax the amount for war use each year. The government tolerated it because they knew the government would get the last word. When she died, the government subtracted the amount of unpaid taxes she had refused to pay while she was alive, and the government got the amount due and the penalty fee.

Although citing times by which a single person is financially discriminated against in his/her way of living is a joke, it does have a serious side of bias, but not so great that anyone is going to worry about it. It is true that the single tax payer probably does pay more than his/her absolute share of the accommodations that is used, but no one cares. (It may,however, be an interesting argument to bring to the family values organizations under "unequal taxation", and really watch the struggle.)

I know of no gay who would deny the rights of taxation for children, schools, playground, lunch menus, scholarships, etc. Even without children, the gay person realizes how important it is to have an educated, directional society, so none of this should be taken seriously, although it is fun to speculate.

CAN I BE TOO GAY?

Of course. One part of your life is your sexuality, and it may affect other aspects of your interests. Sex is not an end in itself. It is a means to get to the desired point of personal satisfaction.

Unfortunately, some gay men and lesbians become so involved in their own sexuality and their personal sex drives that they are completely dominated by gay sex talk and gay subjects and little more. They have to build a life aside from their gay minority; interests of being gay should be only a part of their interests and should not completely dominate their minds and activities.

Look over stacks of gay magazines and newspapers, each person writing a little differently than the next on the same subject; what is happening that's gay in my community of Chelsea, San Francisco, Chicago or New York. They list the people, the gay bars, the hangouts, the guest houses, the upcoming events, the personal advertising, the gay lawyers and the scene of what seems to be in every larger village in the United States, Canada, and Europe. The hot numbers, the legal aids offices, the politicians that are opposed to or in support of gay issues. Each city is about the same.

There is a personal, psychological point when a gay person finds that if he is HIV positive, he searches out selfishly for any and all information, and this search for his own survival completely dominates his life. It is called "dementia", where he concentrates only on every idea or direction or conversation of opinion concerning the problems of handling and caring for AIDS, his AIDS.

Current publications thrive on new articles and new directions and with a sophisticated readership that understands many of the terminologies of modern medicine, the articles are technical and are free in advice of how you should live your life. They hint that everything from vitamin C through positive thinking can stop the progression of AIDS. At this point, there are still no scientific physical cures, although we seem to be learning how to delay the action. Allowing the mind to become so obsessed with one direction is not healthy regardless of the subject matter.

There comes a time when we have to rebel. "We are tired of hearing about gay things and people, HIV positives, and AIDS, gay talk and gossip. Stop the ship; we want off. We not going to allow ourselves to be dominated only by these ideas. We will read and talk for information, but we will not re-hash, re-evaluate, re-educate, re-align ourselves by being dominated by the subject of sexuality." There is a time to run away.

Check the conversation of gay bartenders, drag queens, your friends and you'll find that some are so completely involved in their sexuality or sex that it is all they know or want to explore or expose. Someone else's sex is not as interesting to you; your sex life is interesting to you.

We all have an associate, call him Miss Doom, and he is the first to shout about, announce, and work out the details of anyone that has died. He is the first with the news and he can quote accurately deaths, obituaries, times and dates. He attends most funerals, particularly those with wakes after the ceremony. He needs a life.

There are ideas and adventures in life if we only take advantage of them, tales that can be woven without thinking about our personal sexuality, or sex for ourselves. Be aggressive. Do not forget that you are gay, but you do not have to live waving a gay flag 24 hours a day. Stop wearing your problems on your sleeve. Give it a break.

Don't give it the "poor me" attitude of constant sympathy. You are responsible for your own happiness and it is much easier to sit back and complain of your problems than it is to get going and do something about them. Christianity and Judaism have taught us how to publicly suffer, and we carry it to an extreme.

THE EXTREME

There are some gays that operate to an extreme of wanting practically everyone and everything to be gay. We have all heard it. Jesus was gay. All movie stars are gay. All athletes are gay. It is obviously not true. These extremists would like to have a gay President , a gay House and Senate, and what a mess that would be.

The gays must realize we are a minority, and everyone will not accept us. The gays must protect themselves, the laws governing their lives protect them against discrimination, but the laws will not give us equality until we earn equality, and maybe not even then. There is the right of the individual to like or dislike whomever he/she pleases so long as there is not illegal discrimination, but the individual has the right of preference.

There is a major emphasis in the gay community in sexual relations, probably as strong as the heterosexual interests in that society. The clubs and bars play to this interest for both gays and straights. The human relationships seem built upon the response. The frequency of the gay attempts at trying to establish a relationship, for many sexual partners, implies immorality that the heterosexual community has difficulty understanding. The heterosexual community is not honest counting the numbers of their own experiences and they appear to be amazed at the gay promiscuity. No one can deny that sex is a basic desire of homosexuality, but there is much more to the gay lifestyle than the mere physical act.

The early religions regarded homosexuality as a way of avoiding reproduction, and homosexual acts reduced the number of acts of heterosexuality, thus, the number of children. Being gay threatened survival of the race, and of mankind. The church feared homosexuals would attract some heterosexuals, and the church fueled homophobia. [8] No wonder the straight people threw the faggots on the fire. In the fall of 1997, at the National Conference of Catholic Bishops, a reinterpretation of previous parental rejection of homosexual children stated that "homosexual orientation is not freely chosen and parents must not reject their gay children." [9] Although sex to reproduce is probably the basis for animalistic heterosexual physical sex, there are more requirements in a relationship or a marriage.

It is easy in the gay lifestyle to get caught up in the name calling and slander of those that do not think as you do. It may be easy for some to have a constant confrontation with those who do not agree. Often the gay will challenge a situation with his/her presence, maybe his actions or drag, and wanting to make a point, but wanting confrontation. We all know the woman liberationist that has carried the flag too long to the wrong places.

The gay person is not wanted in every social event, and a wise gay person will avoid those situations in which he/she is not wanted. Usually, however, they are not unwelcomed because they are gay. They are sometimes unwelcomed because they push being gay, or how they behave, or even because of how they dress. However, the current practically militant direction of some gay groups is to participate in everything, even in those things that you are not welcomed. Relax.

CAN I LIVE UP TO OTHER'S EXPECTATIONS?

Who are the "others"? Family? Friends? Your lover? Yourself? Who has established your sense of values? You.

The gay man or lesbian puts demands upon him/herself growing from not being accepted in a family structure that meets his/her desires or demands. When the childhood dreams of being an adult are fulfilled in the child's mind, the expected values inherited from what the family wants you to be do not meet the demands to the gay man or lesbian's satisfaction. The gay person wants something different, something not realized by the heterosexual desires and dreams of the family unit. The family cannot build in you the dreams and fantasy of a world they do not know. They must think from their own experiences, and their heterosexual lifestyle leaves little room for them to realize more. The parents are doing what they can, and the child is not satisfied. They live in ignorance of each other's dreams.

If the child realizes the parents really want the gay son or daughter to be happy with him/herself, the parents are in a positive direction. (We say this without understanding that there are many parents who only want their children to reflect themselves because they have, egotistically, found the 'right" answer to life.) It is necessary for the parents to withdraw being incapable of satisfying the demands placed upon them by the young gay male or lesbian. Under their sense of child responsibility to parenting, they do not withdraw easily even if they understand that withdrawing may be better for the child. They would rather try to understand the feelings of the gay person than withdraw. Admittedly, they do not know the desires or feelings of their offspring.

The parents of the gay man or lesbian usually build on the other aspects of his/her life, those things aside from the sexuality of their child. Interests like traveling, music, accomplishment, direction, and fulfilling activities for the child's positive evaluation of him/herself produce the best results. Realizing the gay man or lesbian is different is one thing; dwelling on it creates a confused child. Ignoring the child could develop a particularly serious consequence, like a child's suicide.

Many parents of gay men and lesbians do not want to recognize their son or daughter may be gay. They may instinctively question or know, but the parents will refuse to acknowledge the characteristic. They may be wiser by not mentioning the subject that would cause confusion or a difference in the family unit.

Some gay parents with straight children avoid the confession that they are gay to protect the children. "You don't always have to hang out your laundry." The parents assume that if the issue comes up to the young adult, he/she can handle it, and, perhaps, they feel they do not leave as large a scare on the child. A straight child of a gay parent usually becomes aware of his parent's wonderings, and if he does not confront the parent, the behavior may not be a problem to the child if the parent does not confess to being gay.

It is not unusual to hear about long married couples who get a divorce and the wife or husband complains that the other person was really a S.O.B. Doesn't that say something about the mate's choice, how stupid the mate was to choose the person or how dumb he/she was to live together for so long? Why did they marry? Why didn't they get a divorce earlier? Why did one stay in the relationship? How can a loving person become a S.O.B. overnight?

If the main interest of parents is their child's happiness regardless of his/her problems, the parents soon realize there is a time to be concerned and a time to let the child do what he wants to do. The gay man or lesbian will often push this decision of the parents. The parents feel they are protecting the weak, the gay son or daughter.

There is also a time for the newly independent gay or lesbian to stumble before they learn to walk. The parents should have built something more than the sexual animal, and the child should have learned to stumble and walk on his/her own. Americans call it independence. The gay man or lesbian will someday thank the parents for allowing him/her to stumble without their aid and for guiding the child to walk.

Unfortunately, some are lost. They will never learn to walk. They will wallow in their own self-pity, make excuses for their being, blame others, and never take responsibility for themselves. They have been sucked into the system of self-indulgence and pity, and all they really want is to be important to someone else and to themselves. They take a coward's way out. Sympathy doesn't give them what they desire. The parent or parents hide the gay son or daughter afraid to allow him/her to make a mistake. How many gays are still living with their parents or living with one parent for, supposedly, protection of the parent?

Alcohol is the easiest, the least legally restrictive. Drugs are so available and allow you the ease of escape although with the penalty of being arrested. The easiest seems to be non-conformity; living in a liberal lifestyle that will accept so much, and extending the limits to as much as you can get away with, the choice of many. Alcohol, drugs and escape come in combination; an open invitation to self-destruction. All are roads taken of what others expect of you, and what you expect of yourself unless you are strong to stand against destruction.

Establish your own expectation of yourself; what makes you happy. Make it a goal which can be accomplished. Learn to accept it and not fully accomplish the goal. You're only human and the imagined poten-tial may be much greater than the actual potential. Satisfy yourself.

BE RESPONSIBLE

We observe the gay person, both male and female, and the straight woman without children, the old maids, the spinsters, the heterosexual bachelors, the divorced, the widowed and many are awkward at the gay conversations and actions. We talk in stereotypes of the kinds of Americans we are. Few of us are living the stereotype of the happily married husband and wife, the beautiful children, the owned home in the suburbs, and the excellent job. We have had and cherish these goals from early childhood. We accept these values, and we privately admit that we have not reached these goals, and we question if the goals are practical or wise. We change our stereotypes as we mature, but the ideal "made in Hollywood" couple exists in our value scale.

Some people consider themselves lucky not to have children. Parents allow a child to be the center of attention and cannot talk of anything except the child. When a child cries or misbehaves in a restaurant, or cries at night, when baby carriages clog the isles of grocery stores, accepting the heterosexual family is the American direction. It is un-American to say that you don't like children. It is similar to not liking your parents. The gay wanting to be liked by all, cry out to mimic a lifestyle in which they may not easily or comfortably fit, and when they are rejected, they blame their disappointment on being gay. The gay person seldom realizes that there are many unhappy, unsatisfied, unsuccessful straight people, and many of them are fighting for happiness also. The American value scale gives the individual the right to "pursue" happiness; it does not guarantee happiness.

As gays, we do have to use the same values that govern the majority of the people, but we respect them. We are not forced to adopt the same values into our own life pattern, although many try. When the gay man has to marry to be accepted, and the gay woman has to have a child by her husband for fulfillment, the individual is confused although there is a clearly drawn direction. How often we assume that the person that has taken an unconventional direction will not be happy? How often in one generation's behavior considered degenerative only to be accepted in the next? The working woman. The soldier. The often divorced. The married woman who does not want children. The gays.

As gay men and women, we have to get over blaming everything that happens negatively to us on being gay. We have to realize that there are many confused, disillusioned, and bitter gay people. Being gay does not make you right. We must be responsible ...

AM I A FATALIST?

You have been dealt five cards in order to play poker, the game of life. You are not responsible for the cards given you. You did not deal. But, you have the cards, and you have to determine if they are "good" or "bad" cards. In draw poker, you may take a chance and throw away three cards and be left with two, and are dealt three new cards in your new hand. The first game of poker leaves you only luck; the second draw poker gives you a chance to gamble for better. Both games are based on the luck of the first draw.

Many people equate life as a poker game; you are given five cards and it is up to you how you play them. Others believe this draw poker game has an element of chance and an advantage, you can trade three cards for three new ones.

Some gay men and lesbians believe the similarity between poker and life, but one of the cards is the wild gay card which cannot be thrown away, and you must deal with that card. Can it be a threat? Worrisome? Defeating? A looser? A destroyer? Or can it win the game being wild over someone by being higher, making a pair, turned to an advantage? It all depends upon how you play your cards.

The fatalistic approach to living for gay men and lesbians is the negative approach to poker rather than a positive approach of having some faith in your card playing skills. Again, it is like looking at a glass of wine which is either half full or half empty. Many gays are beaten before they even start to play the game; few look at the gay card as an advantage because, perhaps, of a limited amount of advantages and there may have been no one to teach the game.

The fatalistic conclusion is to play the game with the cards you have been given to the best of your ability, and if you lose, you lose; if you win, you win. Cold. Calculated. A lot of credit to chance. That's life.

The fatalistic approach to life is lacking when it takes the human factors from the game; when the five cards can be selected to be played against or in competition with the opponents. In other words, just accepting the cards is the first step. How and when you play each card becomes an individual's choice. A randomly selected card is often a give-away. Who plays first and has the advantage or the disadvantage?

Too many gay men and lesbians hide under the fatalistic approach. They say "These are the cards I've been dealt, and I lose." They don't even try to play the game, but quit.

Others have accepted their five cards and although no better or worse than the other poker player's hands, they make the best of what they have by learning how and when to play each card. They often win.

It is difficult to understand the complete fatalistic approach to life because so many people blame everything wrong in their lives on someone or something else besides themselves, and they seem to give no attention to their own smarts, decision making, conclusions and directions. The difference in the two fatalistic approaches is that the second allows the individual to participate in the decision making, and this can decide who wins or loses the game.

We hear it often in the heterosexual lifestyle; "if I would not have married so young... If only I had waited having kids... If I would have gone to college..." and a million and one excuses.

The excuses for homosexuals are limited, often not supported by other gay people. "My parents made me gay ... It's the environment in which I was born ... My father wasn't home ... My mother was a drunk ..." Excuses. Excuses.

WHEN AM I ADJUSTED TO BEING GAY?

Once you have left your birth family and gone off to college, or work, or the military or whatever, and established your life in a larger city of your choice that has a larger gay lifestyle, and once you have settled into this new surroundings and the people of the gay lifestyle, you will start to feel that you belong.

A college freshman calls home the first term three or four times the first month. As he adjusts, he calls home less because he feels more of the college scene. As a senior, he has to remind himself to call home.

Any new place will be different at first. You will desire the security of your birth family, and if you live near, you may visit your parents or they will visit you quite often. There is a degree of security in family. You'll keep track of your old school friends also. As you start to build new friends, some more similar to you than your home town friends, you will write less, call less, and see your family and friends less frequently. As the years progress, this separation will become more apparent to you, your friends and your family.

A young lesbian realized she was independent from her childhood friends and family when she no longer had a comfortable place in her family home because they turned her bedroom into a guest room. She wanted to return to the city and her new family in the city.

It is a point that we remember fondly, because it is not a sad event in life. It's the realization of independence. With some, it starts when you call your nest your "home". It is the night the young groom brings his wife to his parent's house to spend the night in his original bed. You have broken the cord to your family and often to your friends. It is not that you don't want to see them and be with them and are concerned. It is at your discretion, not requirement.

This by no means implies that you love your family and siblings less; you are just involved in your new world as they are in their own new world without you. The week days get longer and the week ends get shorter as you become involved.

You will probably make three, four or five lifetime friends. That's about all a working person has time for, but these friends will share a common bond. You don't have to be constantly in contact with them to maintain your friendship. Months pass, maybe years, and as soon as you hear your friend or see him/her, the time between the last meeting is unimportant. There is an unstated contract of friendship.

NEW PEOPLE

Realizing you are gay, you move to a larger city where you are employed and you meet other gay men or lesbians of which you approve and are accepted, and you start to establish your own gay family away from your natural birth family. Your life feels pretty full of your social contacts, and the procedure that you establish to comply with your sexuality. You must extend yourself beyond this group of friends.

What are your personal interests aside from those related to your sexuality, your hobbies and areas of concern? Do you sing or play an instrument? Do you want more education? Have you considered taking a foreign language? What training do you need to enhance your job? The direction becomes to push you away, only temporarily, from the security of the created family, the security of your living conditions, and into other activities aside from those sexually oriented into an interest based part of life, organizations, clubs, or meeting places where you can experience being yourself aside from your gay self.

At first, you may feel intimidated by being in a group that is not gay, but your interest in the subject matter or activity of the new group will allow you to socialize, and you will find that you like some of the people without you spilling your sexual history to them. Of course, at first you can easily pass when you find others that have similar interests to you. The intimidation will become less. Hopefully, you'll learn to listen and, to a degree, relate without your sexual confession.

The socialization of a club or organization carries further than the meeting place, and you may find yourself enjoying other activities at their invitation. You can go to a straight party and feel comfortable. You can even date the opposite sex without it being a strain on your own sexuality. You don't have to have sexual relationships with everyone; at least I hope not

Is this presenting a false side of your personality? It doesn't have to if you can listen rather than talk. People don't necessarily want to know everything personal about their friends. There are questions which are none of their business. There are honest answers that you do not have to volunteer, or should you. There is respect for privacy, and if someone steps over the line, you let them know. "That's none of your business ..." or "Why do you want to know ...?" You learn to avoid not because you are ashamed of yourself, but because you would rather the other person does not have that information. The only way they can accurately get the information is from you, and you don't have to tell anything unless you want to. Don't allow someone to intimidate you.

Don't intimidate yourself by telling everything about yourself to someone who could probably care less at that time. "I only said 'Hello'. I didn't want her life history."

We can be our own worse enemies.

If you are in a gay relationship and it does not work out, that's your business. You owe no one an excuse or an explanation. Learn to be your own private person.

Being your own person may mean you will have to start building a wall around yourself, allowing inside the wall only the people to whom you have given the privilege. It is called self-protection and there is nothing wrong with having the wall so long as you are responsible for destroying it when you want. Too strong a wall impossible to scale by no one is also destructive and too defensive. So, you'll have to decide how thick and tall that wall should be.

Meeting new people and ideas also helps when you are away from those sensual years and when you become more mature and into retirement. At 20, gay life looks like one perpetual romp on the mattress, but although many will not admit it as many will not admit their real age, as you grow older, "it ain't". The older you become the more important other aspects of love are to you; the kind word, the tender gesture, the desire to please, the comfort. Life is not "sex city forever", or if it is, a lot of people have yet to find out.

"GRABBERS"

The homosexual community is composed of many people who have run from their family home and friends to a new place where the people are more understanding of their sexual activity and the confusion that develop. These include frustrations, anxieties, and problems that the homosexual personality in this period of a new situation may develop as he/she is viewing the gay lifestyle.

The gay lifestyle accepts a greater variety of morals and actions than the straight lifestyle, and can often allow individual personality differences to develop while the person is still socially acceptable. Behind the problems of the gay person is often an aggressive person who wants to prove his/her own worth through being successful. They are often successful. With success usually comes additional financial rewards, and there are many financially successful gay men and lesbians. This sets them up as a target for the "grabbers", those people who want whatever someone else has, and a person that finds nothing wrong in stealing, either emotionally or physically.

We make the mistake of thinking these "grabbers" are the scruffiest of people, uneducated, with questionable manners and no social graces. This may not be their stereotype. They can be cool, sophisticated, intelligent, suave and proper, sometimes equals, who have their own betterment foremost in their minds regardless of what it will do to you. The "grabber" may be your best friend, or you.

The gay community has a greater tendency to gamble on another person than the straight community because there is less obvious direction for the finances, and the gay has an awareness of another person being misunderstood, perhaps misdirected. Gays often confuse companionship with affection.

The gay person is an easy emotional weakling to the skilled "grabber". Playing with a gay person's emotions is the direction to the target. The "grabber" finds someone vulnerable and plays to this weakness. Sex becomes the weapon. There may be some exceptions, but we really don't believe the 60 year old had a great deal of mental stimulation from the 21 year old. Without gifts or advantages, the younger person would rather be with someone his/her own age.

The weapon is not always sex; stronger and less identifiable is the younger person's interest and direction in his well-being, the free dinners, shows, social outings and companionship, often the same characteristics that are found in a close friend, and the "grabber" can be a friend right up to and after death of the older person.

In reality, some straight couple's relationship are based on the well-being of one person to the partner. There is a limit of physical desire which is demanded by both, and the partnership can be tolerated if the limit of comfort is constantly improved. They are called "marriages of convenience" and the practice is still used.

Into the gay lifestyle comes the "grabber", and his/her morals, attitude, desires and guts may be mild or strong, and success is determined by what he/she can get. Some gays want to be taken, and the "grabber" is there to accommodate them. Most older gays are willing to be taken to the degree they can afford it, or they are complimented by the flattery to a degree that their wallet can stand, or they will tolerate much finding it impossible to turn away from a smart hustler. Some older gays end their lives financially broken, but maintained the expenditure was worth it. Others end up murdered.

Our logic would indicate that we could figure out the whole scenario before we become personally involved, but we don't . The "grabbers" are still there, and the gays with jewels held out to them.

THE MATURING OF BEING GAY

Sodomy is usually defined as oral or anal sex, and it has been against the law for many years. In 1961, all 50 states outlawed sodomy. Six states specifically indicate laws against same sex sodomy (Arkansas, Kansas, Maryland, Missouri, Oklahoma, Texas). 15 states have laws against sodomy for homosexuals and heterosexuals (Alabama Arizona, Florida, Georgia, Idaho, Louisiana, Massachusetts, Michigan Mississippi, Minnesota, North Carolina, Rhode Island, South Carolina, Utah, Virginia and the U.S. Military). In 1986 the Supreme Court ruled that privacy laws are not applicable to those convicted of same sex sodomy.

There are some that feel that the gay person is only unique in the way he/she prefers same sex partners. Practically all gays realize that sex is only one aspect of the gay lifestyle, probably one of the most abused, and it certainly does rank high on the human relations scale of feeling happy. Sex is a tool, a method to get to greater depths of understanding. It is only a part of the gay lifestyle, a part that seems relatively unimportant as greater understandings are built. Yet, the gay person is always aware that he/she is breaking our laws and, to some, the laws of God. Guilt is built into our lives.

Having adjusted to the gay lifestyle, the realizations of the "goods" and "bads" of it for your personality, these behaviors have to settle after being constantly challenged to see if they can work into a healthy, happy life for you. How well you handle the adjustment to gay life determines how well you will allow the adjustment to develop into maturity of life's principles that guide the rest of your life and your influence on other people. To be with direction rather than floundering for answers is a secret of maturity.

TIME

As individuals, we are victims of our time, the days in which we were born and the events that happened during our development, through middle-life to death. As individuals, we probably have very little to do with the changing time during our lifetime, but these events, actions or influences have greatly affected decisions we have made during each period. If there were no war, we could not have volunteered for the service. Where we are, the place, and what we are, a female peasant, greatly influence even our own estimation and reaction to time. A British nobleman will judge the oncoming war differently than a Chinese labor man even at the same time.

All things and events seem to be affected by the element of time. When you walk through the woods, various trees and plants have different life spans; trees living 500 years, plants living 70, animals living ten, insects living only a couple of days, etc. Man is part of the matter and manner of that woods. All things don't develop at the same rate.

As human beings, we are born into a certain time with a certain amount of years to live, and we are born into a woods that has various life spans, some perhaps are eternal. Our lives develop and are shaped through the other life spans, all growing at the same time but at different rates.

Toward the end of the twentieth century many human advances have been made, but they have not been made in a consistent rhythm in time. For example, science has advanced tremendously in the twentieth century, medical science following closely behind. There have been great gains in the use of materials such as new terms as "steel", then "plastic". Things that produce other things seem to have been the direction; probably not the emphasis on the aesthetic things, like art, music, ideas, etc.

It was less than a 100 years ago that the Wright Brothers flew the airplane in Dayton, Ohio, and since then we have put a man on the moon. Medical science can now cure so many of the physical problems of the body (exceptions being the common cold and AIDS). Sewer pipes are made of plastic, and we can reroute underground water supplies. We are working on the problems of bias, prejudice, and hatred, although we have yet to eliminate war. Advancement is not in even paces with time; the maturing of ideas and things operate at differing times, and many physical events are not logical or reasoned events.

We get impatient when we realize that we have been struggling as an outspoken minority of gay rights for the past 30 or 40 years and even much longer, The blacks have been fighting for independence for several centuries. Women's struggle for independence and equality has been going on for as long as the history of women. Prejudice still dominates in many groups and the superiority of one race over another, one religion over another, one sex over the other, one political party over another, one person over another is consistently taught to the next generation. The fight for gay rights is quite a newcomer of the prejudices to the viewing world.

But, the time is ripe. When so many people are fighting for the acceptance of the individual and realize that each individual is of value to himself and his society, when we realize true individual equality, the time in society is ripe to push for these equalities. The push will be spastic; great progress getting through the action it wants, and at other times, it will be stagnant. Unfortunately, some times will be counter-productive, setting the movement back or at least putting the movement on a plateau.

The gay fight is about the worth of the individual and the rules and regulations that protect that individual. We are making progress. Sometimes slowly. Sometimes we have to back-track. As the cigarette ad says "We've come a long way". We have to be cautious not to push too hard, too often, too crudely or we will hurt our cause.

HOW DO I SPEND MY TIME?

A study of sleeping habits indicates that men and women in their 20's get about seven and three quarters hours of sleep a night. Those in their 80's get about eight and a half hours of sleep a night. In theory, the older you get, the more you sleep at night. [1]

In an early study of dreaming, the author theorized there were five levels of sleep, some people falling into the deepest level five as soon as they go to bed and slowly increasing consciousness as morning comes, a second person drifting into the unconscious with the deepest sleep in the morning. [2] He found we dream about every 20 minutes, but we recall the dreams only of the first or second levels, a half-conscious state just before many awaken.

The many studies break down into a very practical decision for everyone. Since we spend a third of our lives asleep, buy a good bed. It is one of the major investments for good, healthy living, and it is sure to be used.

In one study the author found that men spent, aside from the sleep, the greatest amount of time at the job until around the age of 60 and that women spent the second greatest amount of time at the job until around 40. [3] Who does the dishes after the woman is 40? This study is probably not accurate of gay men and lesbians, and they probably spend more time at the job than those with family responsibilities. Also, the career woman not only devotes more time to the job, but also has the house chores and duties.

There have been many studies concerning the amount of time Americans spend at work. Men usually average about 61 hours a week. The working woman averages about 56, but this is increasing.

So the job and sleep take up two-thirds or more of each day which leaves you with six or seven hours of time to more or less relax. Your obligations are part of that period. It is not really the amount of time that is important, it is what you do with the time. There is an old business slogan that states "Give the job to a busy person, and he/she will get it done." Time scheduling.

What is important is what we do with the time we have in which to relax, and if we can relax. We know many people who sit these hours in bars, and that can be a gay curse. We know others who cook, socialize with friends, have hobbies and interests which keep them involved. We know people who use their spare time well, and others who just flit it away.

Unfortunately in the gay life style, we know many people who are bored; bored with themselves as well as with their friends. Another cliche: "If you are bored, you are boring. Make yourself exciting."

Many gays are in the "I wish ..." habit. "I wish I had 5,000 dollars... I wish I could paint or write ... I wish someone would take me away from all this ..." Complaining without doing anything about it. They have created unfulfilled dreams because the person has not done a thing to help him/herself. Stop making excuses and get out and do something; practically anything that doesn't hurt others, regardless if you are good at it. You'll be amazed at what you can accomplish, and how much better you'll like yourself.

Negativism is characteristic of all kinds of people. They allow themselves to be pulled down by others who think negatively. They often pull themselves down. We all know a person who has never felt well a day in his/her life. We fear in asking "How are you?" for the deadly experience of receiving a detailed, morbid answer.

We listen to complaints of "... can't make the rent" over again. This is the "crisis personality", someone always in a state of decision making without ever making a decision, but with the amazing ability to tell everyone. The negative thinker cannot pull himself from his own worries to be positive about practically anything. Combine the "constantly ill" with the "crisis personality" and you have a really boring companion.

Eliminate boring people in your life. If you are boring, purposefully set out to change your patterns by going new places, meeting new people, doing new things. Take a class at the junior college. Write poetry. Take tap dancing lessons. Anything to get you out of the rut you have created. If you know boring people, eliminate them as associates. (It is sadistically good to be around boring people because it makes you appreciate how interesting you are.)

Many people get caught in the "I complex ..." and particularly single gays are guilty of using the word too often. The easiest way to be liked is to listen. Gays like their audiences. Partners use the "we complex ..." "We are doing this or that." There is good reason; many gays are so self-involved with their own sleep, work, and leisure time that they have developed an attitude of not being interested in anything that does not directly involve them. You know how bored you get listening to heterosexuals talk about their children. Why would you subject anyone to every little detail of your life?

Another way that particularly successful gays spend their time is talking about their personal wealth or business. They never ask questions of the listeners. They ramble on telling about how successful they are. They share only with another business person a conversation and they will be quick to admit that the other business person knows nothing, certainly not as much as they do. If you have to tell someone how successful you are, being successful is not very obvious.

Caution to gays who start practically every sentence with "I know..." and he/she continues to top each story with a grander detail of his own experience. Ask yourself that if he knows everything, why are you talking to him? The "I can top that ..." personality soon becomes a bore. No matter what you have done, the talker has done something greater or bigger with no hesitation to tell the story. Irritating. Eliminate.

In college someone in the know would tell the story of a polar bear sitting on an iceberg which broke off from the main iceberg and the polar bear would say "And so did I", and those in the know in the audience would break into wild laughter. There was no point to the story and it was in no way comical, but the laughing group who knew the non-joke could identify the newcomer who would laugh for acceptance along with the knowing crowd. Haven't you heard a joke that you didn't understand? Did you laugh?

WHAT'S IN A RELATIONSHIP?

One of the many studies concerning heterosexual relationships was done of 111 men and women who were asked what they expected from a relationship. [4] They were separated or divorced, and they listed similar qualities, although they differed on the intensity of these qualities. Although this study was of straight men and women, a study of the gay man and/or lesbian would probably yield similar results.

Affection headed the list. Both men and women answered to be more interested in the mental and emotional aspects of a relationship than the physical aspects. The women put more emphasis upon what they thought the man wanted. Applying this study to the gay lifestyle, does the aggressor put more emphasis upon what he/she wants or upon what he/she thinks the partner wants?

The emphasis upon sex for the gay male or lesbian is probably different in the gay lifestyle. The desires mellow as the two people replace and/or build other attributes that seem important. Allowing sex to grow into a form of love is a long term objective of a gay relationship, and relationships that are based only on sex are short-sighted. The gay male takes this short-sighted relationship more easily than the lesbians who may demand more than a physical, one night stand.

The two sexes agreed that attractiveness was important but each gender felt it was more important to the other person than it was to him/herself. Attractiveness in the gay lifestyle is heavily related to the imagined sexual activity of the gay male or lesbian. The cliche: "...in the eyes of the beholder." There is probably less stereotyping of mates in the gay lifestyle, not meeting someone who must be approved by others. The older gay male may use the younger mate as a trophy for increasing his own ego. The stability of the older gay mate may be attractive to the younger.

Many publications showing half-nude or nude bodies seem to be more prevalent with gay males than lesbians, but female models which become role models are more prevalent in the heterosexual world. Our grandmothers never saw an erection, maybe one. Today's grandparents look at pictures.

A severe change in the last 15 years has been the establishing of role models for both gay men and lesbians. What has surprised many is that the gay person is in every profession, every level of life, every society. Coming out of the closets are politicians, singing stars, architects, and businessmen many not in the artistic fields that we have labeled effeminate. Reversing, many of the occupations that we have accepted as having a large gay contingent are owned and patronized by straights.

In the study, emotional support was more important for women than men as was acceptance. Emotional support seems to be very important for gay men and lesbians, although acceptance seems to be much more free and open. The relative ease of ending a relationship is much greater in the gay lifestyle. If the gay man or lesbian is not emotionally supported, he or she moves on.

Most straight people thought that honesty was much more important for their mate, more important than for themselves. All people probably know themselves better than they know their mate, and they can identify their own degree of honesty better than assuming the degree of honesty of the mate. I doubt if there is much difference between the expected level of honesty of the straight mate or the gay mate, both recognize sexual infidelity.

In this study, the women had the difficulty of recognizing the relationships of their potential husbands to other women, seemingly a jealousy trend. This is not true in the gay lifestyle; same sex relationships fearing little from the opposite sex. Lesbians competing with other lesbians, or gay male competition is severe because there are few rules and laws. A broken hearted gay male or lesbian can be vicious opening new scars where old ones have healed.

Enthusiasm among heterosexual relationships is an expected quality, but there certainly are more social obligations of planning a wedding, selecting clothing, invitations, receptions, etc., of a straight wedding. Enthusiasm can be in an understanding between two gays, but it is less public. Some gay males can get enthusiastic after a one night trick. Enthusiasm as a major quality of the gay relationship is low except for the two people involved, because the gay lifestyle has seen many combinations of people and their relationships are their own business.

The expectation of intelligence and communication, the interchange of ideas and relaying of ideas, is essential in the heterosexual wish list, both men and women feeling it would be difficult to achieve. In the gay lifestyle, communication is that glue that adheres two people since the liberal lifestyle easily allows two lovers to split without the social restrictions of legal marriage.

In general, the study of heterosexual expectations extended to the gay lifestyle points to the restrictions, obligations, and protocol of the straight which exists differently in the gay life.

SAME SEX WEDDING AND MARRIAGE

No one can oppose a relationship between two people who love each other, confide their desires and limitations, and devote themselves to understanding and being with the another person. This is the height of human involvement and respect. When two people commit themselves to each other, the union must be respected. If we mean by "marriage" the understanding and commitment of two people, physically, mentally, and spiritually, it is the major idealistic goal of every person.

No one can be against the relationship between two people, but many straights and gays are against the terminology that could have been avoided. The same sex marriage issue grows from the public writing of people concerning discrimination which is "prohibitive on the basis of gender" and is gender directed. There are only two genders: male and female. Gender is usually not considered by law unless it has been used as discrimination or used as a tool. Confusion in this book is the constant "he/she" and the term "gay" to refer to both genders, the term "gay male" or "lesbian" to differentiate the genders.

If you mean by "marriage" the understanding and commitment of two people, other terms like "domestic partner", "partnership agreement", even an "understanding " or "significant other" break down the heterosexual confusion of defining "marriage". The heterosexual stereotypes of "marriage" mean non-attractive implications such as divorce attorneys, alimony, children, legal responsibility, tax returns, to discrimination issues. With the term of "marriage", not the concept, we have opened a wide range of technically difficult problems with complex answers which put more emphasis upon the legal position of "marriage" than the union of two people.

The taking of heterosexual terminology offends the straight community because of many ancient stereotypes of marriage in the world, meaning the marriage of male and female. Straights become confused and are against the term of "gay marriage", not necessarily the relationship between the couple of the same sex.

Some gay people want same sex relationships to be registered by law and have the same legal rights of a heterosexual marriage. Only Hawaii has made an active attempt, much of the legal discrimination writing uses heterosexual language in defining gay situations. If one says he met a nice "couple" last night, most people assume a man and a woman, not a lesbian and her girl friend or a gay man and his boy friend. Most states have elected not to recognize same sex marriages, and have established laws protecting opposite sex marriages. Why didn't we call the understanding between two people something else?

Why is there a need for a gay couple to be recognized by law? There is a need for the physical responsibility to the other, but this can be accomplished legally through a contractual agreement. Another reason is inheritance, but this also can be accomplished by a Right of Survivor agreement or a Power of Attorney, or a will. There is a Right of Survivor on Medical Decisions and a Deposition of the Remains. There is even a legal adoption that can be used by those over 18 or 21 years of age. Vacation times, emergency benefits, insurance beneficiary payments, etc., can be contracted by a benevolent employer. There is no legal documentation that is held between a wife and husband that cannot be held between two people of the same sex with the exception of a marriage license. The legal means are there for gays, but many gays selected the term "marriage".

The problem is that gays don't use the means available to us. We want the marriage license because it is denied to us. Firstly, the many previously mentioned papers are agreements that are not often signed because one of the parties does not wish to take the time to sign them or he/she is cautious about signing them. Are we aware we can create an inheritance will, and many people will not? Does the gay couple want to create a fuss, a publicized function advertising their relationship? Does the couple want the public to know of their commitment?

Utilize what is already available to us. Don't give attention, time, and effort to something that is already available in our laws. Why try to mimic the straight terminology and language?

If we have same sex marriages, we will have to have same sex divorces, same sex distribution of wealth, same sex responsibilities for the other person, and many other legal specifics that are covered with a straight wedding or a legal document. We are right back to "Who will get the dog?" The process is endless, and the lawyers get fat. What has been accomplished? Better spend time on something that has a greater benefit to the gay movement, and watch out for the palimony suit.

If we define marriage as the expectation of child bearing, there are many straight marriages that really cannot be considered marriages in-so-far-as they want no children. Should we differentiate between the marriages that want children and those that don't want children, those marriages of traditional family values, and those of gay marriages? What a mess we're getting ourselves into.

A gay wedding is an announcement to friends of the union of two people of the same sex. The spirituality of the wedding is between the two people; the audience is just watching. Announcing the union may be fine, but it does not have to be done in a church because, like it or not, the church may recognize the union, but the law does not.

Give a cocktail party. Let the information be known by what you say and how you act. If you must have a legal agreement, have it drawn up. Don't get caught in the confusion over parroting the heterosexual lifestyle which is only half successful at best.

Look at the confusion with gay marriages. Will a gay marriage in California recognize "common property"? Will there be a domestic-partnership law? How long is "common law"? When can I sue for palimony or alimony? Did I change his/her life for better or worse? How about fidelity? Can I just live off my x-mate's checks?

IF WE'RE GROWING APART IN A RELATIONSHIP?

Be sure you know why you and your significant other are growing apart, and consider that the difference between you may just be part of the maturing understanding of each other. If not, identify the problem. Don't lay blame on the other person. Talk about the problem and see if there is the desire for both of you to solve it.

Can you or the other person tolerate the problem to save your relationship? Do you want to save the relationship? Does he/she? Did he/she say so, or are you indulging in wishful thinking? It is strange that any relationship problem is always the other person's fault. Is the problem anyone's fault, or is it just an adjustment problem? Do you want to continue your relationship?

Can you sustain in the relationship with the problem? Is it worth it? Can you both take fault for the problem and not blame the other person? Is this problem so great that it overshadows what the two of you have built together? Can you forget who faulted and forgive or be forgiven? "I'll forgive it, but I'll never forget it" is an incomplete answer.

Growing apart in a lover relationship does not mean that two people are not spending time together. As a relationship matures, the lovers may spend considerably less time together, each having the emotional security and understanding to realize that each needs his/her own alone time.

Growing apart does not mean that each does not have individual interests that are unique and not shared by the other person which can be a healthy relationship. Has each maintained their individual identity?

Separating from the lover does mean that if they have accomplished their goals, they need to establish new goals. The lovers may have become comfortable and contented and are no longer growing to take on new challenges and directions, and some people would call that contentment. Each has accepted his/her role in the relationship and they are satisfied, the largest goal of life.

If the relationship is unhappy or boring, if there is no longer consideration for the other person, if companionship has become routine rather than exciting, if compassion dies, understanding lacks and directions are foggy, two people may have grown apart.

If there is no energy or desire to dissolve what they have created, they are content, but they may not necessarily be happy. Settle for being content.

IF SEX BECOMES DULL ...

Your first consideration must be yourself and then your same gender mate. Before sex becomes dull to you and to your mate, sit down and have an honest talk. What can you do to make sex more exciting for yourself? What can you do to make sex more exciting for your mate? This should result in knowing at least you both understand the problem.

One person may want to do a certain thing that the other person does not want to do, or vice-versa. This discussion is not calling off the relationship. It is only clearing the understanding between people. If you are not allowed to do something you want to do, just be patient and, maybe or maybe not, it will come about. If you are wanted to do something you may not want to do, the other person has to be patient. Neither accepting a sexual act or denying a sexual act is going to break up what you have established with the other person.

There is an old hooker's gag line of "the list of things that I wouldn't do gets shorter and shorter and shorter".

It is possible for two people never to reach a conclusion, never change the status quo of living together, just forgetting the sex part of the understanding. If this is true, your lover has turned into your roommate. Do you want an old lover as a roommate? No matter what happens, the newly discovered roommate is going to block any other emotional and physical ties you attempt to make, as you will try to block his new friend. If you are no longer interested in a sexual meaningful relationship, you can try it, but the situation is bucking into danger. If sex is no longer a part of the understanding, and you want some kind of understanding that involves sex, either live with the situation as miserable as it may be, or go out on your own and try to find it. Relationships when smashed are rarely mendable. You can try.

THE FAILURE OF A MEANINGFUL RELATIONSHIP

Why did you get into the relationship in the beginning? Do you know what a relationship is? Where did you fail once you've decided the relationship is over? You must be sure that the relationship is over. There are no more common goals. There is no future, little understanding, no growth. It is done. No going back. Over.

If there are any contracts held in common, rules are in the contract to dispense it. There are some things you own, some things he/she owns. One of you or both have the lease on the apartment or the mortgage on the house which includes how to dispense of it. There are some things that you have bought in common including gifts that were given to both of you. There's the dog.

It is much easier for homosexuals to end relationships than it is married heterosexuals who spend days, months, sometimes years negotiating who should have what. Don't drag down to that hassle.

Without additional contracts, under the rules of law, you are two individuals, each separate, unless you want to go the legal route of palimony. If you have sat down with your lover and discussed ways to mend your relationship and that has failed, and if you cannot come to agreement as to what to do with the things you have in common, make a list of those items with a dollar estimate of each. Split the choice and value 50-50. Give your friend first choice to pick any item; then you pick an item so the conclusion is about equal in money. If you and your friend are not talking, you both are lacking one of the most important elements of a meaningful relationship, communications. Appoint someone else to take your place; someone else to take his/her place.

Withdraw only your half (not what he/she may owe you) from the checking account and/or savings account and eliminate your name.

If you are sure the relationship cannot work and you fear the split will be unhappy and nasty, move you and your things out as soon as possible. Find another place to live without telling your friend. Don't dally with indecision or with convenience. Make the move fast preferably while he/she is at work. No big scenes. No fights over things. Although this advice seems cruel, and it is, the faster you or your partner can do the split, the more respect you will someday have for each other.

When you no longer have a relationship and have moved away from the person with whom you thought you were going to live the rest of your life, continue your life with your other friends as usual.

GUIDELINES AFTER A SPLIT

1. Never say anything bad about your past partner. It only shows bad taste on your selection.

2. Never discuss with your friends the division of your material goods. This is none of their business.

3. Do not get into discussion with your friends of what they report your past lover is thinking about you or talking about you.

4. Try to remain friends with your past lover, but don't allow him/her to be a telephone buddy.

5. Never again discuss with your past lover what went wrong in the relationship. That chance is gone. You analyze the situation without help from your friends.

6. Do not avoid your past lover. You had him/her as a friend when you met and became lovers with the hope of a meaningful relationship which did not work, concluding in again being friends. Don't lose the friend by turning him/her into an enemy regardless of what is said by others that he/she said about you.

7. Never compare your relationship to anyone; not even your next potential lover.

8. Give it time. Remember that he/she is probably just as hurt and disappointed as you are, and say nothing that would harm more. Cuts heal. Some have scabs and some don't. Some heal rapidly; some don't. Forgive it, and go on with your life.

DO I SUFFER FROM GUILT IN MY SECRET DESIRES?

You probably do, but that answer is too simplistic. Currently, we define "guilt" as something bad, and there is a negative connotation to "secret", something mysterious.

Prior to adolescence, the child senses he/she is unique to the parents who control his/her life. The parents are disturbed when the child turns into a sexual being, and this child is disturbed, confused, and bathed in anxiety when adolescence approaches and he/she feels that confusion of not being able to meet the demands placed upon him/her by the parents, and guilty of disappointing them. The gay man or lesbian hides the guilt in secrecy.

There may be positive attributes to guilt. When a person feels guilty, he constantly re-examines what he feels guilty about, and this leads to a clearer understanding of what he/she wants. The gay male or lesbian may rectify his understanding of what is wanted. He may rectify guilt by feeling more strongly about what he believes to be true.

The gay does not want to feel alienated from his parents. Gays risk that alienation when they tell their parents they are gay. The consequence is that many young people leave the security of home and the family relationship because they are gay and have exposed something that the family did not want to hear. Or a gay may hold his guilt in secrecy.

With the guilt of not pleasing those who are making the greatest impression on your personality, and keeping the guilt secret, other personality characteristics are challenged. Self-esteem may be affected by not being honest. Loneliness. Shyness. Lack of communication. Religious guilt of non-approval. The feeling of being a "bad" person. Guilt can also manifest itself in day-dreaming and pretending.

The guilt of being gay is delivered in the personal confession, usually to the parents, brothers or sisters, or a close friend. The gay is attempting to satisfy his own guilt by telling someone of his true feelings often to not-listening ears who don't have the slightest idea of what the confession means. The gay feels more isolated and alone. He/she feels that he is the only person in the world that thinks and feels as he does. As the physical body is crying out during adolescence, the mind is suffering in pain.

If there is physical sexual activity with the same sex during this period, women have a more difficult time adjusting to the guilt than men who fear they will be caught at the indiscretion. Women tend to be more socially aware than men. The female will vow never to be indiscreet again. The male will forget it or set it into his subconscious mind so long as no one knows. Some will get strong hints that they may be gay.

The sharing of secrecy between two people in a romantic situation may also have a positive effect upon their relationship. In some manner, the two people join in their guilt to share a part of them that is the most vulnerable. Their strength comes from each of them knowing the other's most delicate concern. This could tighten their bond to each other.

We have always had gay men and lesbians. There has always been gay relationships. How we handle those relationships depends upon the time in history. The two old spinster school teachers that have lived together 50 years. The young friends who have remained close, closer than usual, through marriages and divorces. The military buddies who share more than combat experiences. Society accepts them because their lives are clothed in secrecy.

There are relationships between two men or two women which are not physical relationships and society considers this quite natural. Two people of the same sex can love and respect each other, but their lives are heterosexual. The love is a natural outgrowth. Yet, if the two have sexual relationships, their friendship is "unnatural". The youthful experiences of kid's masturbating groups often become adult straights understanding that the activity was one of youth. The inability of so many to have same sex friends is hampered by the fear of allowing another person of the same sex to get emotionally close. Straight brothers are often competitive.

Our current generation requests "... so tell the world I'm gay." Parades. Marches. Demonstrations. Television talk shows. Magazines and books. The exposed confession. Truth.

It is difficult for the gay community to accept that they are not accepted by all heterosexuals. No one is trying to convert heterosexuals to homosexuality. Gays will argue that they are just like straights except they prefer their own sex. What they really mean is that the gays want the same freedoms as the straights without bias of their sexual preferences. There is a great difference between the heterosexual lifestyle and the homosexual lifestyle, and a difference in the rules of society toward each.

It is amusing the way we look at religion. We are taught that all religions are equal. Yet, my religion, say Catholic, is just a little bit better than all the other religions. Isn't that hypocrisy? We send missionaries into the jungles to teach our values, and they are killed. Not all things are compatible; some are competitive. Oil and vinegar do not mix. They combine, but not compatibly. One can not practice the religion of being a vampire here because it is not compatible to other American religions. No wonder we get confused when we think that homosexuality and heterosexuality are compatible.

HAPPINESS

Simply, happiness is accomplishing personal goals. These goals have been established in us through our family, and we expect that accomplishing many of the goals will bring us happiness. From learning there were weaknesses in our parent's happiness, we decide that countering the ideas of what has not brought our parents happiness, will bring us happiness. In other words, my parents yelled at one another which brought them unhappiness, so if I never yell at my mate, I will be happy. Idealistically sound reasoning, but it lacks practicality.

We continue behavior which brought us unhappiness. Many parents of child abusers were abused. We also fantasize what will bring us happiness with no guarantee, and these fantasizes are often physical and financial. "If I win the lottery ..." "I want a cabin in the hills ..." "I want a new bedroom suite ..." Accidental, short term financial gains seldom bring long term happiness. We are left with a family history of what is happiness, a revision of what will make us happy, and a fantasy of what happiness is when it happens.

There are some concepts that seem to have remained constant over the years and over the generations. We want good health and to be happy. We know of many cases where bad health has led to pain and suffering which has led to unhappiness. Health and happiness are closely linked.

We want a productive job which pays adequately. Since a third of our day is spent on the job, we want to be satisfied in the work place and appreciated for what we have done.

We want to be loved by our friends and we want to have the ability to express our love, and we want to love ourselves. We want a mate who enjoys what we enjoy, who is a partner to similar goals, who shares, someone in which we can confide. Many want a sense of stability, a family, direction, a home, and a sense of accomplishment and contentment. We want to be proud of ourselves. We want to be confident in our decisions.

There was a study of 18,000 subjects and concluded that the happiest group was married women, followed by married men, single women and single men. [5] The study did not measure gay men and lesbians in the study conclusions.

If we were to apply the conclusions to the gay lifestyle, we would probably conclude the happiest group is lesbian couples followed by gay male couples, the singular lesbian and the gay male, but this distortion of research is questionable.

HOW DO I ACHIEVE HAPPINESS?

Primarily, you must appear satisfied to your mate or to your friends. Your attitude toward yourself is reflective to others. If you give the attitude of being stable, you'll reflect others who are confident or who are at least playing the same show game of displaying stability. If single, be happy with your status.

Minimize those who are constantly unstable. Don't allow them to pull down your happy attitude. There will always be those who carry the whole world of troubles on their shoulders, those who want to take every moment of your time to express how broke they are, troubles in relationships, personal confusions, and ego set to talk only of their own problems. Your job in life is not to solve their problems; it is to make your life the best possible and happiest, and that may mean getting away from their problems.

You do not go through life with rose colored glasses seeing only the pleasant side. You are not floating on pot. You are selfish enough to understand that desperate people pull down your attitude, and you would rather be positive. Discourage unhappy people as bores.

Most satisfied people fill their lives with short term and long term goals or objectives they feel will further support their own positive attitudes. Make a list.

The short term goals are those that give you immediate enjoyment, the kind of music you like, sports, the dinner party. These immediate goals can give you pleasure every day of your life. If you like to read, read. If you like to fish, fish.

Too often the gay person does not meet his own demands for time and space in which he/she can reach those everyday goals which give satisfaction. If you have a significant other, you still need your own day-by-day goals. A relationship is not based on 24 hour domination. Gain your own time to support your goals. Don't be jealous if your partner's goals are not identical to your goals. Why should they be?

What happens is the gay person finds him/herself in a rut, doing the same thing day after day. "I work eight hours, I sleep eight hours, that leaves eight hours for fun" and the "fun" becomes a nightly search for someone else or something else.

Try to avoid routines. We know that sleep is a routine and that work may be a routine, but the remaining hours do not have to fit into a specific pattern. Try something different. We know the cliche: "Born, pay taxes, and die." If that is all there is to living, we are not living very interesting or happy lives.

Find a challenge at work or during your spare time. Do something that you have never done before, something that challenges your skills as you know them. Don't be afraid of failure because we all fail except for the person who never challenges himself. Paint the kitchen. Plant roses. Don't just put in you time at work; find other ways of accomplishing the job, easier ways to do it, faster ways. Take on additional responsibilities, more challenges. Maybe even work an hour later without getting paid for it.

Take care of your body and your health. Go out for a run down new streets and new places. Look while you run. With the American trend toward healthier bodies, you'll be amazed at how many people are exercising by running and never looking up except at cross streets. Listen to the sounds. Many wear ear-phones to drown out the wonderful sounds of an alive world. Join a class of aerobic exercise or go to the gym. Play volley-ball. Challenge your body as well as your mind. One of the few exercises in which you don't need training; take a long walk.

The mind needs challenging. Don't become stagnant. Take a course at the high school or college about something that you know nothing about. Get a new skill and new information. Education can never hurt unless we stop learning. In furthering yourself educationally, you are increasing your self-esteem, and you are more satisfied.

The gay person has difficulty building self-esteem. Coming from confusion concerning their sexuality, raised in a value scale different from their background, challenged as to who or what they are, pushed for survival into a gay lifestyle, contending with much of America that does not understand them and many who do not want to understand so they disapprove, the gay man or lesbian must like him/herself above all to respect himself, to feel he has worth to his society and to himself.

There is a difference between self-esteem and self-importance. Self-esteem is personal and is really the way a gay person looks at himself. Self-importance lacks humility and is a public display of society's values that may have been accomplished. Self-importance is displaying how many gold necklaces, telling the value of the car, pushing the position held with a company, announcing the membership in the local golf or country club. Self-importance is based on insecurity and is public knowledge without humility. "Look what I have done." Self-esteem is fragile and personal, how you really feel about yourself.

The insecure gay person and the straight man often confuse self-importance wanting self-esteem. He plays with the wrong toys, the memberships, the cars, the socially correct companion, the two children because the national average was two-point-four per family and then one-point-eight, and he can't work it out, the never satisfied ego. He lacks importance for himself. Going after self-esteem the wrong way, he accomplished only self-importance. So do many people.

One value of happiness which is more prevalent in gay life than in the heterosexual life is probably the value placed upon money. Many will disagree. The heterosexual lifestyle is on-going with a family, and the financially successful husband and wife turn their attention from making money to making themselves happy, to the off-springs. The gay relationship may build a family with the two people, dogs, cats, and friends, but it is not on-going with the same sort of socially acceptable pride as the typical straight mother and father. There are usually no descendents.

The singular gay person builds his/her family around friends. He has an every changing adoptive family. Many gays take on the responsibility of the parents' care, not only because they can afford it, but because they do not have a socially accepted family themselves, and because the brothers and/or sisters have established their own family responsibilities which dominate their life. The gay person living with someone else for 20 years as a same sex companion is still considered by many of the family to live alone.

In our society, money is important. The extremes of no money verses great wealth has built into it the acceptance of what we need to be happy. Another cliche: "I can live better with it than without it". Maybe. You certainly can't live without it.

Most people feel a relationship with another person is a necessity for happiness, a relationship that is sharing and honest, but this relationship does not necessarily have to be a sexual union. Pregnant teens, single parents, fathers and mothers; there are many different kinds of relationships including gay guys and lesbians with children. Does that mean the lack of sexuality hurts the relationship? I doubt it.

In no way do we doubt the intensity of a sexual relationship with either homosexuals or heterosexuals, an intensity that can build to become practically a spiritual unity. But, this spiritual unity is not common for either group. We attempt to measure happiness by years spent in a relationship rather than the intensity of it. They are happy because they have been together 30 years. Caution. The 30 years may have been just "so-so" years, not happy but not miserable.

If faith is something greater than man, call it God or Jesus or whatever, it is needed for happiness, a faith in "good" over "bad", justice and, probably, the after-life which becomes our optimism of the future. All people believe in something.

Not differing from the straights, gay people seem to be quite religious, but not necessarily in the sense of joining an organized religion. Since many religions or individual churches do not believe in the gay lifestyle, they don't welcome gays. Their parents are embarrassed by their children's lack of acceptance. The parents and many religions have turned their backs on gays. The gay's faith comes through their understandings of the Christianity, Judaism, or a religion which emphasizes a "non-prejudiced God", "a child of God", "a fair God", "acceptance", and "God is Good and Loves You."

Growing in the last century, religious organizations such as the Metropolitan Community Church have aided gay people, although many will argue the socialization of the gays had dominated the religious teaching. Others will argue that a gay religion is just another top heavy business. Some established religions have specialized instruction or classes for gays. Other religions refuse acceptance of the "abomination", those people condemned to "live in hell".

The valid expression is "man is responsible for his own destiny". If the gay person wants happiness, he can have happiness if he/she is willing to search for it; if the gay person can look in a mirror and actually see the image. The gay person can be satisfied and happy with the God he has accepted. Most important, the gay can live by the principles that God put forth for us.

CAN I TRUST?

The person that you probably cannot trust is yourself. Have you ever had a secret and asked someone to share your secret and swore them to silence? You are the one that has broken the trust by sharing the secret. You cannot trust yourself or you would not have shared the information. Do you become angry when someone else breaks the secret? A secret is one person's knowledge, not two or more.

The average gay person, and there may be none, has questioned the personal trust of other people, and, being disappointed in the inability of others to be trusted, seldom looks at him/herself to see if he is trustworthy, if he/she can actually retain a secret without sharing it. Not trusting yourself sets you up for not trusting others.

Gay people are sensitive to others around them, particularly in the young, growing years. The sensitivity of breaking from the traditional creates mistrust in yourself as well as the trust of others. Some personalities are able to throw it off and not allow the disappointment in others hamper them. He/she gets little pleasure and few rewards for being "apart". It is not uncommon for the gay man or lesbian to be a "loner", more satisfied in his/her imagination and playing alone in a fantasy world of desires.

With a sensitivity of trusting, the gay person matures and maintains sensitivity, and it hampers the gay person in the work place and personal relationships dealing with a significant other, as well as straight friends. The gay person lacks the trust in others that he/she desperately wants even of himself.

Females, lesbians, have a more difficult time with trusting than males, gay males, because the male is taught more of an aggressive behavior pattern. Currently, males are taught to be or show themselves to be less aggressive than years before. Today it is common to see fathers emotionally involved with their children, a tender side of the male. Women's liberation has aided the females to be more aggressive. It probably helps in the development of the lesbian who has a more worldly view of trusting and who is certainly more aggressive than her grandmother. Does she trust her convictions or herself?

CAN I BUILD FRIENDSHIP?

As a single person away from your birth family, you should have a desire to build friendships with both the gay community and the straight community. You will start to build your new family in the gay community, a process of accepting and rejecting that will continue most of your life. If you are on friendly terms, you will have contact with your birth family, your parents, brothers and sisters. You will develop a heterosexual link, usually job related.

Your gay community will change frequently, and you will constantly be adding friends. New people will come into your acquaintance. Some will move away. Some will die. Some will change to the degree that you are no longer close. Most people feel that if you make three or four friendships that you can hold for your lifetime, you have been very lucky. These will often be relationships that you have established when you are young, a high school or college association made during the period when both had little except friendship to offer. This is the steady type of closeness that time and/or distance does not seem to waver, people or a person with whom you can be totally honest and completely free, and some of these early friendships last a lifetime.

As you grow older, you'll establish associations with people that are not really friends, but people of interest to you, and this can be selfish interest, but these are not close friends. The more mature and comfortable you become, the more difficult it is to have associates turn into friends because you have acknowledged your own biases as well as become aware of what the associate may want from you. Neighbors have lived beside one another for years and one family moves and they never keep in contact. Besides, building a friendship takes time, and you don't have that much spare time if you are personally active.

Beware of the person who states that he/she has lots of friends. Chances are, the person has lots of associates, probably few or no true friendships. If a person has to brag about the large amount of friends he/she has, the person is insecure and may need friendship.

If a person proclaims friendship and he/she asks to borrow money, it is probably only an associate or less. In the gay life as the straight life, more friends turn into associates with the borrowing of money. Don't ask your friends for money; don't loan money to your friends, and hesitate before loaning to your associates. Always get a contract or note in writing. If your supposed friend dislikes giving you a contract, don't loan. An honest man is not afraid to show his intentions in writing. The only thing a friend wants from you is your friendship, not the things of your life.

If you as a gay person have been lucky enough to have established your birth family, brother and sisters, etc., as friends, you are very lucky. They have known you longer and sometimes better than anyone else and, usually, because you are family, they can often overlook your differences. The whole "blood is thicker than water ..." stuff is usually true. The bond of being a brother or sister or parent is often so strong that little can shake the foundation of your friendship. They may not completely understand you and your motivations, but they tolerate you because of this bond.

As you grow older as a gay person, you and what remains of your family grow closer and more tolerant of each other, and closer in your friendship because of the shrinking family. The straights can even empathize with you although they can never fully understand what your being gay means to you and to them.

Your heterosexual friends that are not part of the family bond hold many of the same feelings. They will accept you to the degree of friendship so long as you do not bombard them with self-confessions and attempting to sell your way of life. A gay person may have difficulty communicating with a straight person if they haven't found a common ground of topics in which they both are interested. Most straights are not specifically interested in the gay lifestyle. Don't sell it.

It is very important for the gay person to have straight friends or at least associates because it keeps the gay person in touch with what is happening to people aside from his/her little group. It is easy to get caught up in the gay lifestyle and begin to believe the whole world feels sympathetic and similar to your ideas. When the gay man or lesbian that lives in a gay neighborhood and lives a gay lifestyle returns to the small town in which he/she was reared, the gay person is amazed at how unworldly and unsophisticated the small town can be, and the United States is packed with small communities. The small towns are surprisingly naive to the gay lifestyle.

Hopefully, the greatest friendship that you will ever form is with your mate, an honest, giving, and caring friendship that will take you through tough times, as well as a variety of fine times. This one friendship may be able to last beyond life.

The difficulty of a friendship is not in the building of the relationship, the good times shared by both, the trust and understanding, but the difficulty of the friendship having an end. No one takes rejection well. Even though misunderstandings, preferences, negligence, or death, when a friendship is over there is a void which is difficult to fill. It is like losing a part of yourself. You cannot recall a beautiful sunset or make a wilting flower bloom again.

With as much time as we spend on working and acquiring things only someday to find that this process does not bring us happiness, you would think that we would eventually get smart enough to concentrate on building friends. But we also realize that to have friends, you must be one, and few of us take that much time.

CONFIDENCE, COURAGE, AND HUMILITY

Confidence in decision making is the ability to analyze a problem from all possible sides, and draw a conclusion based upon your analysis. Some people are very skilled at analyzing a problem, but they fail to come up with a conclusion. The ability to conclude is directly related to the person's ability to have the courage to stand behind the conclusion regardless if it is popular or unpopular. Humility is the technique used to present the conclusion, particularly if it is an unpopular conclusion.

The person who admits to himself that he/she is gay has taken a large step in drawing a conclusion. The gay person has analyzed him/herself, and has dug into his/her own psyche. A gay person has read whatever he can about the lifestyle and he/she has analyzed the many directions. The conclusion is when the puzzle finally make one clear picture, the point at which the person is emotionally and logically in touch with himself, and the result may be that he/she is homosexual or heterosexual.

There is no room in between the two extremes because making room is the failure to draw a conclusion between the two extremes. During this time, he may have bisexual activity in experimentation, but he will draw one of two conclusion. He/she is either straight or gay. Failure to draw a conclusion results in frustration, and the supposed bisexual is caught in that frustration. Usually happening in adolescence, the realization of sexuality is that awkward time of self analysis, information, and questioning that must result in a conclusion. The conclusion is more than the satisfaction of the physical sex drive.

What a person does with his/her conclusion depends upon his/her courage. The easier road is to be heterosexual like the majority of people, but that is sometimes not the conclusion. If he/she is gay, he must take the less popular, a minority conclusion and, hopefully, the person is aware of some or many of the complexities. Being a minority is not the end of life. When a person finally admits his sexuality regardless of the conclusion, he/she is released from hours of self-analysis and has taken a major step toward maturity.

It may seem that homosexuality and heterosexuality are based on the realization of maturing sexuality. Many of the other differences are social and/or learned responses. A straight person learns to live a lifestyle of how to act according to what is expected of him and his knowledge seems natural to him. For the gay man or lesbian, some of the learned differences and protocol are what separate the gays from the heterosexuals.

In Victorian times as before, the term "homosexual" was rarely used because the actions and behavior of the gay person met most of the social standards, and only private sexual experiences were evidence of homosexuality. The Restoration fop was certainly effeminate, well trained in manners with powdered wig, but he was not necessarily gay. Social structures developed and social lifestyles reflected the minority emphasis and the sexual interest. We assume some individuals will be happier within the minority with others of similar sexuality. The assumption is rarely questioned.

An individual who realized he/she is gay could have the courage to choose not to participate in the minority and to withdraw from sexual activity. But, why in today's world? That is like wanting to live only a portion of your life.

It takes courage to stand behind your decision. The majority does not understand most of the complexities of the gay lifestyle and the parents of the gay man or lesbian are filled with expectations, dreams, hopes and fears for the siblings. We should not expect them to understand. Often, the first inquiry about a gay person's curiosity about being gay is discussion with the parents or parent, and the parent does not answer "Wonderful. I hope you are happy."

It takes rebellion and courage to live the gay lifestyle, although there is more happiness than living in a community that does not understand you and usually resents you because they do not understand you. An advantage of the gay lifestyle is that you can select from it what aspects you want, and not select those ideas which do not appeal to you.

Decision making to a conclusion and the courage to stand behind your decision is an everyday event, and a road to being accepted by your friends. It does not mean you must be dogmatic, bull-headed, stubborn or aggressive in your presentation. Use humility in your approach. Everyone likes a person with humility.

AM I AN ACTIVIST?

An activist is a person who demonstrates his/her support for something in which he/she believes and, to that degree, we are all activist in supporting anything, from mellow conversations to demonstrative marches. The term "gay activist" has taken on a more radical meaning. A gay activist is usually a gay person who actively participates by marching, standing, writing, or speaking in support of any issue, bill or backing any politician that advances gays or is actively against anything that threatens gays or the gay lifestyle.

Most people feel that raids on gay bars, laws against drag, harassment, etc., led to rebellion. The gays stood up to the police with the gays demanding their rights in front of a gay bar in New York, Stonewall 1969. Since then, there have been gay marches, gay pride days, gay Olympic games, and an onward and aggressive campaign to demonstrate the presence of gays in our communities. There has been open confrontation of politicians denying gay housing, unequal employment rules and regulations, mate benefits, etc., and there has been exposure of "closeted politicians" that are thought to be gay but have worked against the gay movement, the "outing". Currently the religious right and family values are the battle fields.

Some people view the differences between gays and straights as a war, and they join the side in which they believe with full support and a desire to win the war. Some gays are fully supportive and even hostile in their aggression that a gay person is obligated to support his own; others are more passive. Some feel the aggression has gone too far; others feel it has not gone far enough.

There are individuals that join a gay band wagon for personal recognition. In a field of limited study and research, their opinions can be heard. Some are "crusaders", wanting a cause, practically any cause, because they want recognition and they need a cause to draw attention to themselves. These are people who need something. They become authorities in a subject without many authorities. (They often categorize themselves as bisexuals so as not to offend any group.) Following close behind are those that will find a way to make money off of anyone's sexual situation, sexual exploitation.

You must decide to what degree you want to participate in this clash of ideas. To what degree you want to be exposed to the public? Is the war your obligation? Are you really changing people's minds?

Although usually in larger cities, demonstrations expose you, maybe to your straight friends, your boss, your parents, and you must decide if you want and can afford this kind of exposure. The dedicated may lose their jobs, their straight friends, and their own positions to push their beliefs. These are the penalties for support.

Years ago the police took license plate numbers, names and places of employment and published the information in the newspaper if you were parked in front of a known gay bar, and you lost your job. Today, gays join the hundreds, often thousands, marching down the street with the gay flag . It has been a very changing world.

The gay activists are not only interested in a change in the perception and governing of gays. It finds the black movement of change and the woman's liberation movement as allies in the fight for individual independence. All are accused of immorality. The same arguments are used against each minority; unhealthy, unclean, and mentally incapable or distorted. Hitler used the same arguments against the Jews.

Another problem which is going to hit the blacks of America is the constant threat of AIDS using the same arguments of the diseased gays. One study says by 1997, the leading cause of death for black men statewide which will exceed homicides will be AIDS. [6] Another indicated an increase of 55 percent of reported cases for AIDS among racial and ethnic minorities in 1993. [7] In that year blacks had five times the amount of new cases compared to three times the amount for Hispanics per 100,000 people. Statistics and figures will be used as propaganda against the black and other ethnic minorities. The development of the three drug cocktail has currently confused all statistics with the possibility of prolonging life, hopefully until a cure is found.

Even the background of the American black, the Afro-American of a country riddled with HIV positive people presents undefinable problems. They will find there are difference types of HIV positive patients, maybe several different levels where the disease kills at various rates of speed.

Maybe it is the law of survival that man picks upon the weak, and it is also the procedure that somehow the weak survive to become strong. We will always have gays, and we probably will always have prejudice and hate. We still carry the scars of the Holocaust. The activist is not isolating the gay movement from the struggles of the black minorities or the changes in the women's move toward equality. The struggle is for equal laws based upon ability for all people.

If someone were to ask "What is the greatest invention of man that has changed his life?" there would be the temptation to answer the "wheel" or the "arrow" and you can go on with many items that have allowed man to progress through one century into another. Least considered is the "birth control pill" and although it does not seem very revolutionary today, neither did the wheel or the arrow.

The introduction of the birth control pill in 1961 allowed the population to have more control over their destiny; it allowed the woman to choose if she were going to have a child. That seems hardly revolutionary since women have always had children, but it became so because the woman had the rights to choose when to have a child.

Up to this time, pregnancy was either an accident, a way to get a husband and security, a "divine gift from God" that was difficult to rationalize at 14 years old, or results of rape. Historically, the male baby could carry on the good name, reputation, and wealth of the father; the child was a father successor of posterity. Hardly. Children were born bastards, aborted, even murdered and it was usually at the hand of the mother. The Chinese made laws forbidding mothers from killing female babies in the last quarter of the twentieth century.

By taking a simple little pill, the woman can rid herself of the responsibility of having a child at that specific time, but she can also plan when she can have children, the original purpose of developing the pill. Having children became her choice. She can plan her future knowing when it would not be interrupted by pregnancy.

The woman was given voting rights and a degree of equality, but her life was dominated by her reproduction timing, and with the pill she could control that. She became more equal to the man, and she learned from the so-called male qualities as aggression, strength, and dominance. She competed more freely with him than ever before in history. The woman broke the stereotype and has ventured into every field or vocation proving herself competitive to the best male minds. She is raised from a second class citizen. She is liberated, and she is proving her value. And it seems to be because of a little pill.

When we talk of the gay men and lesbians in the United States, we must talk of the tremendous accomplishments of the American woman who has come further from expectations than the gay male who has indulged himself in his superiority. Go to it.

The gay activist takes on many different arguments in his crusade for legal equality of the homosexual which include fighting the same types of hatred toward blacks, women, and Jews. He/she fills an important role in our society, often with the job on the line to fight for minority rights when many of the rest of us will not, or cannot, fight. Although at times embarrassingly aggressive to other gays, it is important that the activist is forward on the fighting line.

STRESS, ANXIETY, AND FRUSTRATION

The medical field and science are based upon what is known as fact at a specific time. Through research we find that some knowledge that we may have considered as fact is not true, and facts change from one period of research to another. We accept what is fact at one period of time. Tomorrow, new research based upon what we believe to be true may develop a new set of facts. At one time everyone accepted the world was flat, and as new information developed, we changed the old fact for a new fact.

At this time, we accept a great deal of medical information which we feel is factual, and we are constantly re-evaluating and challenging established facts to establish new facts. Victims of time and place. We consider medicine a science meaning we can break it into pieces for investigation and analysis, and put it back together.

We have studied and considered the emotions (or mind) a science because we have learned to break the whole into sections for investigation. We look at the physiology of the brain, and we develop theories which may become facts that certain pieces of the physiology affect certain behaviors. We have learned few facts about the emotions, perhaps a product of the brain. We are slow in repairing the brain.

Most medical doctors are aware that there is some relationship between the emotions and physical science, but we are yet to know what these relationships are, where, how they develop, and how they are physiologically demonstrated in the individual's behavior, and we don't know how to treat them.

This theory will become clear when we find the facts of the emotions and when we know more about the relationship of the emotional to physical facts. In the future, we will know much more about the interplay of the two, and we have simply not grown to that level of knowledge. We will someday find there is a strong tie between the two, a heavy dependence and inter-dependence between the emotions and physical facts. There will be an interchange in a new science of the emotions and the physical body including the physical brain which has already started.

We have learned some things about the emotions, particularly with our interests in drugs of many kinds. If we accept that the emotional can be affected by the physical, a certain drug can lessen high levels of stress, anxiety, or frustration, but it is currently difficult for us to separate these three qualities. We can say that by eliminating stress, we lessen anxiety and become less frustrated. Or is it that by eliminating anxiety, we cut frustration and become less stressful? We simply do not know.

Some attribute death to a direct relationship to stress by stating that disease affects stress and stress affects the immune system.[8] Some believe that women have less stress than men, thus, live on the average of seven years longer than men. The figure is now down to six years longer than men since the woman's life has become more stressful. Of the ten major diseases, men lead in early deaths for each one: 1. heart disease, 2. cancer, 3. cerebrovascular illness, 4. accidents, 5. lung disease, 6. pneumonia, 7. diabetes, 8. suicide, 9. liver disease, and 10. hardening of arteries. AIDS is 15th.[9][10]

We wash it all away by accepting that a healthy body produces a healthy mind (although we know many healthy bodies that are emotionally sick). We take the opposite approach when it pleases us. A healthy mind produces a healthy body (and we know healthy minds with sickly bodies). Although we recognize a relationship between the two, the physical and the emotional, we don't know what this relationship is ... not as yet. When we try to add to this simple triangle of emotions many other emotions that we experience as human beings are exposed. Our knowledge of facts becomes very complicated. What effect does love have upon stress, anxiety, and frustration, and upon our physical bodies?

We shake down our knowledge of the emotions to a list that passes in stupid simplicity:

1. Keep a healthy body. (They don't say where.)

2. Try to eliminate stress (for which we do not have a concrete definition.)

3. Try not to be anxious (although we know of brilliant conclusions that have been born from anxiety).

4. Do not become frustrated (and you'll lack passion and become very bored and boring.)

5. Keep mentally healthy (Who knows what that means?)

Perhaps the question breaks down to the control of stress, the control of anxiety and the control of frustration. It is certainly more interesting to live with them, than without them.

There is the old Ben Franklin's advice of moderation in everything. It creates a dull person. Had he taken his own advice, he may not have had so many illegitimate children.

SHOULD I GET HEALTH INSURANCE?

In your teens and early twenties, you feel almost invulnerable; you'll live healthily forever. There is the constant threat of AIDS and venereal diseases, the problems of taking drugs, and their reactions, the possibility of an automobile wreck. It will happen to someone else, but not you. It is not true. You are vulnerable. The "when" of health insurance should be that you are never without it. If you have been on your parent's policy and it fails to carry you once you are 18, see if that company will write you a continuation policy. If not, investigate other companies.

You cannot afford to be naked; not covered. Although the subject is dry and uninteresting, although insurance may be expensive and you are financially weak meaning broke, although insurance is something you cannot touch or feel, obtaining health insurance will give you a sense of security. There are few tragedies that can happen that are as critical. The accident or illness can wipe out any savings account and force you into relying on your parents, friends or the public. Don't set yourself up to be humiliated. Get health insurance now.

At this time we as a country are debating the qualities and quantity of public health insurance for all Americans, but many will get sick or have an accident before these plans are defined. Now.

Your employer including a health package with your job will increase your wage by up to 30 percent, even though the cost may not be in cold cash. If you don't have the cash for insurance because it has been deducted from your check, you can't spend it.

American medicine appears to deal with the symptoms of a problem rather than the disease itself. As an example, if you have the three day flu, you can get rid of the running nose, the sore throat, the upset stomach or the shakes, but the three day flue has to run its course. The symptoms have been attacked, but not the source.

American medicine is affected by popularity and whim and, like any new direction, often misdirected. 50 years ago, death reports listed "heart attacks" as the cause of death and although the heart did stop, that may not have been the source of the illness. At one time "old age" was a cause of death. Prostate cancer and bypass surgery are popular today, and although physicians will deny falling to current health or death fads, they do. "Complications from AIDS" means what? At least, a second or third doctor's opinion is necessary. Don't forget. Doctors get ill and die also.

This is not an attempt to degrade medicine and medical science. There have been some wonderful discoveries and miraculous advances and many theories have become truths and the truths have gone through testing. But, there is much more work to be done as all will admit.

The Pure Food and Drug Law was passed in 1906. The purpose was two-fold, to take remedies of fraudulent medical claims off the market and to check adulterated foods. They fully check their thousands of complaints and, unfortunately, this is often a lengthy process. There was a tonic sold that seemed to give older people more vigor, and it was discovered the tonic was 98 percent alcohol, and it did give some old timers more vigor, but the labeling was misleading.

The basic premise of medicine is biology, and humans are similar, but they are not all the same. Medical doctors are adding into the science of biology more psychological factors such as frustration, anxiety, physical genetic difference, gender uniqueness, etc. as influences to basic biology.

We now have a national Office of Alternative Medicine (OAM} whose function is to examine unique medicines, those not based on the biology or the way we once examined the scientific truth that all people are alike. One third of Americans use alternative medical practices or medicines. The once regarded cure for a cold was "... hot chicken soup, plenty of rest, and sweat it out " and some swear it works. "Eat garlic at least once a week …" if you want to risk your friends, "… eat garlic once a day". What effects do the mental, emotional, and spiritual aspects have upon our biology?

It is difficult to tell unconventional treatment from pure quackery. As we investigate those aspects of our lives aside from our biology, we will find that our physical bodies are influenced by many different aspects, some of which are physical and include those that may not be physical.

In the gay lifestyle and growing deeply into the straight lifestyle is the threat of AIDS. Most AIDS research rests on findings of being HIV positive or negative, the biological approach to this dreaded disease. For anyone who has dealt with a dying HIV positive person, he/she knows there are many ramifications of the illness, perhaps some apart from the biological explanation.

One aspect of the HIV positive person is his/her medical expenses and his/her ability to pay. Health insurance companies can be tricky; they are in business to make money and not spend money. Exceptions on insurance policies are common. Some health insurance companies exclude medical care for AIDS, cancer, and heart disease, the three largest health killers. Insurance companies are mercenary and a 30 year old gay male will find it more difficult to get health insurance, or at least more expensive, than a 30 year old, married, straight man.

Having a medical insurance that helps your financial condition in case of illness lessens the stress and may help your physical condition. Can we also have a medical plan that gives financial support to the expense of mental problems?

A MEDICAL NOTE

A medical note is a plan of what you want done by whom in case of a medical need. It is an emergency plan as well as a longer term plan until proper directions of your demands are found. It is a simple, one page statement that gives someone your direction in case of an emergency, a simple piece of paper to be put in your desk drawer, your check-book, your diary, the place your friend will look first. The medical note is just a starter to a more serious medical insurance, an initiation to the volume of forms. You need specific names, and the information should be readily available to someone close to your

172

lifestyle that sees you on a permanent basis, and knows where the note is. The information can be fun.

JUST IN CASE...

If I am hit by a beer truck this afternoon, my legal name is _____.

My doctor's name is _____, who can be reached by phone at _____.

My medical insurance company is _____, phone _____, and my insurance identification number is _____.

I live at _____.

Expect _____ to answer the phone.

Relationship:_____.

Please contact the following:

_____ Phone: _____

_____ Phone: _____

_____ Phone: _____

Anything financial will be attended to by _____ Phone: _____

In case of immediate plastic surgery, I want the

body of _____

hair of _____

face of _____

personality of _____

Aside from _____,

I'm allergic to _____.

Signature:_____

Although this information seems flip, it is needed by someone who has your interests at heart. You should have discussed with someone what should happen if you lose consciousness. Someone should know your preferences and be legally authorized to speak for you.

LIFE INSURANCE

Call it "death insurance" because you are not insuring your life unless you cash in your policy. You are insuring enough money to pay for your burial, you hope.

Death insurance can be expensive; the insurance companies are there to make money. If you put away one dollar a day from the time you are 18 until you are 60, you'll have over $15,000 plus interest but, of course, no one can do that.

On whom would the cost of your burial fall? Your parents? Your lover? Saved money or assets? If you have absolutely nothing when you die, and few gay people do, on whom would the burden fall? If you don't like the answer, perhaps you should consider death insurance.

Most gay men or lesbians do not evaluate death insurance as very important because they will not be around to enjoy the money of it. The disposition of the corpse is of little concern. Although there may be a desire to be buried at a certain place or cremated and have the ashes thrown in San Francisco Bay, it's usually not a big priority and it is expensive. Most often, to whomever you leave your assets, allow them to have your burial bills. (That is called "getting even".)

Your desires for what you want done with the body after you die should be spelled out in some type of legal document, a trust or will. Writing what you want done is not much help to you, but it may take a tremendous strain off the person responsible for your body after your death.

INDEPENDENT AND INTERDEPENDENT

The balancing act is between being self sufficient and self serving. It allows your emotions to expand so that you are aware of and value your relationship to others, your mate, friends or family. It is a constant juggling of your trust in yourself and your trust in other people.

Many attitude poles will agree that Americans are too materialistic and too independent as well as individualistic, wanting to make their own statement about themselves regardless of any previous rules and regulations of the protocol of a society. Particularly gay men and lesbians want to stand apart from the crowd "listening to their own drummer". The non-conformity separates them from the masses. Some gays feel that since their sexual morals are not conforming to the majority of people, other ideas such as basic honesty, social acceptance, and behavior do not have to conform. This is not true.

Just because a person is gay does not mean that he/she can re-define all of the values in which we have been raised. There are some gay people that are against anything and everything because they have been bruised in their own development. But, even bruises begin to fade away. Too often, they have made a statement of themselves in disliking everything, everyone, and impossible to please with the lack of being interdependent. These are very unhappy gay people.

Interdependence is the ability to be sensitive to others, to value the human relationships, to develop and nurture the relationships with others from a roommate, lover, or just friend. It is the interplay of caring about someone else and the knowing that the other person cares about you. In a way, it is a form of love and trust, a meaningful relationship to both parties. In the gay lifestyle this interdependence is often with someone of the same gender and usually gay, but it doesn't necessarily have to be. The other gender or even an understanding parent or sibling can relate interdependently. Being sensitive to individual rights, responsibilities to others and social concerns is a part of interdependence. Brothers and sisters often fulfill this role.

Most gays are sensitive to and feel they have failed their natural family by not being heterosexual. They are not living up to what is expected of them. Some gays feel they have too much of a gay lifestyle that they are failing the gay lifestyle by backing away or withdrawing for a while. A broken sexual relationship is a failure. The inability to deal with the straight world is a failure.

Of course, no one likes to fail, but we have rarely been taught to accept failure, understand it, understand ourselves, and go one. We loudly announce our achievements and hide or deny our failures, or the failures dominate the successes so we can see only the failures. We do not accept failure well.

A BORING AND ROUTINE LIFE

We associate the two words although they have very different meanings. Routines, having a pattern of action or activity, does not mean the same thing as boring, uninteresting, an attitude judgment.

A pattern of behavior that allows a healthy body, a productive interesting employment, love and friends may be a routine, but it does not have to be an unproductive and an uninteresting pattern. We have been taught routine in all of the things we feel are important to happiness. We daily eat breakfast, lunch, and dinner. We work eight-to-five or three-to-11. We do our laundry on Saturday. We watch certain television programs that air at a specific time. We pattern our lives to accomplish those same chores that are necessary to be accomplished, day by day, week by week, or month by month.

The chores may not be terribly exciting, but we do them because living without the routine would not accomplish the way we want to live. Some routines cannot be exciting, ever changing. How many ways can you iron a shirt? In reality. We like the results of our routines. "I may not like to do dishes, but I love the results of a clean kitchen." There is satisfaction in doing the routine for our everyday pleasure of living.

We don't appreciate routine, although it gives us the satisfaction of the end result. "I struggle in the garden, pour on the fertilizer, water; all labor of which seems worth it once the roses are in bloom." We plan to break the routine, and the laundry piles up and there is nothing to wear. Some wait for the age of retirement, and once retired, go back to the routine of the job. We are victims of making ourselves happy and we accomplish it by planned activity.

Many of our happiest hours are while we watch someone else in a routine. You can remember your mother fixing dinner, your lover in the garden, you going to school or work? The little everyday patterns of living are insignificant in themselves, but do make you and others happy.

We develop bad routines, those that through habit bring us satisfaction, but those that do not bring us much long term happiness. "I always stop at the gay bar after work and usually have one too many, and I'm sorry the next morning." The routine is only momentary satisfaction with a headache aftermath.

Single gay men and lesbians have less difficulty in establishing meaningful routines than couples simply because there is no one else there to depend upon for the routine being accomplished. Single gays also have more of a tendency toward establishing routines that are not worth the result, or they rationalize not doing the routine. Probably single gay men are less structured than single lesbians.

We should be more aware of the pleasures of the routine involvements, the pleasure of accomplishing a goal that brings us happiness, and we should not label it boring, although with some of our many routines, they do become repetitive. Maybe repetition creates boredom and happens are the same time.

Boring means doing the routine so often that you find little pleasure in accomplishing the end result, a weak or bad routine. Life becomes boring when you can guess the conclusion, expect and get the same results with declining satisfaction, rather than look for the pleasure or satisfaction. We are looking for no satisfaction in completing the job. Like it or not, doing laundry is boring and routine.

The biggest complaint in the heterosexual married community is that the wife or husband becomes bored with the routine of living without showing appreciation for the accomplishment and without expressing it to his/her mate. Some people call it the lack of communications; others term it appreciation.

There seems to be good communication in the gay lifestyle because the gay man or lesbian realizes the importance of communication, how it was lacking in earlier years, and exerts specific emphasis upon communication and, hopefully, develop the tools to use direct communication, conversation and listening. This is one of the tools the gay singles and couples perfect more than the heterosexuals, to make gays excellent parents to children, the ability to communicate directly and honestly. Same sex couples and single parents are more aware of the demands made by society on them. Their children develop more freely without strong demands. It is a learned skill necessary for survival in the gay lifestyle, one molded out because of a lack of clear communication in the gay's background. Of course, there are the many exceptions of gays that cannot communicate well to either sex, to children or adults.

AM I RELIGIOUS?

Religion has always moved in cycles. One phase usually referred to as the Great Awakening started in New England with the work of Jonathan Edwards of Connecticut in 1720. This emphasis presented a benevolent God, one more merciful, caring and away from the Hell and damnation of Christianity to a more progressive belief in something larger than human beings. Many new religions sprang up and down the New England coast with a more liberal religion not so strict in interpretation of the way to communicate to God. The "right" path gave way to "many paths", and many different procedures of the Christian-Judea religions.

Another movement happened in the Midwestern United States with an understanding and awareness of alternating realities, becoming aware that something greater, or many things greater than the way the human being was living, made the essence of existence.

"There is no one road …" Through this phase the transcendentalists, the Spiritualists, the Theosophists and the Christian Scientists became aware of the power of the mind over matter at the starting of the twentieth century.

The third phase started later in California, but soon encompassed the United States. This phase was purporting the individual's spirituality, the ability of the belief in a person or object to carry natural powers of healing and of opening the individual personality to turn to his/her basic origins. Not surprisingly, the movement broke into many directions of spiritual healers; the food faddists, the homeopaths, the astrologers, the mediators, and the crystal gazers. The force of God was in or related to the physical elements.

The fourth event has been happening in the United States for the past hundred years. There is a new respect for meditative contemplation through our war experiences and through the amount of diverse ideas we have allowed to infiltrate our country, and through extensive traveling of all countries. There is a new respect for Maharishi Messiah Yogi, the founder of Transcendental Meditation, a respect for Buddhism, the gurus of Hinduism, Taoism, and Zen. The Dali Llama won the 1989 Nobel Peace prize. Even the martial arts of Tai chi and aikido put emphasis upon spiritual meditation.

We have started into the fifth phase of the learning, an awareness of spiritual healing communities, mind and body medicine, an appreciation of the natural environment and a lust to save it, the power of prayer, the values of human relationships and loving attitudes, a sensitivity to history and native cultures, the aspects of true value being our own unconscious minds, and a respect for the meditation and devotion of the variety of Oriental religions. There is an awakening of consciousness, a personal commitment and a selflessness to find and refire the quest for our relationship to God, or to ourselves, or to Nature, or to Soul. The books of the Torah, the Koran, the Tao te Ching, the Bagavad Gita, the Christian Bible support the truths of a new spiritual life.

It is interesting to look at various faiths and specific religions to see how they currently view the concerns of gay men and lesbians. In some more loosely governed religions, each individual church or temple may have a somewhat different handling of a gay issue; others are more tightly linked in philosophy.

In Buddhism the individual's karma should protect the individual from causing hurt to himself or others, and a person's actions are self-centered not god-centered, and the sin is against what he has done to him/herself. The individual has the responsibility of what he does or does not do, and no action is actually a sin against any god. Homosexual acts are only as important and good or bad as the individual they affect.

Judaism believes that gay acts violate the laws of God, but many branches believe that homosexuality is inborn with no punishment, and they applaud the uniting of two gays into a union. They are quite liberal in interpreting gay actions and relationships.

The Islam religion also finds an inborn cause for homosexuality, and although gays can not be part of the religious belief or the clergy, the religion prefers that prayer and fasting help the gays not to practice sex. Like other sins, homosexual acts have Mohammed's curse and are against God.

Most American Christian religions have developed specific philosophies of approval or disapproval of same sex marriages, homosexual acts by member of the religion or the clergy, etc., and each religion seems to differ slightly.

In the United Church of Christ seems to be most liberal concerning gay issues allowing each church to establish their own rules not forbidding homosexuals from being ordained, allowing church ceremonies for two same sex gays, and ordaining gays. The Unitarians believe in similar values and procedures. Some Episcopal diocese are also as liberal, but their control is congregation by congregation and some do not allow practicing gays to be priests.

Many of the Christian religion accept homosexuals in the congregation but frown on any kind of sexual gay activity by seeking forgiveness in prayer, and the religion will not accept gay activity in the clergy. The Roman Catholics ask for chastity in an act that is "contrary to nature" because homosexuality does not promote having children. The Presbyterians are more strict saying that no one in a church office or ordained should have sexual relations aside from marriage, gay or straight. Lutherans are equally as strict, but have a place for all, even those who do not meet their requirements, and all Evangelical Lutherans should abstain from gay sex. [11]

Probably the most strict about gay issues are the Baptist that have some ideas congregation-to-congregation, but are more dramatic is their denunciation of the act of homosexuality. The Latter-Day Saints considers gay sex to be "deviate", against God's will, "an act from the devil", and want no practicing homosexuals in their congregation, their missionaries, the ministers, or church officials. The Baptist are probably the most vocal against the gays of the various American religions.

Although many gay men and lesbians have been raised in religious families, active aggression toward homosexuality has closed the church door on many gays, and the rise of the Metropolitan Community Church, a predominately gay congregation or, at least, an "understanding" congregation, has been developed in many larger cities. Sometimes there is a direct relationship between the religious dominance and the community's attitude toward gays. A heavily Baptist community background will be less tolerant such as in the Southern United States. A Catholic background such as in Puerto Rico is heavily anti-homosexual as demonstrated by the Latino-Latina Lesbian and Gay Organization meeting in San Juan in 1997 and the hostility is obvious by laws of anti gay matrimony, police regulation against employing gays, gay sex as a felony and punishable by ten years in prison. [12]

At the same time, psychology and psychotherapy movements of Freud to Jung to Otto have infiltrated into the Judea-Christian philosophy of American life. From true superstitions to native spirituality particularly with the South Americans has been a search for the quality of human beings and their relationship to a Supreme Being. The advent of a new interest in alternative religions opens other doors.

We can only guess about the future. There will come a new outbreak of a form of religion that will encompass the thinking of Americans. These new religions will be based upon the experiences that America has gone through, a respect for the power of the various states of mental consciousness, a higher consciousness that uses science as a tool, the measurements and computers which cannot replace a respect for the environment and the development of human thought. The human individual's mind becomes reality to him/her.

At the turn of the century, we are facing a massive group of conservatives which we have roughly titled the Christian Coalition or the Republican far right being quite conservative in their approach with Ralph Reed as their spokesman for "family values". These religious groups started out with a political agenda. The group was against birth control, homosexuality, capital punishment, etc. After two marches in Washington, D.C., the group claimed they have no political agenda, but wanted to return to the value of Christianity with the mostly male marches. Bill McCartney, the founder of "Promise Keepers" organized a huge march on Washington, D.C. emphasizing that the control of families should be by the husband. Meanwhile, Ralph Reed organized his own political group called Century Strategies which is a political active group reflecting similar groups as the Christian Coalition. [13] Careful.

To the gay man or lesbian, the problems ahead are much greater in scope, more important in meaning, and more exciting than simply satisfying sexuality. The gay lifestyle will be filled with various religious theories because they are educated, thinking, and relatively guiltless group of non-conformists that have adjusted many of their lives to the time and the place, and won the award of relative happiness

If we do not allow our heads to be covered in sand, if we do not allow concentration on our lifestyles to so dominate our thinking, the gay communities could be some of the most exciting, intellectual gatherings we have yet to see. From the masses should come great leaders of ideas.

A SPIRITUAL PERSON

Religion is only a small, practical part of a greater belief in a spiritual God. To discover your spirituality, you must look beyond the physical interpretation of the body, the physical interpretation of your relationship to people and to the things of the world including your own existence.

Spirituality consists of the recognition of rules or ideas that are larger than our existence on a physical level. It is a belief in something bigger and grander than us, a controlling force or energy, basic rules by which we live beyond our time and place.

It is more than just the practice of religion, the belief in the power of a God. Religion is a practical format in which we can capture some of the qualities of spiritualism, but it only hints at the greatness of believing in a system which is universal and beyond. Our God, regardless of the religion, carries the practical applications of spiritualism to people through religion.

Spirituality is a belief that there are many rules beyond the scope of man; the creativity of growth of a plant or a child, the universal plan of seasons as in Nature, the understanding that man is both perfect and imperfect, the belief in values much larger than man's contributions, an understanding and a faith in yesterday as well as tomorrow. It is the constant striving to be better, to fit more closely, to interpret more accurately. It's fulfillment and peace even into death. It's love, hope, understanding, and charity.

Most Americans have been raised in a religion even though they may not play lip-service to the religion by donations and church attendance, and the members of the congregation have inherited the religious ideas, only a part of spirituality. We are mostly what our parents have taught us. Even atheists have a no-God as a God. There are probably no true agnostics, because the lack of an answer is the answer to their God's existence. Agnosticism says simply "I don't know".

Anyone who can see a sunrise, the grandeur of a sunset, the birth of a baby, the changing seasons, the maturing of a mind can understand a power or force or the existence of something much greater than human beings, and that recognition is called spirituality.

Organized religion is only one path to realize spirituality. Many will question if it is a very good path because it often gets tied to self importance and materialism. With only one fifth of the world being Judea-Christian, there are many other paths, many directions leading to spirituality that we do not know. The American interest in the Oriental philosophies has opened new doors to many. Understanding primitive cultures has enlightened others.

How small our individual sexual habits seem compared to the spirituality of the world. The gay man and lesbian has been chastised for not following "God's word". Which God and what words? Kindness, compassion, understanding, loving and praise are spiritual objectives. Hate, pain, disease, oppression, bigotry are spiritual negatives.

There are few gay people who are against the values of the family; in fact they imitate the values in their own created unions. Gays are against those who try to distort the values of the family by insisting only heterosexuals can have family values and any values shared by gays should be eliminated. Some egos find only one path to spirituality; their path.

It is impossible to love without spirituality, the belief there is something much greater and important than the human being. If love is expressed in sex, the complete climax is not satisfied until the physical expression moves into spirituality.

The oppressive early years of gay men and lesbians has built on a sensitivity to believe in something beyond the human being. Bias, prejudice, values, giving and disagreement with organized religion and procedures often exclude them. The bias of most religious leaders exclude the gays; the Pope excludes them. Gays should be laden with guilt because of their inability to march with the masses, and the American Catholic Bishops re-defined their previous strict rulings by saying that Catholics should "love their children even if gay", but the Church has never condoned the sexual act but tends to admit that being gay may be out of the control of the gay person. "Good" or "bad" is determined by what you do. With this small digression from the Catholic Church theology, more Catholics may be better able to understand and protect their gay children. From these thwarted backgrounds of being gay have come sensitive, talented, creative people that have used their disjointed backgrounds to bolster their personal drives. They can think beyond the day-by-day procedure to greater goals.

Can heterosexuals have spirituality? Of course, but they have to learn to live by the more humane qualities of compassion, understanding, tolerance, and love, and they have to fight the negatives of hate. There are increasing numbers of straights that have opened their hearts to the gay community and lifestyles and enjoy the positive aspects of the gay lifestyle as well as the lifestyle of a heterosexual.

THE ABILITY TO CHANGE MY FAULTS

There is within humans the ability to do practically whatever he/she wants to do if he is willing to take the sacrifices or changes that will happen within himself, and only if he/she sincerely feels that he has fault. It takes a great deal of spirituality, moral fiber, patience and time, but it can be done. The question becomes "Is my fault worth changing?"

What you consider a flaw or fault at one time in your life may not be of consequence to you at another time in your life, if you use that aspect of your personality and/or behavior to compliment your life with happiness, the ageless goal. Without question, certain flaws are more difficult to change than others, all along a continuum of difficult to easy. Some flaws may be physical, others are psychological, but both can be corrected. If I want to give up smoking, a physical and psychological or a combination addiction; I probably can if I really believe that I will be healthier and happier, and if I can break the physical addiction.

There are some basic drives which are very difficult to alter, and maybe altering the addiction is too great a risk to other factors. "Can I give up homosexuality?" Yes, but is it worth it? You'll fight a basic drive of "am I being true to myself?" Are you trying to give up homosexuality or is someone asking you to give it up…but why?

The Catholic priests take vows of celibacy and, although we read of the exceptions, many are celibate. Some people can live without sex. Monks, nuns, and many oriental religions deny experiencing sex. Yes, you can live without sex, but you can also live without much human involvement, but why?

There is very little we cannot change about ourselves if we are willing to change. Today, my gender can be changed, my race can be hidden, my education can be increased, my age can be disguised, and my body can be nipped and tucked so I appear youthful … but why? I can eat only vegetables, I can live on coconut milk, I can pop a thousand pills, I can gulp down a quart of wine…but why?

I am responsible for the way I live. I am responsible for the way I act. I am responsible for what I believe. I am responsible to myself, firstly, and then to others. I am a breathing, thinking American human being with some flaws that I am capable of changing but prefer not to change because the flaws hurt no one. I am a person who is of value to myself, my country, and the world. I am also gay. I hold my head with pride. The responsibility of the well being of the person is on the individual.

From my bias, I'm not going to get into a discussion with someone who supports the inequality of women, the lack of birth control, the hierarchy of politics in religion, rules and theories that don't recognize human growth and development, and a mass of unsubstantiated assumptions that are backed by fear.

IS MY SCOPE OF INTERESTS TOO NARROW?

Sometimes we can get so involved in our lives and the problems that we lose sight of other interests and activities going on around us and throughout the world. The homosexual may have worries if he/she becomes so involved with gay problems, so involved with gay friends, and so caught up in gay work that he concentrates on little else. The gay man or lesbian's world centers around gay issues and he/she becomes swallowed by gay themes. This narrowness is an easy trap because our profession, our money, entertainment, and lifestyle are aligned with our sexual behavior, and this packaging makes a very specialized person.

All people should expand their interests away from their own personal problems, confusions, or insecurities to looking at a larger picture, something detached from the person's directions, goals. Try an interest in politics within the locale, the state politics, national politics, or politics of the world. One can build an interest in art, music, or literature. Specialities like the Inca Indians, dog breeding, real estate, etc., could lead into another profession or hobbies. A healthy gay person must give vent to his/her interests and develop other interests or hobbies from stamp collecting to raising rabbits. The world is full of ideas, some of which may fascinate us.

We give up too soon with excuses like "I can't draw" before we have even tried. A person can do practically anything that he/she wants to do, but he has to star someplace. Enroll in a class. Study with a friend. Take part. There is a line from "Auntie Mame" that is something like "...life is a banquet, and most poor sons-of-bitches are starving to death." Get involved. There is a bad tendency for a gay man or lesbian not to be involved in things outside of the gay world. Don't let that hold you back.

Because of social acceptance and insecurity, the gay person is hesitant to expose his/her interests outside of the gay lifestyle, his security. When you do, the gays do it in mass; not every local Republican meeting can handle 15 gay Republicans in mass. You can get involved alone, even without your partner. The worse that can happen is that you will feel unwanted, and that has happened before, and you can handle that.

Go back to some of your personal desires as a kid. A guy in Chicago collects antique dolls. She always wanted to know how to hunt, and now she is learning how. She loves to refinish furniture. Why can't a woman fix a car? He collects stamps. Expand your interests.

Many gay people are interested in only what gays are supposed to like, the stereotype of conventional minority interests. Let some say "I don't like drag. I don't want to sit in a bar all night. I dislike eating at fancy restaurants and mundane chit-chat. She is much too piss-elegant for me. I don't want to camp." You can be your own person.

GROWING AWAY FROM RELATIVES AND FRIENDS

You have changed considerably since you were good friends with many of the kids you grew up with, and the relatives that you had to like because they were a part of your parent's family. They have changed also. Most have reflected the heterosexual lifestyle as had your parents. They have raised children and will soon be praising their grand-children. They probably have not had the adventuresome life that they expect you have had, even if your trips have not been so wonderful. Your friends and relatives look at you as unique. You have never had that common factor that binds your relatives together, the heterosexual family, friends and relatives. You have become an outsider.

A family lived beside another family for 25 years, and they both raised their children who were the best of friends. The husbands worked together. The wives shopped, laundered, cooked, cared for the other's kids, and they were all good neighbors. The kids grew up and were off starting their own families. One couple sold their house and retired to Florida. The two families never kept in contact.

Being gay, keeping contact with your parents or maybe even a brother or sister is a very dutiful obligation, one the gay person easily takes as responsibility because he/she has left unfinished business and there is always some sense of guilt. The lack of a traditional family leaves the gay person who has learned responsibility and who has not married, as the leading contender to care for the parents. Even with the responsibility of a meaningful relationship, the gay person can rarely refuse the care of his/her parents.

Notice the reactions of your gay friends who return to their parent's home to attend a high school reunion or a college reunion. Few are not left disappointed because the situation repeats the feelings they had in school when the gay person was not as aware of himself and the world around him/her. Usually, the gay male or lesbian is glad to return to their new home where they have established their family, even if they prefer not to tell old classmates about it.

40 TO 50

Well, maybe not exactly at the age of 40, but around that age is the time when a lot of common circumstances have taken place among you and your friends, and you begin to have physical changes which strike emotional changes, or vice-versa, and there can be a great deal of re-evaluations of your desires, drives, and where you place emphasis.

We know the woman goes through the most obvious physical change, menopause, a period where her reproductive body is changing to one which is no longer able to conceive, although through science this period of carrying a baby is extended. We know that 91% of eligible men get married before 44 years old.

By 40 to 50, most of the wanted children have been born and mostly raised. The wife and the husband suffer from how well they have accomplished their child rearing task, both usually resulting in some disappointment as well as pride. In the future, we imagine that same sex couples who have adopted children will suffer the same feelings of inadequacies and adequacies. The children start to leave the family unit.

If diverted in a career as well as raising the children, the woman must re-establish her relationship with the husband. We know that some mothers must re-establish their time from raising the family unit to their careers. A same sex couple raising children must pay more attention to the lover once the children are gone.

The husband's life has changed. The burning passion of getting ahead when he was young has mellowed, and he has learned his limitations. The demand for raising money on which to rear his family has ended in acquiring many things, but less time and appreciation for the things. He has become aware of how important his children and mate are to him. Ignoring his wife or mate is no longer tolerated. The aging man becomes aware of his his personal business limitations and he cleverly hides his short-comings. In an attempt to appear satisfied, he becomes frustrated. He has gone up the success ladder and he can see the top of the ladder, and he questions if it is worth taking the next steps.

What has happened is that many years of expected goals, of failures and successes, of compromise have gone by and the mere weight of being 40 to 50 years old with, perhaps, a questionable future has taken the toll both mentally and physically. It has affected the straight husband and wife, the married gay couple with or without children, the single gay person and even the closeted gays. 40 is a mystical age and a created line of measurement, a time of self-evaluation, perhaps a time of appreciation, maybe a time for a change.

The gay man or lesbian has similar experiences of reaching goals, but less structure in the lifestyle to accomplish each step at a particular pressured time. If alone or even with a mate of similar age, the gay person is seldom ready for the realization that may accompany the artificial measuring point of 40 to 50.

There is much emphasis placed upon the appearance of youth for the gay male. He dyes his hair, builds his muscles and pays particular attention to what he wears and the exposed labels of success. He hedges at the talk of age. He fluffs the hair over the balding spot on his head. He sucks in his stomach. He wears the style of the younger generation, usually unsuccessfully. He is desperate in his attempt to be the romantic lover and the appealing sex symbol, too often he gets tired too early in the evening. He wants to be Don Juan, but he is only Don. He buys the red convertible, flashes money, and boasts of his success. The poor guy is just fighting getting older.

The single lesbian at 40 to 50 has given attention to building her nest with the thousand and one gadgets. Although she is still afraid of success, she is at last getting someplace at her job. She feels she's on the right track. She may decide to adopt a child, a late attempt at a family unit. Secretly, she like her counterpart, the gay male, is still prowling and looking. Hoping. Maybe, this time. At least a family.

The same sex couple has completed their nest and are constantly redoing in hopes of gaining more into the relationship. Some have simply adjusted to the opposite person allowing him/her to do whatever he wants; others complaining the whole way regardless of what the mate wants. They have to re-establish their relationship with each other as well as friends while they have been busy either building their things or raising children. They have to re-establish their understanding of each other, clarify the rules that have happened, and decide if they want to continue with each other. Those with children usually want to continue their relationships; some without children will give it serious thought for a change.

40 to 50 and the children gone from the house is the time that the closeted person realizes that he/she wants a different form of life than what it has been in the straight family unit. It is not unusual for the adult to open the closet door. What a bunch of confusion when he/she approaches the gay lifestyle beyond prime.

Those lacking in friends past 40 to 50 will find it difficult to establish new gay friends of the same age group, They often obtain a younger person and pickup the bills, less tolerance for late hour parties, a greater sensitivity to breakfast, lunch, and dinner, and more tolerance with themselves and two martinis. The work schedule will often be increased because of the insecurity of "I might as well be making money as spending it."

What really marks the difference between the gays and straights at 40 to 50 is that the straight men are adjusting to their gray hair and getting fatter while the gay male is using plastic to correct the nose, lift the eyes, and pin back the ear in an attempt not to adjust to the changing years, but to hang on to youth. There is a line of "... if I knew I was going to reach 40, I would have taken better care of myself."

Hopefully, the gay male or lesbian establish in an employment where he/she can grow and be interested with the securities of health insurance, savings, and the possibilities of advancement. Hopefully, the person lives within an income structure with time and money to travel. Often, the gay person has re-established with the natural family and has taken responsibility. The gay has created his own family of friends and associates, interests and activities that are vital to him/her.

Gays without children lack watching their children grow, accepting their mistakes, and guidance of their interests. Single gays find the supposed change of life difficult, more than same sex couples or straights. Single gays, however, are usually still in search for someone, now to accept their real self rather than their youth. The gay's fading youth and the impossibility to stop it makes them desire the youth they are losing or have lost.

Every age has it frustrations. The years after 40 to 50 have no guarantee of being serene or peaceful. They can be filled with unanswered questions. Do I have enough money to retire? Should I take early retirement? How do I plan to live and how do I plan for my death? Questions, and some answers. At 40 to 50, you are only half way there; it is not over yet.

OTHER GAYS

There are some people who realize what the gay lifestyle means to them and move into other kinds of lives. They will not admit, perhaps even to themselves, they have experienced the exposure. It appears impossible to measure how many people have participated in the gay life and have decided that the gay lifestyle was not their choice. There is a difference between choice and desire. They have decided for whatever reason not to be part of the gay lifestyle.

Some of these people are loners, they dislike any type of organizational pattern which may interrupt whatever it is that they want to do. They prefer to go their own direction and care little or nothing for their emotional surroundings, except to be alone. They want no commitment to anyone or anything except themselves. They really want being alone from personal preference or from the amount of problems that have mounted and seem to overwhelm them to conclude they want to be alone. If their reason is personal preference and they understand why they have made this choice based on sound reasoning, fine. Allow them to be alone.

These loners account for the constant travelers, hoboes, street people, drunks, hermits and other sub-groups which may be living singularly happy lives. We imply that all homeless people are not in that position because of their own choice and some are not. Many, however, prefer the lack of restrictions and conformity and they have found many willing to allow their individual preferences of being singular and alone. They have become professionals at their style of living, although there are many problems of alcohol, drugs, emotional instability, and various forms of perversion. We can allow the non-conventional style of life, but we have little patience with the crimes they commit.

However, if being alone is only for the perpetuation of a lustful, sexual gay activity, the alone person may be in a serious mental state of causing harm to him/herself or to someone else. Some psychiatrists feel that a person can degrade himself to the lowest form, and that could be gay. In other words, the toilet faggot that has nothing more than his sexual activity, has serious mental problems.

Having experienced the gay lifestyle does not mean that you will slip into a disastrous position of being an alone bum. It does not mean you will become an active degenerate, or have mental problems. You would just rather withdraw from the super activity of gay life, return to a physical and mental direction that you may prefer.

There are some men and women who have experienced the gay lifestyle for a while, and decide not to participate and return to a straight lifestyle without much sexual confusion. Some gays return to the heterosexual lifestyle to be excellent mothers and good fathers, and they control their fantasy desires if they have any.

Don't confuse the issue with being "latent". Everyone is a latent something, latent meaning some fantastic idea that has never matured into action, some dream. I am latent _____.

Age and maturity have the ability to change your sexual energy. When you are 16 and horny, you may look at the gay lifestyle as exciting. At 40 to 50, when you may feel that life is mostly over, the gay lifestyle is interesting but not too exciting. At 60, the lifestyle may be boring, and some gay men consider taking a straight wife as a companion. There are "different strokes for different folks at different times."

Time has changed the manner in which things can be done. The current straight younger male can wait longer until he marries. There are plenty of single mothers that no longer face a social stigma, both straight and gay. There are straight and gay divorced fathers raising their children. There are gay men and gay couples with adopted children as well as parents who select a medical procedure for having their own biological children. Lesbians are having children. It is possible for a woman to conceive without the presence of a man. The "family", thus family values, depends upon the definition of a family. The definition of a family is up to the individual.

BISEXUALITY

Opposing a common, popular belief there is a sexual deviation from homosexuality and heterosexuality, there is no separate and distinctive sex called a bisexual. There is bisexual activity. The term "hermaphrodite" has lost its meaning in human science, and it is usually used to refer to an animal or plant that has both male and female organs. There are two sexes, male and female. There are many sexual activities from sadistic to masochistic, from leather drag to female impersonation. All activities are done by either a male or female. Even a celibate is a male or female. Those who call themselves bisexuals are either male or females, either gay or straight.

The term grows from Freudian studies which were inquiries into sexual activity and the early Kinsey reports followed by Johnson and Johnson which were also based on physical activity of having sex. If homosexuality and heterosexuality in the United States is based only on sexual response, one may be able to support a bisexual category. However, both the gay and straight procedures go beyond the purely physical to a gay lifestyle and a straight lifestyle.

As commonly understood, a bisexual is a person who can have sex with either a male or a female with equal attraction and affection Granted, there are some heterosexual men that can have sex with females and males, as well as heterosexual females that can have sex with both males and females. There are some lesbians and gay males that will have sex with heterosexual males and females. The bisexual category implies that a bisexual has sex with his partner, a straight female on Monday, a gay man on Tuesday, a lesbian on Wednesday, a straight man on Thursday with equal emotion and fulfillment.

There are many lesbians and gay men that have had sex with both straight men and women, but they are certainly not bisexual. There are some straight men and women who have sex occasionally with lesbians and gay men, but they remain straight in their own values and lifestyle. Many gay's early experiences are with the opposite sex, but they are not straight.

Simplistically, you are the lifestyle you live. If you live by the rules of that group, you are what that group is. If you live the gay lifestyle, you are gay. If you live the straight lifestyle, you are probably straight. Over simplistic, but probably true,

There may be a period in a person's life where he/she is experimenting with homosexuality and heterosexuality that he/she does try both. There are more people that call themselves bisexuals because they are after something more than just the other person, whether it be association, fame, a bed to sleep in, or, more than likely, for pure financial benefits. The sexual response of the bisexual is not for the enjoyment of the sex, but rather for the benefits. The bisexual is using sex trying to find himself. He/she becomes a sex machine, and sex has become an end in itself, not a means to an end in a human understanding, but in obtaining the person's goal.

It is true that through a lifetime, a person may prefer a heterosexual relationship rather than a homosexual relationship, or vice-versa, but this different lifestyle is based upon qualities of the lover or supposed lover at the time. There is a more convenient time to raise a family, a more convenient time for companionship, a more desirable time to increase financial assets, a time in your career that is important to you. You may personally select a different lifestyle.

Why would a person want to be called a bisexual? As you know, it takes courage to "come out", and often pain and confusion. By calling yourself bisexual, you imply the sexual pattern not to be judged too harshly by the gays or the straights. Public figures often use the term to support their desires to be at least half liked. Straights find the term an introduction and acceptance into the gay lifestyle which may offer them opportunities for being acknowledged, or liked, or to gain. The bisexuals linger with gay public acceptance, "someone understands".

We can define sexual activity in a variety of different ways. Do we imply an effeminate man is more female than male, a masculine woman is more male than female? When we talk of a pedophile, do we know if the male or female attack is upon a boy or girl? We know only it is a child. Does beastialty indicate the sex of the animal's partner, or even of the animal? Is sodomy directed to one sexual activity of which sex? Does necrophilia indicate the sex of the perpetrator? Does an orgy tell you how many people? Why should bisexuality be a category in itself?

Conclusion: There are two sexes, male and female. The two sexual activities can be divided into homosexual or heterosexual. Their sexual procedures can be many different things.

HOBBIES ASIDE FROM MYSELF

Sitting at a bar cruising is not a hobby. Walking the streets hoping for a trick is not a hobby. Getting drunk, doing drag, ironing clothes, and many of the other things we do each day are not hobbies. To present ourselves better to someone else so someone will want us is a necessity. A hobby is an un-personal, unselfish interest in something besides you and your personality. The only way in which you are involved is your interest in the subject matter; not the conclusion or result of the interest which benefits you, but a true interest in the subject itself. Gossip is selfish. Tricks are often more fun in the conquest than the actual performance. Alcohol has its down side. Drugs are only temporary.

Yet, somewhere inside you is an interest apart from you, an interest in something in which you are not involved, in which you can gain nothing, and which does not feed your ego except in the accepting of the information. These can become your direction of interest because they are aside from you, a non-selfish direction apart from the self. It may be an interest in witchcraft, collecting butterflies, working at the Salvation Army, donating time to the less fortunate, building clay, painting or practically anything which is not personal to you.

We become obsessed with the words of "I", "me", "my" and "ours" to the point where we never think beyond our own self-satisfaction, rarely think of the millions of ideas and experiences that are beyond our lifestyles. We tunnel into ourselves for understanding making ourselves the object to be understood without listening to the other tunes being played by the band. The world is full of "me", and we fail to look beyond. The question becomes "What are you doing of interest for someone beyond yourself?" It is not an easy question to answer unless the answer is "nothing".

Get involved in hobbies that you personally like but hobbies beyond your personal self; something in which you can have an interest in collecting the information without personal involvement. Broaden your world. Don't aim to broaden your ego.

People never stop learning for it seems there is always more to know, and it does not decline the older we get so long as we keep ourselves interested. That is our individual goal; keeping ourselves fresh with new information and the investigations of our hobbies. Sameness is boredom, and boredom leads to the lack of interest and the lack of interest leads to death of the mind and the spirit.

A CAT OR DOG

Gay men and lesbians are some of the most kind pet owners. They take on the responsibility of caring for animals readily and well. It gives them a sense of well being and protection. If the gay person is alone, the animal is the start of the family unit that he/she wants to build around himself. It is caring and, supposedly, it is being cared for. A dog or cat never says "you are wrong".

In the young years of a gay person's life there is a lot of changing of roommates, changing apartments, and changing locales. Be sure that you are close to settling before you select an animal. If you have a pet and a roommate, you must be sure the roommate knows who is the owner of the animal; joint ownership ends with one person's feeling hurt for lack of affection from the animal. Establish ownership.

Make sure the well being of the animal is the first consideration. Don't have a dog if you are often out of town. Substitute friends do not replace you. Don't have a dog unless you have a yard, a park or area close by to walk the animal twice a day. Be willing to take the responsibility and understand the necessity for the care of the animal. Do not walk the dog with hostility.

To many people, a cat seems to be less responsibility for a metropolitan community, but even a cat needs affection and attention, but not as much as a dog. Cats tend to be more selfish demanding to be fed and praised. Cats are possessive as are dogs. The discussion is not dog verses cat; the subject is responsibility.

Understand what you are doing. You are attempting nest building by raising a family, even if it is a dog or a cat. You are needed. Birds, fish, and other pets may give you similar feelings of being important to someone or something. To be needed is a feeling of contentment, and we all, particularly the gay man or lesbian, need the security. Even if you have a lover, the pet seems undemanding, and you eagerly take on the responsibility of caring for it. I'm not sure you can love a boa constrictor in the same way.

What you are trying to do is to make your nest, either alone or with a partner, a place of harmony and understanding and of love. Anything you can do to satisfy that craving within you for contentment is worth considering. There are few rules to follow except for your own desires. Right now, happiness to you would be _____. It is probably not things, but attitudes. If you don't try to make yourself happy, no one else will. You are responsible.

When you are growing older, get something to love aside from the pretty little guy or gal down the street and unavailable to you. Studies of older citizens in homes or wards indicate that the companionship from an animal leads them to a much more interesting and interested life, a reason to push on..

THE CRISIS

One of the most fascinating unscheduled event of living is that time of crisis. It always happens at an awkward time, but a crisis is not convenient. There is not an appropriate time. It just happens, and you may be old or young, healthy or unhealthy, in a good emotional state or in the dumps. A crisis is completely unpredictable. Sometime along living, it comes like a hurricane. There can be several or just one. No person lives without some crisis.

Living is like a stock car race. Some cars, the gays, get off the starting line very poorly with a great deal of handicaps, but get caught in the traffic and catch up to the leaders. To others, the poor start means immediate defeat, and they pull their cars over to the sidelines losing before they start the race.

There are pit stops along the way, places to make you aware of what is happening and time for you to fix the engine, to realign the wheels, to gas, change the oil, to rotate the tires. Then you are back on the track but with the knowledge of what better your car can do. Some drivers junk the car at the pit stops. Some drivers never make it out again or pull over long before the end of the race.

Others get more energy. Since they know the car better than before, they know how to drive it better. They know when to apply the breaks; when to give it gas. They look toward the finish line with gusto, and some get more energy and race across the finish line.

The pit stop of life is crisis. It is the drastic event which can change your life, each event differing in importance to each person. A death in the family. Personal illness. Loss of a business. Death of a loved one. Finding out your are HIV positive. These are crucial moments that may change your life tremendously if you do not make the right decision, and there is no clear right decision. Whatever may cause the turning point in your life, that time of crisis, you identify it as such. You cannot continue as usual. You must stop, re-evaluate, and hopefully continue your life understanding what has sent you out of the pits and off into a new direction with more appreciation.

The pit stop can only be a warning; one that should scare you, but one from which you can recover. Someday, maybe without warning, there may be a crisis from which you cannot recover. You may have no desire to continue the race and without the desire to continue, you will die. You give up.

HALFWAY TO 100

There is a time when youth has passed quickly. Falling in love and building a family is finished. You've experienced buying the new car or the new house, when you're settled in your job knowing that you probably won't progress much further to making big decisions. You are satisfied with the day by day routine of the job and the people and the pressure from upstairs, and you have found you can live comfortably, maybe not extravagantly, on your income. You push back a few bucks for growing older, a time when you are over halfway to 100. It is not a lightning, sudden realization, but rather a comforting, easy pace of being satisfied. It is like resting after a good dinner, satisfied and comfortable.

At 50 to 60, the house or apartment is quiet, the telephone doesn't ring as often and sometimes you won't pick it up anyway. The monthly bills are paid as usual. There's gas in the car. The dog has been walked. Television is boring and you sit looking out a window or staring into space.

The dreams you had as a young kid, the ambition and the drive to get ahead, the energy for the kill, the cocky attitude, the confidence in your choices, the strength and pride in your approach to others, all have rested. The imaginary huge office has settled to a desk pushed against the wall. The mansion has digested to a pleasant and comfortable house or apartment. The career has settled down to a job. The energy of making those great decisions is gone because no one asked you for your opinion. The great romance of your life is the person finishing the dishes in the kitchen.

What happened to the fireworks? Where were the flashes? The car? The clothes? The big mansion? The success? The praise? The honor? Like soaked and wet sparklers, they were never lit; the fireworks never went up.

Yet in the darkness, alone, you would not say that your life was a failure. True, you didn't meet some of your greatest plans, too early for some and too late for others. You didn't acquire all you wanted, but you seem satisfied by the bit you obtained, and you used it well. They probably would have liked you at your thirty-fifth high school reunion, but you were busy that night and did not attend. It made little difference anyway; most of your high school class is not as happy as you are. Did you lock the garage door?

The future looks pretty good. Probably wise to take the early retirement; probably forced to. With good investing, there will be enough money to do a little traveling. You've always wanted to do a garden. You've got medical insurance and in a few years you'll get social security.

You are only a little more than halfway ...

PREPARING TO BE OBSOLETE

At the turn of the past century, a man would work his entire life acquiring little except food and saving nothing, perhaps his major lifetime investment being his home and paying back a 30 year mortgage before he retired. If he grew too old to work, he would become dependent upon the humanity of his children.

In the 1930's, our government set up a system which would automatically subtract from our pay checks and save the money for our old age; a system called social security. With the government's wisdom, they declared that a man or woman who has worked until he/she was 65 years old should be able to withdraw some money to help him/her when he grows old, enough at least to keep a roof over head and food. Later they passed laws that said he/she could withdraw 80 % of his savings if he started withdrawal at 62 years old. The U. S. Government created 62 years old or 65 years old as the start of the working person becoming old.

This has been complicated in the last tight budget 20 years when business has realized it can hire two or more people for the one top level position, an offer called early retirement. The plan was to buy out the higher position and eliminate the higher salary, not working for one company all your life, and it cut the company's expenses. Sometimes business tactics are not kind, and they are powerful. A 55 year old will find it difficult to get another job in a market that prefers less expensive salaries which usually demand youth.

When do we become obsolete? 55? 62? 65? (The government is still attempting to define the question they asked but never answered. They are repeating the question, but only in the hopes of getting an answer which will save money in the economy.) Business seems to feel that a person of 50 plus can be replaced. Social security states 65 or 62. To save money, someday the government will increase the age of retirement to 72 or 75. We're living longer costing more.

There was a change of values and attitudes of the working men and women. Why should we work so hard for a boss that could fire us whenever he wants? Through this struggle of the working classes grew the unions, that were suppose to represent labor; not management. The unions attempted to help guarantee a "good life " of values for the laborers, minority representation, women's liberation, child labor laws, women's rights and restricted working hours, days and conditions. Union grew from the support of the working class to become "negotiators", and the wealthy were usually "right", and the unions tumbled having changed some things but bowing to management and the cost of having a union.

The original seven and a half million people when social security started in the 1930's grew to today's 34,000,000 people, and it will continue to grow to an overwhelming 61.4 million as the century turns. Not only are people living longer, supposedly they are living better. (Politicians, be quiet.)

Retirement is not the age of adolescence; quite the opposite. At retirement we have accomplished our objectives and gained most of the things we have wanted or we have learned to get along without the things, and now we only have to worry about replacements. We've accomplished our goals. Most families are raised and gone from the home. We have adjusted to ourselves, our mate, our friends and our interests.

We don't look at ourselves as in loneliness, but rather in a moment of being able to rest a little and do the things we want to do. We know what to do to make other people respect us. There is no isolation; we want our own place to live away from the children. We want our independence and a piece of society that the younger ones are now building. We want our say. We want to give them our wisdom, and they are often willing to take it. We want to know how to retire.

These are the golden years. Of course, it takes more than just the social security check to live, but most have planned for that. The senior citizens have learned that they are in a whole new political, social and economic game of experiences, and they have the energy, intelligence, and wisdom to appreciate it.

For gay men and lesbians, the golden years may mean marriage of the opposite sex or continued good living with a lover or even being alone, the lust and passion of youth having stepped aside for the maturity and availability of a partner or the strength to be alone. For the 1.6% of our population with assets over half a million, woman are wealthier than men. [14] Since women live longer than men and women have more wealth than men, a female straight partner for the next several years may not be a bad idea for a gay male, certainly a more comfortable lifestyle. The gay, polite, sensitive man without children is desirable to some. However, most gay men stay single constantly making new younger friends. The lesbian has the company of straight grand-parents in her age group and/or her mate of similar years. Although older straight men do not appeal to young lesbians, older non-demanding straight women do appeal to some gay men.

We have to accept the aging cycles and learn to appreciate each one for its own beauty. These are often the struggle-less years. Behind is the confusion of adolescence, the problems of building a family and vocation, losing your job in the social structure, raising the kids with ideals, doing without, seeing that the kids make it, worrying about their mates and children, retiring, your crisis, your energy for the future. Now, it's someone else's turn.

THE WISDOM OF BEING GAY

From understanding your background, realizing you are gay, adjusting to it, and maturing your ideas may develop some kind of wisdom about life in the old search of "What is it all about?" Wisdom is more than adding; when two plus two equals four. Wisdom is when the total of the parts is more than the sum; when two plus two equals five. The extra point is wisdom. It is when you have not only lived life, but when you understand and appreciate it.

An authority studying age cited his definition of wisdom as sound judgment, insight, and perspective, the ability to measure conflicting values and to have a technique to produce problem-solving. [1]

UNTIL SOCIAL SECURITY

The money from social security is not that great of a financial crutch that we thought it would be, although some people do live on the fee. The few dollars have to be stretched many ways, but you've done that before.

While you were in your forties, maybe earlier, you should have gotten a small piece of real estate, a house, an apartment or condo, and attempted to pay it off during your working years. Real estate does hit plateaus, but it seldom declines in value. Make sure the property was adequate; certainly not elaborate or ornate for the coming years. You should have crowded the nest with the things you like, but your major objective was to own it free and clear before you thought of collecting social security. Buying a place to live was often like saving money in case of an emergency; it could be sold or refinanced.

There are also other assets you have. Jewelry? Clothing? Antiques? Loans that need to be recalled. Don't hesitate to recall a loan from your children; that's just good business sense. Sell the car or the house. Cut down on the expenses.

Beyond 40 to 50, don't be ashamed of slowing down a little; of not donating all your time and energy to the job or to your family. If you have been forced out of your employment in the new business ethics, find yourself another job even if it does not pay the salary of your original employ. Your goal during this period is to balance income and output, at least until social security can help.

Don't be afraid of growing older, and don't try desperately to hide your age. Pounds of plastic, make-up, and jewelry hide something that you are not. You are not ashamed of your age and consider it an asset, and sell it. Who is judging anyway?

Put into a new job the same sort of spunk and a little less energy than what you had on your favorite job in out-smarting your competition with your experience. Work part-time if necessary or more comfortable. Approach your job with the idea of you are not only getting older, but also better. Have confidence in your own abilities. Increase your effort to please your boss. Something that the younger generation has not learned, don't complain. Your boss has rarely seen an employee like that.

Be prepared that your boss may be a woman. Men can work for women bosses also, but they must learn to curb their aggressive male humor which the new woman finds offensive. The older woman often becomes an ideal to the woman boss.

Continue to be creative in your employment. Take some of your previous working experience and apply it to the new job. Utilize your own talents. You may have to learn to use a computer, but you can do it. Don't under-estimate yourself.

Don't be afraid of the new challenge, but approach it as a new game thinking clearly through what the boss wants to the strategies that will give him/her the desired goal. Don't assume. Ask. It may clarify your boss' objectives to himself when he explains them to you.

Watch carefully of your amount of references to the past. Don't bombard him/her with your history. Come up with the strategy or idea and, if interested, he'll ask you where it came from. If not, forget it. You are working today; not ten years ago.

Continue to maintain good store conduct and office procedures. Be on time. Be attractive (not necessarily glamorous). Be pleasant. Do the job. Even the most naive boss today knows that an employee does not work beyond his/her work schedule without compensation. Know your limitations.

Don't be ashamed of getting older. A 15 year study concluded there was no measurable difference in body decline until age 70 and very little until 81. [2] You've got many good, healthy years ahead.

Don't ask about the benefits package until you have an understanding of the job. Your boss wants a job done and you may feel you are qualified to do it. He/she is not hiring you because of the advantages of the benefits package and your approaching golden years. If you have physical, disease related symptoms, get medical attention. Don't wait until a medical program chimes in with your age, because that may be too late.

What is your alternative? Is it to be shut up in some nursing home with many people your age, to wait for the Sunday afternoon visit from your friend, to write letters concerning your physical ailments and what you had for dinner? That's not living.

WHEN THE LOVER FANTASY FAILS

Somewhere in growing older when the individual looks at him/herself in the mirror, the image that once gave him pleasure, the tight stomach, the flock of hair, the personable smile has dimmed. The gay no longer is the great physical specimen and now even the person's naked eye can realize it.

All the plastic surgery and lies in the world, all the tucking and reshaping of our bodies, all the creams for lines and lotions for shadows cannot trick our vanity into being younger. This country is so obsessed with age, obsessed with staying young and virile, that we do not grow old gracefully, but rather with gallons of age hiding creams and techniques. Many seniors fight age. Growing older does mean you are losing your attractiveness, but gaining the attractiveness of growing older. Lesbians approaching the golden year are under the same illusions as gay men, desperate attempts to re-capture attractiveness.

Staying young implies that we are staying with the same dreams and aspirations, hopes and desires as when we were younger. One of our favorite dreams is that important someone someday will come around and sweep us off our feet and solve all our problems. Of course, he/she never comes, or maybe we feel the fairy tale ending as a San Francisco lesbian comedian stated "... she had ridden by and swooped me up in her arms and dropped me on my ass". Reality indicates that the body has sagged, the energy is lessening and the dream is gone. Mr. or Ms. Wonderful is not going to come or has come and left. The heroes from imagination have faded. Now, it's just you. What is there left to dream about?

Plenty. Get rid of your total self-satisfying pity and get some spark in your life. Stop worrying about yourself (you've been doing that most of your life) and start worrying (if you must worry) about things that are more important than you. Yes, there are many.

You have made your bed. You have loved. You have made mistakes. You've done a lot of good. You've made a lot of associates and a few very dear friends. You've seen people grow and die. You've seen an ever changing world. You have made yourself what you are. Be proud of it.

True. The heroes from the past, the lover that will take you away, the person that could have given you more than you could give yourself, all were dreams of expectations, and only a portion of those qualities came true. No. You cannot re-live the years gone by. You don't have to live in those years either. You don't have to give much concern to the years ahead because you have reasoned what that will be. The secret is to live for now, the "live every day for the pleasure of the day" approach.

It will be more fun for you to live each day one day at a time if you live those days a little dangerously, just to prove to yourself that you still have a little devilishness. Tell your friends that you are going to join a nudist camp. Have two slugs of liquor in your nightcap. Double your prescription from the pharmacy. Keep them guessing. When you go to bed at night and try to get that pleasant dream about your hero, and the dream won't come because you've grown older and the illusion has faded, think about how you kept the younger ones guessing today.

Remember back also to the wild day. Although the young male today might not remember before the advent of AIDS, there was a period in the sixties and seventies where there were male bath houses, gay steam rooms where practically anything physical and homosexual could happen, and did. The older gay seniors have something, memories, that it is going to take the younger gay people a lifetime to accumulate. Have fun remembering the memories. You can even join SAGE (Seniors Active in a Gay Environment).

ELEGANCE

Since we all start from some place and work our entire lives trying to make a higher step on the social and economic ladder to success (not necessarily happiness), we have put values on physical things as gauges of our success. When I buy my car, my house, my vacation home, my silver, my fine clothes, all those things of refinement are currently beyond my level and no longer important. When you have acquired what you could acquire and gone beyond your expectations, you may have arrived at a sense of self satisfaction of elegance, a refined grace slightly beyond your limitations.

The attitude of holding your body erect and composed, of knowing what to say and, equally important, what not to say, of presenting yourself with assumed standards of conduct and social position all are attributes of elegance, but it is even more than the attributes. It is the wisdom and the manner in which one carries the wisdom and releases the knowledge that he/she has the wisdom. It combines humility, tolerance, knowledge and tact. It is a respect you get from other people concerning their attitudes toward you.

American society is quickly losing a factor of elegance by losing respect for growing older. New ways of doing things, new ideas and products, new methods for handling people and promotions, the changing world has left many with little or no respect for what has happened prior to them. We have lost respect for old age and the wisdom of some in old age, and the seniors often play the game of pure elegance, the maturity and wisdom to look beyond the current situation.

How often the older Americans, those not so physically alert, perhaps mentally slower than the younger minds, more concerned with people and ideas than advancement, are pushed aside. With the breakup of the whole family living together, husbands and wives, grandparents, children, aunts and uncles, the family unit has become much smaller; indeed, sometimes only one person. The new family does not have the opportunity to learn from the previous generations. The younger ones do not learn from the older. Age alone does not guarantee wisdom, but it is difficult, if not impossible, to have wisdom without age because how would the theories be proven?

With a respect for age comes the appreciation of the elegance of the older generations. It is like dancing with your grandmother or grandfather, an elegance they have been there before and know what to do and what has been done and why. Their taste in dress, furniture although old, refinement in manners, habits, literary skills, etc. smack of a grander life and lifestyle although they may not have lived it. It is so great of a feeling that it also has a smell about it, a refined, subtle aroma and a cloud around it of an all encompassing feeling of social protection for those older in years and wiser in wisdom.

For some reason, the gay man or lesbian is strongly attracted to the senior person and it may have something to do with the all accepting reflection of wisdom and elegance. Gay participation in senior citizen's homes and nursing homes is tremendous expanding beyond themselves to help others.

WILL I HAVE WISDOM?

Wisdom is based on something more than just the number of years old you may be. It is based upon experience and the older you are the more experiences you will have, but it is the inter-relationship of the knowledge of the experiences plus time that allows some people, but certainly not all, to draw generalizations that are applicable, valid and true and can be applied to each generation and/or all generations. You develop wisdom with time, but time alone does not guarantee wisdom.

Researchers in Europe have been studying the aging mind and have presented some interesting qualities of a definition of wisdom. [3] Wisdom is a factual and procedural knowledge about the trends of the world and human growth and psychology. It closely links the knowledge of how humans deal with their own personalities, and how the personalities deal with the scientific truths. While recognizing the uncertainty of the human condition, there is an uncertainty and appreciation of unanswered questions. Involving thinking, emotion, and motivation of the person and the society, wisdom is knowledge of the self and generalities that involve our society and other cultures.

Wisdom incorporates human generalities with cultural generalities, time and creates it own truths to be bantered about for their lasting qualities through time. It shows us the strategies to apply the knowledge to our specific situation. It is more than information; it's the rules behind the information that allow the information to be digested into our minds of the application, strategies, and the substance of the information and a grander whole, what we call truths.

As long as the mind is growing and it should be allowed to continue to grow with new experiences, the greater the chance of establishing new wisdom. A biological approach to a disintegrating physiology implies wisdom stops when the person dies. For most, wisdom has never started because of the American belief of the decline of our physical bodies, but we are slowly pulling away from that interpretation.

American business does not seem to have the time to wait around from 62 to 65 to the end of life for the employee to gain the experience of the wise man and to utilize his wisdom They would rather read a book about Mr. X who started Y company which Mr. X wrote many years after he left the company. The reader's conclusion is that things are like that today; the lack of application of wisdom.

With the AIDS scare, many gay and straight lives have been cut short from the lifetime expectancy figures (78.6 for American women; 71.6 for men, and no statistics available for gays and more recent figures indicate woman's life expectancy is six years rather than seven years different from men's life expectancy). Many have learned that adding a few more meaningless years to their lives without comfort or progress in curing the disease is senseless. They die sometimes by committing suicide. This trend will continue; it is the quality of life, not the quantity.

AGING

There has been has been a great deal of testing of aging and learning in the United States. [4] The many studies agree with the results of an 8.4 million dollar investment grant expense concerned memory loss as well as retaining knowledge while aging. [5]

One study finding includes seeking variety, flexibility and finding peace within yourself to maintain a healthy mind. [6] In childhood, you should eat correctly, get stimulated in an enriched environment, and stay in your educational pursuit. The author felt a young adult should make friends, find a mentor, marry someone smarter than yourself, and continue your education. As a middle aged person, you should develop expertise, save or invest money, achieve lifetime goals, enjoy the bustle of business and your private life, and not get burned out. After 65 you should seek new horizons, feel a sense of purpose, take daily exercise and control mental apathy and deterioration.

Researchers rather scoffed at the misconceptions of learning of older people. In one study of 1,583 persons from 25 to 92 years of age, they found that a quarter to a third of subjects in their eighties performed as well in math and reading comprehension as did their much younger counterparts. Most older people retain strong mental skills until at least age 70, but over a fourth of those continue past that age without significant drops in brainpower.

Some felt the dangerous age was not 40, but 50. Around 50, people of similar ages began to differ in their mental performance. Some of this was related to the person's training and his concepts of growing old and losing mental ability when growing old. The researchers realized that the recording of events continued to grow and not deteriorate, but it became more sophisticated with each advanced year. They equated the smarter older people with "above average level of education, complex and stimulating lifestyle, and being married to a smart spouse."

REMEMBERING

The greatest fear of many senior citizens is that they are losing their memories and forgetting things. The loss of memory is a fear of not being able to handle money to wondering who will care for the older person. Many older people worry about not remembering,

The fear of losing your memory is the singularly most important cause of poor memory. Aside from the dreaded disease, we joke about old-timer's disease and about not remembering. Your memory or mind carries about 30 or more years of events and experiences and, naturally, some are more clear than others. The best advice is to keep venturing into new ideas and new directions. We've never had a full brain yet. [7]

The Dana Foundation grant found that "... most types of memory loss should not be considered normal and could be treatable". [8] Other researchers repeated the study and implied that maybe senior memory loss or forgetting is simply a way of avoiding responding, and there may be no physical proof that age increases poor memory or remembering so long as it is not a disease. [9]

When we fear talking about memory and remembering, aren't we really hiding the subject of becoming dependent upon someone else for our well being? Aren't we really asking, "Who is going to take care of me?"

You have been caring for people all your life and the answer to that question is obvious: you are going to take care of yourself in the manner in which you want. It is possible that you may need some assistance. There are many help groups from religious organizations to Hospice for that kind of help. There are also plenty of fine homes for senior citizens and they are no longer like the old folks home up on the hill.

There are activity centers of people your own age, often from close to where you have lived, sometimes people you know that you can re-meet. There are daily activities and exercises and games and recreation. It is not falling back, but it is going ahead into action and activity. You are usually not confined, and many people enjoy the comfort and security of the retirement home realizing and proud that they are not being a burden to their children or family.

Will you grow old gracefully? Hell, no. You have not lived gracefully and why would you want life to be that dull? I would hope that the senior retirement home could be a lot of fun for you, and allow you to continue to grow.

There will always be the fear of running out of money. You will have enough. Your family and friends won't let you down. Hopefully, the government won't let you down. You won't need that much.

You have had over 50 or more years of managing money, and you have probably missed few meals. Besides, in living alone or in living in a retirement home, there are few social restrictions on you. You can do what you like to do. You can stay home or go to the dance. You've stayed home before and enjoyed it. Or, you can go to the dance. Your experience in budgeting has made you an expert, and you undoubtedly manage money well.

Don't start being a pessimist now. Don't use the words "... but what if" because no one knows the answer to these questions and sometimes they have no answers. "But...what if I die?" You are going to someday anyway and you've lived a large chunk of time not worrying about that. The children are going to be happier and more satisfied if you spend your money on yourself if you have raised them correctly. Besides, it is your savings; not anyone else's savings. There will always be the vulture cousin; he doesn't get what he has expected. Your kids will adjust; the vulture cousin never will.

What the aging question demands is for you to worry about those things that you can do something about; don't worry about things you cannot control. Notice that the burning question of sexuality has not been discussed. When you have reached the happy golden years, no one really gives much of a damn about your past sex life, and don't believe the ads; sex after 90 is not better. It is just rarer.

Above all, enjoy yourself. These are the years that you have been given that have only recently been enjoyed by other generations because they usually did not get the opportunity to enjoy the senior years. Modern ideas, modern medicine and living, they are all for you to enjoy.

There is only one thing you must do before you are ready to let her rip and have a good time. You must have your legal affairs in order. You should have done it years ago, but now you have to do it. Since so much of your life has been lived with common sense, you must now take the final steps in being responsible.

AM I RESPONSIBLE?

Like it or not, we are not responsible to ourselves presenting problems that we could have solved had we taken the time. We procrastinate. We put it off until tomorrow; maybe never. We can find a thousand excuses not to do what we don't want to do. Then we are sorry we didn't do it.

Even with HIV positive gay men and the limited few lesbians feel indispensable and they will live forever. So many have not taken the few minutes to complete a few forms to make the arrangements in case they become ill or for use when they die, and we are all going to die.

The surprise of the AIDS plague is that it affects the young, those not ready to make mature decisions about death, and it establishes the reality that any one of us can die of many things at any time. Sometimes the crisis of our life makes us realize that death is a possibility. Somehow we exclude ourselves.

If we do not do the paperwork, we cannot expect our wishes to be filled. These legal contracts are so simple to complete and so necessary to do if you have any respect for those you love, but you must face the fact that all people die, including you. These contracts are not just for gays, but the legal and simplified versions were made inexpensively available out of the AIDS crisis and the demands of the dying young. It only takes a couple of minutes, and it saves others hours, maybe days, and it settles many of your loved one's questions.

John and Bob were friends from grade school, but not related. Each had given and taken the responsibility for the other. When John became ill, Bob could make no decisions for John because he was not a blood relative of John nor did he have legal papers.

Mrs. Smith lost her son and although she was legally his heir, she wondered for years if she had made the right decisions for his burial that he would have wanted.

Sue and Betty lived together for 20 years, and everything was in Sue's name. There were no legal attachments. Sue died. Betty was not allowed to make any decisions concerning Sue's death wishes and, although Sue had not seen her family in 20 years, Betty was left penniless.

In a situation where you have a significant other person that is not your blood relative or to which you are not legally attached, and if you want to be, make sure you cover yourself with the correct legal papers. (These rules differ from state to state, but a simple phone call to your AIDS center, and they can tell you what forms are necessary in your state. The center may even have the forms. You do not need the expense of an attorney.) What you need in forms will include:

(1.) Your Power of Attorney. Be cautious. The power of attorney means that you are giving to someone else the rights you have to your cash, your property, your checking account, and anything else you may own. He/she just has to show the document and sign, and it leaves you completely vulnerable.

For the gay man or lesbian, giving your power of attorney to someone else implies you trust him/her completely, and it becomes a game for the con artist. There are too many cases of broke old men who have given their power of attorney to a hustler that has cashed in. Some will say give your power of attorney to your lawyer, but I can not. Consider your brother or sister, but maybe not. Consider your partner, but maybe not. Consider your parents, but you'll probably outlive them. It is a very difficult decision and one of the most important legal documents you'll ever sign.

The power of attorney gives control over your financial matters and it is not to be confused with the Power of Attorney of Medical Decisions, a separate legal contract.

(2.) The Power of Attorney for Medical Decisions. This form is also called an Appointment of a Health Care Surrogate among other things, which allows the appointed person to make medical decisions for you when you may not be able. As an example, if you are unconscious and the doctors feel your leg should be amputated, the person you have appointed could make that decision.

(3.) Living Will. Another legal form allows you to select the medical equipment, medicines or machines, that you want or do not want to be used on you should you become ill. If you are unconscious, and you have specifically stated that you do not want to be placed on a respirator, and the doctor is aware of the legal forms, he has no authority to place you on that piece of machinery. Without the form, he can do anything to save your life. Do you want morphine? At what point is your body and your mind dead?

There are some living wills that include your desires to donate your body to science, a procedure that is becoming increasingly popular and necessary as we learn to substitute parts from one body to a second. You can write in your requests in this document, and you can also carry a card showing you want to be an organ donor should the situation present itself.

(4.) Deposition of Remains. This form indicate what you want done with your body after your death. (State laws do not allow for you to have your body bronzed.) It should indicate where you want buried, under what religious faith if any, special and personal requests of the deceased. Cremated? Ashes where? Obituary? (Do you really want to get the last word?)

(5.) A Will. Should you have a will? Of course. The cost of a will form in any stationery store is under a dollar. A will allows you to direct where your things go when you die. It is a protection of your desires. You don't even need a form; a signed and notarized hand written yellow sheet of paper will do just as well.

Many people will rationalize "Well, I don't have anything anyway" and never complete a will. Who knows what will happen in the years to follow that decision. The person marries and his/her mate legally leaves him a million dollars. The stub in her dead body's pocket won the lottery. Who knows? (If a person is hesitant about doing a will, promise him/her you will leave all earthly possessions to his/her worst enemy. They'll get a will.)

Any legal document can be challenged, but the challenge should not imply the challenger is going to win. Any will can be challenged, so be sure to include all brothers and sisters and your living parents with a minimum of one dollar to prove that they were considered rather than forgotten.

These simple five contracts will take care of you at a time in your life when you may not be thinking clearly. Once the five forms are completed (and it often takes an unbelievable amount of pressure from your friends to get you to taking care of your own business), do not sign the forms until you take the forms to a notary public. Banks often notarize free if you have an account.

Completing these forms may seem like a major project to you, but it will not take you long to complete them; much less time than it will take someone else to figure out what they thought you wanted.

1. Complete the five forms.

2. Have the forms notarized with two witnesses (some states require three witnesses.)

3. When notarized, write on the original where it can be found. (Example: Original in apartment, lower left desk drawer.) Put it there.

4. Have several copies made, and mark them "Copy".

5. Give a copy to your doctor.

6. Give a copy to your lawyer. (He/she may be angry if he missed the fee.)

7. Give a copy (and a blank copy for him/her to complete) to your best friend.

8. Put the original where you said you would put it. (Not a "copy.")

Completing these forms is part of being responsible. The reward? The great feeling of independence when you have all your bills paid for the month. Pride in your ability to watch after yourself.

If you have acquired a larger sum of money, property, or assets, you may want to consider a trust. A trust is a separate company aside from yourself of which you are the President and only you can withdraw from the account. Should you die, the person you have appointed as Vice President becomes the President and the assets go to him/her. This also means that your will (which is included in the trust papers) and the trust does not have to go through probate court, and the whole process takes only a few days.

The United States Government has established the rules and the USA Financial Publishing Corporation, 708 12th Street N. W., Canton, Ohio 44703, publishes How To Set Up Your Own Living Trust to Avoid Probate for a fee of around 25 dollars and you have the forms to complete and have notarized. (A lawyer will gladly complete his forms for several hundred dollars. Gamble for the booklet first.)

These procedures will take a short period of time and it will give the living the satisfaction of knowing that they have done what you wanted done.

THE PLAGUE

There is probably no time in the history of the humans that there hasn't been someone to profit from the misery of others. Wars make millionaires. The strong dominate the weak with taxes. The biggest and strongest, not necessarily the "right", wins. Money buys power, and power buys more money.

Unfortunately, there are many who make money from the gay lifestyle, many that are not gay. The bars and guest houses are not always owned by gays. There are those that state they can cure gays of their "problem". There are those that are self-appointed authorities on the gay lifestyle. There are the publishers of gay books and magazines. There's "gay day" at Disneyland. There are those that demand the spotlight no matter what the subject may be.

Out of every crisis, someone makes money. The American dream.

Someone is manufacturing and selling the jewelry red ribbons showing our support for AIDS victims, and making a profit. Newspapers freely advertise the buying of death insurance policies of HIV positive patients at reduced insurance settlements and quick money for the buyer. AIDS doctors own pharmacies and drug production companies. A doctor proclaims a cure. The army of volunteers string blindly behind some overpaid AIDS employees. Someone must always make a buck. The loser's plague.

A couple of hundred years ago, London experienced the black plague where hundreds of children, men and women died from being sick inside their stomachs, and many people were sure that the black plague was an action of the Devil. Someone miraculously decided to chart the city's deaths on a city map, and they found that people were dying around certain wells, watering holes that serviced a specific community of London. Investigation of these wells found them infested with dead rats, and the conclusion was drawn that the dead rats contaminated the well water and the people drank the water causing the black plague. Amazing.

In 1918 when the United States was entering World War I, more Americans died here than abroad from a disease called the Spanish Influenza, a pneumonia that touched about every family in the United States. More people died of the disease than died in World War I.

A few years and many deaths later, the plague seemed to lessen. Although medical assistance was minimal, more people were living. Later, the plague was over and the United States settled not ever knowing the remedy for Spanish Influenza.

Today, the United States is going through another plague; the plague of AIDS, and it is affecting the world. After a 15 year struggle, we know only the tragic effects of the disease of death, not really the physical causes or all of the symptoms, and few concrete answers. We are still looking for a cure to the disease, if it is a disease. The three pill "cocktail" of the middle 1990s seems to prolong life. The Food and Drug Administration is allowing more and faster experimentation.

There is hope that AIDS may run its course as did the Spanish Influenza or that we will find a simplistic cure as discovering dead rats in a well, but these may be idle dreams.

HAVING FUN

We have been given a new era in our aging process compared to our grandparents, the period between retirement and "falling apart", from our sixties to our nineties or maybe beyond. These golden years were not appreciated by generations before because they did not have the golden years while they were working constantly until they died.

Some seniors want work to continue during all their lives. They don't want to stop work because they feel they have a great deal to give, the wisdom they have stored. The stories are many of men and women who have lived well into their nineties still working at their jobs or professions, and still loving the work. They usually own the company or they are self-employed because they are often without a boss that tells them what to do.

One aspect of the golden years is that there are no longer bosses for many. Either the one time bosses have died or lost control, or you no longer are responsible to the boss. For some woman, that boss was her husband. For others, the husband was the constant companion for which the woman lived. For some, the loss of a lover may have been the loss of a boss. Regardless, the boss is gone. Now the senior can do anything he/she wishes to do without someone overseeing and regulating. The golden years are freedom.

Usually, there is a freedom away from the building of money. You know what you have and you've learned to live on it. You are not making great demands upon investing for profit unless it is a game. You can pretty much afford to do the things you want to do, or you want to do the things you can afford. You want to enjoy yourself.

The list of activities you can enjoy is endless, everywhere from going on ship cruises to romantic island settings to large cities, and you don't have to feel, nor will you be alone. The tourist industries are well aware that the senior has money to spend, and the salesman is more than willing to find you outlets for your money. Dude ranches to Paris apartments to American train trips. The American Association of Retired People number in the thousands, and they are ready to go. There are no more crying children at home, no job responsibilities, often no home except for an apartment to care for, and even the animals sometimes interfere. There are two words for the seniors; "Going" and "Fun", and they are ready in mass.

Of all the periods of your life not to be bored with the routine of living, the seniors have the freedom, the spunk, and the desire to venture into new ideas and places that continue to keep them alive and well. There may be a little more patience needed with wheelchairs and walkers and a slower pace, but they are not fighting the war of time and hurry-hurry.

They are beyond the period when they care what people say about them. They want to do "their own thing" and they can think of many things to do. They are not willing to sit on the back porch and knit unless they want to knit, and they reserve that right. If they are interested in politics, we'll hear from them. The Senior Citizen vote of AARP members is heard in Washington, D.C. and numbers in the thousands. There are no barriers held against them, few restrictions to what they can and what they cannot do. It is their best time. It is their golden years. Paul Newman, the actor, said upon turning seventy "I don't have to worry about being something for somebody."

For the gay men and lesbians that have reached this point, life can continue to be exciting if the individual wants it to be. It is now the senior's choice. In the gay lifestyle and community, there is a respect for age and a kind of consideration the younger give to the older, the younger realizing that someday they may be in the same position as the older. A gay organization for seniors over 50, SAGE is available in some large cities of retirees like Fort Lauderdale, San Francisco, Los Angeles and New York. In many cities there is an "old farts bar" where the seniors can collect to exchange stories and directions, and they call it "God's Waiting Room" and they are usually entertaining bars.

There is probably no other period in the development of the human being that is more interesting, comfortable and fun than the senior years; a period of little pretense, a worldly appetite, usually the means and energy to do what the seniors want to do when they want to do it without answering "Why?"

HONESTY, REALLY

When we are young and we give our word and providing we do not forget that we have given our word, we appear to be totally honest. Wild horses could not pull us from our trust, the information which we possess, so long as we remember. As time goes on, we become less aware that we have given our word. When other interpretations infiltrate into our knowledge, our vows to secrecy and giving our word seem to mingle in a hazy memory. We remember our word, or has our word been forgotten? Do we no longer remember what we've promised?

A widow in the Hamptons promised on her husband's coffin that she would be with him soon, and 30 years later and two more husbands, she was buried alone in another cemetery.

There is always the concept of timing with honesty, that you promised to do something at a specific time only to forget what you promised. Lawyers dealing with wills are familiar with the concept. "He told me he was going to leave me his life insurance. He never mentioned the big house? She said she'd take care of me." Not only forgotten promises, but the lack of following through which was more important to someone else than to the person making the statement. He/she may have meant to keep the promise, but just never got around to it. Maybe the statement was false from the beginning without intention of fulfilling it.

It was a promise to comfort the moment, but nothing on which you intended to act. That's where "really" comes in. All the good intentions in the world, all the promises, all the satisfied people who someone has pleased at a specific time, may not have been the intention of the person making the promise. "Really" makes it come true; the lawyer is called, the will is changed, the transactions are recorded. The honesty has been given some substance, but this rarely happens.

The person promising doesn't really mean to go back on his/her word; it is just that the first time the statement is made is more meaningful than actually carrying out the promise. How many nieces have heard "I'll leave this necklace to you in my will." That's the end of it. Meaningless conversation to get a positive reaction and hopefully some conclusion. "Let me get back to the office and see what I can do about that." Nothing happens.

Combine dishonesty with "the check is in the mail" plus a friend promising to give you back the ten you loaned him, and "eating carrots improves your eyesight" and you'll soon learn to trust no one; and maybe this includes yourself. Maybe you are not to be trusted; maybe you are not honest. Really.

Not trusting is an awful way to face the world, but it is a negative quality that is necessary for survival. A lot of nice guys finish last. Is there some kind of justice to the scheme of the world? We believe in someplace beyond life; someplace where someone can work out this whole mess that we have made of us.

When someone promises you a fortune, follow the conversation with a question, "really?" and get your lawyer.

DIVIDING THE ASSETS

If you are fortunate enough to have cash, property or assets, your problems may become how to fairly give this wealth to your heirs. You must realize that what you consider fair may not necessarily be what your heirs consider fair. We all seem to reason from our own financial advantage.

There are probably several personal requests for your things of life that you have promised. "If anything happens to me, I want you to have _____." It is respectable and nice to honor those requests. There will be the bleeding niece that wants everything and will never be satisfied.

Some people will want to put a value on the personal requests to be subtracted from the total cash allocations. Others will think of just forgetting the personal items and dividing up the cash. Someone will complain. "That ring wasn't worth $500" and his cousin will say "That ring was worth more than $500". There is no way to satisfy everyone.

There have been more families split because of inherited money than what we like to believe, much more has been spent and/or wasted beyond the value. Once a person dies, some of the relatives become birds of prey over a fresh road kill. The common line is "What did he/she leave me?" and there is no way to please everyone or, perhaps, anyone.

If a person dies and leaves his financial gains to a charity or institution or organization, the family and friends gang up against the deceased questioning the deceased's previous mental condition as well as the charity's intent. Sometimes the deceased ends up with the entire family disliking him because his estate settlement went to his favorite charity.

Toward the end of your life, you will probably start getting the monetary worth from the property, stocks, etc. that you have acquired. It seems easier to divide cash. You have enough financial sense that you are aware of how much money you have, although you may not demand that much on which to live. You always had that "kitchen money", that financial reserve behind or in the cookie jar. It is kinder that you turn your assets into cash since you know the history and value of your assets, than to allow the person who inherits to turn your things into cash.

There are several different ways you can handle the distribution of your wealth. You can give it to an outside source. You can give it to your relatives and friends that you feel are deserving of it including a value of the items you have left them and subtracting that from their cash inheritance. You can ignore things you have given them while alive and have the cash divided equally. You can have everything put into cash and divide that cash equally or proportionately to what you feel the person needs and expects from you. You may want to have a trust account particularly if you have real estate holding. Regardless, any way that you want to arrange the distribution of your wealth, there will be hard feelings. I hope not verbal complaints. One woman put a stipulation in her will that should anyone contest the will, the assets to that person were void, but I doubt it held up in court.

The gay male couples or lesbian couples have a particularly difficult time in dividing his/her worth considering a living mate and family money. There are incidents of inherited family wealth where the mate had little to do with acquiring the wealth, and the deceased may have felt that he/she should not share family money with a lover. A lover or lifetime companion or meaningful relationship has no legal rights to the deceased person's assets unless it is in writing, such as a palimony contract. Should the deceased have written into the will that he/she had considered the mate and left him/her only a token? Any judge would give this statement some validity. Of course, wills can be contested. Someone could claim palimony, but that is a difficult and expensive road to prove.

It is much more common that lovers do not plan far enough ahead with the understanding that one will someday die, and their lack of doing the legal planning, leaves the living lover without assets. Sometimes, this can be tragic. Gay men and lesbians are not invulnerable to death or to weak planning.

The gay man or lesbian must understand that if he/she leaves assets to the lover, the family will never understand and there will always be some selfish hurt feelings. The lover who receives nothing from the death of his friend will also have to answer or ignore what appears to be a selfish act on the part of the deceased lover. There is nothing that can be done about either case.

AND DEATH

When we read a book, we start with the beginning and measure the length of the content with our right hand indicating by feel how many more pages we know are left until the end of the story. Someone should write a book with the last 20 pages blank indicating that we never know when the end of the story will come.

From the wisdom of maturity and the deserved award of a happy life of being gay, death becomes an adventure on the other side of the bridge, or a new adventure ahead. Dying is the final step of the physical body giving up.

Hopefully, there will be many aspects of life that live beyond the physical body; the great love of friends, the goodness, the understanding, maybe even the deeds. These go beyond the mere physical deterioration.

I want to be able to look back over my life and say "It was a hell of a good time. I lived it." Few sorrows. Few regrets. "I was true to myself."

NO LONGER ASHAMED

What continues to amaze is our long history of homosexuality through every age and the refusals of admitting its existence. For those that did admit it existed, it was usually thought of as a "crime against nature" and punished by death or imprisonment, then a "degenerated sexual perversion" and banned by religious organizations, then a "mental disease" operable by shock treatment and lobotomy, then as a "social disorder" after protests from other minorities, and now we are questioning it as "a possible genetic imbalance."

We know that homosexuality has existed probably as long as man. We know that other animals have dual homosexuality and heterosexuality, but some humans cannot accept a similar characteristic in humans. We know that homosexuality crosses cultural lines and racial lines, and that it was as prevalent in the frontier days of America as it was with the American Indians. (Read Gay and American History, Lesbians and Gay Men in the U.S.A.. by Jonathan Katz, Avon.) We know that homosexuality is not just a period of our lives of sexual activity, but is a way of life that may dominate our lifestyle.

Yet, we are hypocritical, refusing to study it or talk about it until the last 50 or so years. It seems strange that the Chicago Society for Human Rights, founded by Henry Gerber and chartered by Illinois in 1924, probably the first male organization, and the Mattachine Society founded by Henry Hey in 1948 mark the early organization of gay men. The Daughters of Bilitis (DOB) founded by Del Martin and Phyllis Lyon, an organization for lesbians was started in 1955.

In these short amount of years there has been a tremendous amount of recognition of the gay lifestyle with churches, travel groups, social groups, activist groups, etc., that have answered the gay calling. The Human Rights Campaign is the largest gay male and lesbian political organization. The Gay and Lesbian Alliance Against Defamation (GLAAD) watches inclusive and accurate media coverage. There are gay marches and gay organizations in practically every city. We are no longer ashamed to say the word "gay" or "lesbian". What took us so long?

I am painfully aware that there are thousands of adolescent kids wondering why their world is so different, why their thoughts are so strange, why no one understands including themselves, kids that cry themselves to sleep in their confusion as I did. The kids do not realize their closet door has a lock on the inside of the closet for them to open.

Ignorance may be the best answer. Fear from the heterosexual another. Lack of recognition of the minorities. Hatred based on fear fed through generations. The lack of the gay man or lesbian to stand up for himself. The lack of gay pride. Fading into the other problems of the world. Lack of leadership and organization.

What is the future of the homosexual? Hopefully, bright. Elimination of bias. Education. Recognition. No fear of extinction. No teen suicides. Equality in employment and through our laws. Pride. Individual self esteem. Homosexual happiness. Contribution to ourselves, our country, and our world.

A short article in the newspaper by a high school graduate of 1994 titled "The Last Socially Acceptable Prejudice in America", an opinion that was surprising coming from a young lady that must not have been much more than 18 years old. [1] Her statements of "homophobia is ignorance", and those concerning the intolerance and prejudice practiced by some Christians is what the gay movement is all about. So long as we have thinking young people who are willing to support individual rights even among those who do not think exactly as they do, there is a chance of freedom for all. Thank God for logical, young mind.

As Citizens of the United States and Judea-Christians, our strength is with the young people passing laws that make first class citizens of all minority groups through understanding and education. Women are getting closer to being equal in all aspects to men. The blacks are still pushing for their equality as they have over the last hundred years. The American Indians seem forgotten. The Orientals are a new threat to some. The gays are uniting and becoming a stronger force.

WHEN THE SCOOTER BROKE

Every kid had a scooter, regardless if it were a homemade one of a board and two roller skates or a bought one from Sears-Roebuck. You either had to have a wagon, a scooter or at least a pair of skates, and if you had skates, you had a scooter with very little mechanical fixing. The whole flock of kids, scraping, yapping and screaming, would swing up the street with their combinations of wheels. There was always someone whose skate, or bike, or wagon was broken.

Some products seem to be made better than other products. They ware longer and they are tougher and they don't need repair as often. Strange, you never saw a completely broken skate, bike, or wagon in the garbage; they could always be repaired. Kids are like their toys, easily repairable and usually ready for action. We only knew of two kids that could not be repaired.

Growing up, our toys fell to the next group of kids to use, but we always seemed to be repairable. After high school and the early child rearing years, we lost a couple more of the neighborhood kids because of parts that seemed not to wear too well, but that was expected. We lost too many in the wars. We lost too many in automobile accidents and work accidents. Many just disappeared and we never knew how long their parts lasted.

When you push that old machine of a body to the maximum, when your body is so tired you think it can never be repaired, when you feel its usefulness is done and it is due for the garbage, somehow, it seems to get repaired, and you are at it again. The body seems to make it through each crisis, through each period of life. Sometimes when there is little hope, it needs a little oil. Sometimes it needs new parts. Sometimes it just needs attention. The old machine, the skate, the wagon or the bike, seems to pull through.

There comes a time when the sharp edges of the gears are worn rounded, the cogs don't fit smoothly, the chain catches, the wheels waddle, the handle-bar slips, time when the old machine is just getting old and worn, a time when it should be thrown into the garbage, but it is put at the back of the garage for someday, someone younger will pull it out, fix the parts, and give it new life, and it can give wonderful enjoyment to someone from the next generation.

There comes a time when our bodies just wear out, but usually long before our minds start to get old. The elbows don't work as well, there's pain in the knees, the fingers ache. The inside gets confused. Some doctor calls it cancer, or heart trouble, or circulation problems or one of the million other names. We only have the wheels, maybe the steering wheel of the scooter or bike to go wrong. Sometimes it can be repaired, and sometimes it can not.

When the skates, bike or wagon get worn, maybe broken, it is wise to see if they can be fixed for a couple of more times around the block, but sometimes they cannot be repaired and it is a waste of time to try.

HOW ARE YOU?

"Thank you for asking that. No one has asked me that for at least five minutes." Does an older person have to give a minute-by-minute report on his/her mental and physical condition to everyone who asks? The question makes you want to answer "none of your business. If you were 90 years old and all the parts didn't work, and your mind gets a little foggy now and then, and you don't know or care what day it is, how would you feel?"

Older people are aware of slowing down, of the physical body and the mind not being as alert as they once were. They are much more aware of a direct relationship between mental health and physical health putting neither superior to the other.

Physical medicine has developed rapidly with the creation of new methods and drugs to avert the symptoms of a disease or eliminate the disease itself. Few die of syphilis today; tuberculosis is curable, only the common cold seems to avoid the medical scientist's eyes. They eliminate the symptoms, and let the cold run its course. Medicine is certainly not an exact science, but it has developed and saved many lives.

The average age of the ancient Egyptian was 37. Romeo was only 14. Modern man can expect to live into his 70s, maybe 80s, sometimes into the 90s or beyond. (We are talking quantity; not necessarily quality.)

Mental health has also developed and psychology can now give us many of the answers that were previously unavailable. Mental health doctors, the psychiatrists, psychologist, philosophers and even social scientists have used the tools of medicine, the mind controlling medicines and pills of science in their work on the mind. Common knowledge considers the many sides of the personality of an individual, the pressures of guilt and stress, the anxiety factors of living and with these discussions have come education, research and reasoning. Every honest physician will admit that he has only limited knowledge of the physical body, and something beyond his help and knowledge must take over the healing process. We will soon see the day when the physician is well versed in psychology and the psychologist is well versed in medicine.

Being recognized as compatible and related field, the physical study of modern medicine and the study of the workings of the mental process are closer and will result in a compatible working arrangement for the healthy person. In reality, the medical physician with their physical cures and the mental psychiatrists with their proven theories, do not represent opposite sides as imagined. Both theories today agree that the mind affects the physical, the physical affects the mind. As older citizens, we can vouch for the effects of both.

A favorite game of nursing homes is to play "the disease of the day" where you name symptoms that everyone has, but there is always someone there from "Can You Top This". Psychological games are fun also. If you don't want to be disturbed and someone is bothering your peace, just start to repeat the alphabet, and they'll leave. Of course, you get the reputation of being a little screwy.

We like a routine. We worry about the most important events of the day being breakfast, lunch and dinner, and we avoid the conversation when it turns to bowel movements and regularity.

We are living now in the time when an older person can list in a living will those precautions, medicines, drugs, and machines that the ill person does not want to be used on him/her. There must be respect for the person that obeys the ill person's wishes. Something must be said about the person who is so physically ill with no chance of recovery and with not enough energy to help him/her acquire death, and help is needed.

Perhaps most difficult to the senior citizens, the gay man and lesbian that have lived their lives as fully as they could, the many talented, creative young that die each year both mentally and physically from AIDS, the slow crumbling of the soul and the body. Most seniors would gladly trade places, but that is not God's plan.

No one that has died without a belief in something beyond man, a faith in something yet to happen, or a belief in a complete "nothingness". Only a few have died without gratitude for being on earth.

The seniors reach a point of caring for their physical malfunctions but more aware of their mental readiness to take the next step. We never read a death certificate that says "She was tired ..." or "He was old ..." but we always have to give scientifically significant reasons such as "heart failure" or "stroke". That time to give up will not come until the person is ready, and some seniors will fight to the very end.

THE WILL TO GO ON LIVING

Many people leave the last quarter of a football game knowing that the end is coming and they have to beat the crowd to the parking lot without the conclusion of the end, anticipating the final score. But, the fourth quarter can be deceptive. When one side has quit trying, the opposite gets a shot of energy unexpected by either side, and only the final minutes determine the winner of the game.

The game of life is similar. Some people leave the stadium long before the end of the game. They anticipate the final results. They guess at what they have won or lost, and they adjust accordingly, but they are often not accurate, They leave before the final touchdown is made. Much more than admitting defeat or victory, they anticipate the final score and choose not to enjoy the game for itself, and prefer not to watch.

There is, by self-training, the ability to watch, anticipate, and play the last few minutes of the ball game to the very end of the clock. Some people live and die by the clock, and, surprisingly, they gain the ability to stretch time until they have seen enough. They wait through the last seconds of the game until the stadium is still, and then they go. They have the will to stay with the game even beyond its time. It seems to be inherent. The drive. The will. The controlling desire to follow the idea beyond the end of the game to the historical conclusion.

Each language is not complete with exact definitions of one to the second language. There are subtle nuances of a definition that may be captured in one language, but not the second.

In the Yiddish language the word "moxie" and it is difficult if not impossible to translate that word in its full meaning to American English. It is more than selfish aggression, more than personal perseverance, more than self motivation or self survival. It is that push to continue to squeeze every ounce of juice from the orange. It's folding a five dollar bill in your left hand while begging for five with the right hand.

If we had a term for "moxie" in English, it would include people of all religions, ethnic groups, races, and social levels, but there would not be a great number of them. This rare quality of survival is held by a few whose life seems to have been toward the end a couple of times, whose circumstances have been less than ideal, who have overcome disadvantages with a willingness and a power to go on, regardless.

What makes these individual fight and succeed beyond what they can endure? It's a motivation. It's a drive. It is larger than the physical, stronger than the emotional. It's a power to accomplish. In Christian-Judaism faiths, we like to think that it transcends death, perhaps a view from the other side of the river. Perhaps a view of life as it progresses even after the person is deceased.

Death has been described by many as drifting away from the physical body, of being above it and viewing the whole scene that is present before it enters a tunnel toward light and the millions of scenes that have been lived to get to that point where the body is little more than changing a shirt. Most believe, a kind of intelligence lives on, and we call it soul. The soul of the person remains on earth maybe for hours, days, or weeks until it can be set free.

Contrary to all medical reports, the power of will is all-encompassing, and it cannot be scientifically analyzed by psychiatrists, psychologists, or physicians. But, it does exist; it is. Some people believe that it is greater than the mental world, greater than the physical world, which would categorize it in the spiritual, meaning beyond understanding.

We see it in all kinds of situations; the writer who will not die until his book is published, the school teacher who wants to survive until her son graduates college, the cancer patient who must make his next birthday, the orphan who must find his father. Many times this desire becomes so strong that it dominates beyond the expected rolls of health and medicine, beyond human expectation, beyond what doctors can tell you of your condition. It is an energy to live, a dynamic drive to continue.

Poor Van Gogh. He painted all his life through hellish situations, through struggles of his own mind and heart, and he sold only one painting to his brother. Years later, his paintings sell for millions. Franz Liszt was tortured through the church and ended half crazed in a monastery, never to achieve happiness, but bringing the world the magic of music. There is no guarantee of life being fair.

The ability to go on living in spite of the odds, the "moxie" to persevere, the drive to continue has helped many. God somehow gives a peace and satisfaction to those rare people who have dared to live greater lives than the average. That is the real meaning to inward peace.

It is reflected in small ways. That poor, little, old lady who is sick and disappointed awaits her daughter to come and visit her. The little old man takes pleasure in the imaginary scenes of himself and his wife. Someone waits for the postman. They are not yet ready.

PAPERWORK

Since you have planned most of your life, or maybe you have allowed your life to plan you, at least plan the last paperwork that accompanies death.

Write your own obituary and keep it with your hospital papers, but not with your will which will not be read until after you are dead. You know yourself better than anyone. You know the things of which you are proud. You know what have been your high points as well as your lows. Another person looking at your life may not evaluate your life like you can. Do it. Write it out. Be careful that it is not too long and will cost too much money. If you don't want an obituary, say so. It is really your chance at "... the last word".

Have enough respect for the living to strongly suggest that you have a brief mourning period, not one that draws out over several days or weeks. Judaism has an interesting concept that a person must be buried within 24 hours of his/her death and "shiva" is a seven day remembrance, the wake. Many religions and funeral parlors purposefully drag out the burial ceremony. The living individuals need time to heal with your death; give them that time by being rapidly buried rather than prolonging their suffering.

Currently popular in burial ceremonies is the "affirmation of life" get together three or four weeks after the person has died and been buried or cremated. Some find the occasion morbid, non-constructive, and often a stage for public display of mourning. To them, the event is re-tearing the wound that has started to heal.

Don't be afraid to talk about the person that has died. That is his/her living memory which should go on. Talk of the fun times, the silly times, the laughable times as well as the serious times. Let everyone know how the deceased was an entertaining, fun loving, happy person. The largest compliment the deceased could give you would be for you to go on with your life and always remember him/her. That you can guarantee.

HAS EVERYTHING BEEN ACCOMPLISHED?

Paul Newman approaching 70 years old said, "And I have seen a lot of people who go to their graves without ever getting in touch with what it is that's the core of them."

Everything accomplished? Not at all. If I were to go on living I would _____. I'm proud of what has been done. I'm proud of what is happening now. I'm glad I could stick around to see so much change, and it has made me a happy person. I'm going to be more proud of your future.

Is there a dance I have not danced? Many.
Is there a song I have not sung? Thousands.
Have my dreams been met? Never.
Is there a bed I haven't slept in? Millions.
Is there a body I want to hold? Yes.
Has everything been accomplished? No.
Am I satisfied? Oh, yes. Thank you, God.

THE FANTASY OF THE SCAB

At any age, we make up little stories in our imaginary world while daydreaming or before going to sleep. These stories are little dreams about ourselves and our world of freedom, but they are more pleasant little indicators of what we want or wanted to become, or what we want or wanted to happen in our lives when we were younger. They were and are pleasant little ditties which set humans apart from animals, the ability to imagine, pretend, and dream. They were stories of what we wanted life to be like, rather than what it has become. There is always the ability to curl back and allow yourself to day-dream.

In realistically analyzing the content of the day-dreaming, you will realize that nothing so trusting, so innocent, so fresh could have happened to you, but you were willing to play the game in your dream. There was always the house and it became everything from a log cabin to a castle, but it was security. In this house was a person, the all trusting, all concerned, all considerate, all loving of me; the Ms. or Mr. Right. There were plenty of loving things around; the horses in the barn, the cattle on the acres, the dogs asleep, the cats, possums, and skunks, all loving like in Bambi or Snow White. The fantasy of working together with someone you love to accomplish something may be small, but it seems large like world destruction by volcanoes, the slipping ice cap of the North Pole, or the battles with all of South America. As we grew older, the dreams seemed to fade and they are not as easy to call to mind, but the scars of the dreams are still there in an emotion. The scars hint at a fantasy dream.

As you grow older, and go to bed earlier once the television has bored you and reading no longer excites you, and you hope to curl up and allow yourself to dream part of that whole fantasy world you have created, and once the lights are off and it is quiet, and the fantasy dreams no longer come.

LOOKING BACK
I really didn't design my life, but I want the right. All of a sudden, I was. I was born into a place at a certain time, and I attempted to make my friends happier in our world, and I attempted to be happy, and I got a big chunk of it.

The early thirties was a whole world of rules and behavior, "do's" and "don'ts", some of which we understood, some of which we could not. We accepted those rules with which we could agree, but rebelled against the others. We rationalized, made excuses, substituted and denied many of society's rules, and even challenged a couple to make a society of our own, the gay community.

We lived through changes in the world, World War I, World War II, Korea, Viet Nam and into peace with Russia, Japan, and Germany, and the acceptance of China. We've lived through the advancements in medicine from quick cure peddler's bottles and home remedies to operations without cutting the skin. From radio through television to the computer to chips. From neighborhood witches to social therapists. There have been many wonderful and tremendous changes. But, we are not stopping.

There is much more to be done in the future in all fields, but there are many more educated minds working on the problems, and all the problems can be resolved. We know where we have been and we know where we are, and now we have to figure out where we are going.

Our goal is that each gay man or lesbian should have the rights to live to maximum potential in a world free of bigotry and prejudice, a world we are yet to know. We're getting there.

Footnotes

THE FORMING OF BEING GAY
1. Reverend Louis Sheldon, Traditional Value Coalition, Fausto-Sterling Study.
2. Marcia E. Herman-Gidden, University of North Carolina, Pediatrics American Academy of Pediatrics, April 1997.
3. National Opinion Research Center, University of Chicago.
4. Ibid.
5. Robert H. Knight, Family Research Council.
6. USA Today, "Counting the Gay Market," April 23, 1993.
7. Michael Gravois, Rivendell Marketing Company.
8. National Crime Survey Report, Criminal Victimization in the United States, 1990, p.18.
9. Deryck Calderwoed, "The Male Rape Victim" Medical Aspects of Human Sexuality, May, 1987.
10. Warren Ferrell, The Myth of Male Power, p. 165.
11. Ibid.
12. Mel White, News from UFMCC, Key West, Fla., November 1997, p. 31.

THE REALIZATION OF BEING GAY
1. Ferrell, op. cit.
2. Psychology Today, Sept/Oct 1995, p.49.
3. Karen Arno, Sexuality and Homosexuality, NY, W. W. Norton, 1971, p.84.
4. Philip W. Sergeant, Witches and Warlocks, London: Hutchinson and Co., p.12.
5. Sally Booth , Witches in Early America, NY, Hastings House 1975.

THE ADJUSTMENT TO BEING GAY
1. Human Resources Management, Advocate, op. cit
2. Op cit.
3. Ed Mickens The 100 Best Companies for Gay Men and Lesbians, Advocate, op cit., February 16, 1994.
4. Loc. cit.
5. Carol Rosenberg, "Miami Herald", "Clinton sets a precedent at gay rights fund-raiser", November 9, 1997, p. 20 A.
6. S.L.A. Marshall and Jean Elshtain, Women at War, N.Y., Harper and Roe, 1987.
7. Ferrell, op. cit., p. 74
8. National Conference of Catholic Bishops, "Miami Herald", October 1, 1997.

THE MATURING OF BEING GAY

1. Lois Verbgrugge, University of Michigan, Institute of Gerontology
2. Lilly, Dream Institute, University of Southern California,
3. Verbgrugge, op. cit.
4. Barbara Given, George Mason University.
5. Verbgrugge, op. cit.
6. Thomas Juster, Frank P. Stafford, University of Michigan, "The Allocations of Time: Empirical Findings, Behavioral Models, and Problems of Measurements", "Journal of Economic Literature", Vol. 29, June 1991, p.477.
7. Alex Michalos, University of Guelph, Ontario, Canada.
8. Michigan State Health Department, "Advocate."
9. Ferrell, op. cit, p. 181. U. S. Department of Health and Human Services National Centers for Disease Control, vol. 38, no 5, 1987.
10. Ferrell, op. cit., chart, p. 192 quoting p. 435.
11. Accent, The Orange County Register, April 29, 1997, as reported in "The News" Metropolitan Community Church, October 1997, p. 36.
12. Michelle Faul, Associated Press, "Key West Citizen", Oct. 7, 1997.
13. "Larry King Show",CNN, Oct. 7, 9:00.
14. Internal Revenue Service 1990 "Los Angeles Times" August 23, 1990.

THE WISDOM OF BEING GAY

1. Paul Baltes, Max Planck Institute, Berlin.
2. Alvar Svanbord, Gothenburg, Sweden, 1970.
3. Paul B. Baltes and Ursula M. Staudinger, Max Plank Institute, Berlin, Germany.
4. Douglas Powell, Harvard University, Profiles in Cognitive Aging,
5. Charles A. Dana Foundation.
6. Douglas Powell, Brain User's Guide to Aging.
7. Ellen Langer and Judith Rodin, Harvard, Yale.
8. Dana Foundation.
9. Langer, Rodin, loc. cit.

AND DEATH

1. Beth Monchek, "The Last Socially Acceptable Prejudice in America", "The Miami Herald," 1994. An opinion that Jeb Bush running for Florida Governor would not hire lesbians or gay men.